WITH LOVE AS GUIDE

ERATO SAHAPOGLU

Order this book online at www.trafford.com
or email orders@trafford.com

Most Trafford titles are also available at major online book retailers.

Photography by Erato Sahapoglu
Photography for cover page and Author's portrait by Gabriella Bruyère

An excerpt titled "*She is not dead, she is alive*" was first published in Spinetingler magazine in their June 2006 issue.

Note for Librarians: A cataloguing record for this book is available from Library and Archives Canada at www.collectionscanada.ca/amicus/index-e.html

Printed in Victoria, BC, Canada.

ISBN: 978-1-4251-7980-9 (soft)
ISBN: 978-1-4251-7981-6 (e-book)

Trafford PUBLISHING

www.trafford.com

North America & international
toll-free: 1 888 232 4444 (USA & Canada)
phone: 250 383 6864 • fax: 812 355 4082

To Gabriella and Katherine, my loving daughters who incited me to write this book, and to Tito, my childhood pal, my departed companion, my husband, my soulmate, for his continuous love, support and encouragement and in memory of my loving parents Katina and Stavros.

Introduction

In 1985, when my father, Stavros, was stricken by an incurable cancer, I wanted to distract him and make his last months as enjoyable as possible. I asked him to evoke his memories for our family and the archives of our Association of the Greeks of Constantinople in tape recorded sessions. Furthermore, to help him through his last voyage on Earth, I wrote an essay for him – in Greek – where I recalled all my personal spiritual experiences. To make sure he would read it, I asked him to correct my mistakes in Greek. He did, while discussing the essay with me. And it did help him.

The essay also helped very sick friends who read it... They told me it gave them hope and eradicated their fear of death. I translated it into French and English and considered publishing it. But first I asked the opinion of editor-author Jean-Yves Soucy. He gave me an exceptional evaluation report. He told me the manuscript was moving and very interesting, however I should also include my relationship with my father for whom I had written it, and let the readers discover the man that Stavros was. That way it would appeal to all.

Nonetheless, I believed then that my father's life was private and that if I talked about him I would, in a way, betray him. So I let the project sleep. A few years later, I read Mitch Albom's *Tuesdays with Morrie.* This book was magnificent. Morrie's memories were brought to life through tape recordings. The passages made me re-live my taped discussions with Stavros. Far from betrayal Albom's book was a celebration of a man's spirit.

In the meantime, my daughters had asked me to put into writing our family life. So, I decided to do it with the help of the tape recordings with my father.

I am grateful to all those who had read my first essay and encouraged me, particularly Jean-Yves Soucy, my dear friend Eleni Eliadis, and author Mitch Albom whose book gave me the courage to write Stavros' story. I thank Joyce White and Francie Thompson, my tutor at Quality of Course writing school – where I wanted to hone my skills to do an acceptable job – for their coaching and support. I thank Marion Blake, Yvon Paquet and Carol Charley for their thorough editing and Dr. John Rossner and Marilyn Rossner for their encouragement. And finally, I thank Dave Duprey, Kathleen Blondal and Terry Lussier at Trafford, for their professionalism and their valuable help.

Political views and assumptions are Stavros' only.
All the events and names in this manuscript are authentic.
I used, in general, the phonetic version of Greek and Turkish words.

I hope this book will bring to many expatriated Greeks from our native city fond memories about our life in Istanbul and our gatherings in Montreal. I hope it will bring solace to many. And finally, I hope that it will be cherished by my family.

Erato Evangelidis Sahapoglu

September 2008

I - STAVROS

***H**e* asked me to pull the burgundy Lazy Boy chair closer to the patio doors that opened on the golden-red garden. He wanted to enjoy the view of the fall garden, glowing under the early afternoon sun. He sat erect.

I covered his frail legs with a soft, multi-coloured afghan.

I brought him a cup of coffee. After the first sip he exclaimed, disgusted: "This is not coffee! It's just boiled water!"

Has he already lost his sense of taste?

"Do you want some tea, instead, Father?" I wrote on my note pad and showed it to him. He nodded.

I prepared a glass of his preferred *Earl Grey* tea with five spoons of sugar, as he liked it and placed it on the small table beside him. I squeezed his hand. Large, rough, wrinkled, dry, his fingers still nicotine-yellow. Although Stavros rarely smoked now, the pungent tobacco smell had impregnated his clothes and was still part of his skin. I fixed the small down pillow behind his neck, my fingers caressing his thinning, silky grey-white hair that was once a thick wavy chestnut mane.

"How do we start?" he asked.

"From the beginning!" I wrote. "From your parents. How they met, got married, where they lived. When did they come to Istanbul?"

He sighed. Then a smile appeared on his lips as he plunged into his past.

The silence was broken by the click of the recorder, the hiss of the empty tape spooling along, preparing to capture his memories, and by the sound of my pencil on my note pad. He refused to wear his hearing aid – its vibrations and buzzing noises annoyed him more than his deafness.

* * *

"Lung cancer! Generalized. Inoperable."

The doctor's impersonal words sounded my father's death sentence. The floor shifted under my feet, my knees wobbled, my heart contracted. I gasped with pain as this dagger entered deep in my heart. Instinctively I blocked my father's view of the doctor with my body.

"He is completely deaf, don't look towards him. Nothing that can be done?" I asked the doctor.

"Not at this stage. The cancer is all over both lung cavities and spreading to the throat. It has probably attacked other organs too. Chemotherapy and radiation would not help a bit, they would only make the short time he has to live miserable."

"How long does he have?"

"Two to three months, maybe a bit more, depending on his constitution. All we can do is alleviate his symptoms and reduce the pain, as much as we can. In the meantime, he should put all his papers in order and—"

"He has nothing, owes nothing. He only has a government pension. I am his only living relative. I'm not going to tell him. You'll help me tell him that he has a grave case of pneumonia or broncho-pneumonia."

"It's impossible! We cannot lie to a patient. He has to know."

"No, he doesn't. I know my father better than anyone. We've always lived together. You don't know him. Besides, you don't have to lie. Just don't deny what I tell him."

"But he will find out! You can't keep the truth from him. He will hear—"

"He won't! I told you, he's completely deaf! I will make sure that he doesn't find out. I want to make the months he has to live the happiest I can. And that will not happen if he knows he has cancer. He told me once he would shoot himself if he ever got cancer. And I know he would find a way to do it. So, please doctor, for God's sake, listen to me."

"You have to give him the choice of how to live these last months. You have to respect his will. You are upset. I won't tell him anything now. But please, reconsider. In the meantime we'll have to do some tests so that we can decide what medicine to give you for his pain. Liquid or dry morphine probably, later, but we must know. We also need to know whether the cancer has attacked his bones. Meanwhile, make sure he eats well and walks a bit, so that he doesn't loose the strength of his muscles. He will need a wheelchair soon. I will put you in contact with a palliative center—"

"That's out of the question! I will take care of him, to his last day!"

"It will be difficult. As the sickness progresses, he will lose the sense of taste, he won't be able to swallow, to breathe properly. When the brain is attacked, he may become paranoiac. You'd better get in touch with your local CLSC for advice now so that they can help you when you need it."

"What's all the fuss about?" asked Father, pointing to the X-rays on the X-ray reader. "If they are puzzled about the shadows on my lungs, they shouldn't bother. Those are scars from a double pneumonia I had when I was young."

Indeed, Father did pride himself of never being sick, except for a typhus epidemic and pneumonia in his youth. He claimed that the whole glass of olive oil he had to drink every day for tasting – he was an olive oil expert – kept him in excellent health.

"Well the doctor thinks you have double pneumonia now," I tell him in a loud voice, facing him. Then I write down on my pad: "They will have to do some tests so they can give you the right medicine. The doctor says, because you were a heavy smoker all your life, it may take some time to cure. I assured him you have an excellent constitution. He also wants to be assured you have no osteoporosis, so they will check your bones to make sure you do not need any treatment."

"Hospitals! They just want to create tests for nothing. To milk the Government!"

Once home, I fell on my knees in front of the miraculous icon of the Madonna and Child, the only icon I had brought with me from Istanbul. I shook with silent sobs. I prayed that either the diagnosis was wrong or, if that was to be Stavros' destiny, at least that he not suffer any of the unbearable physical pain associated with cancer.

I got a second opinion, from the Royal Victoria Hospital. Exactly the same diagnosis. The tests showed no attack on the bones. They prescribed *Ensure* (supplement) to mix with his food to keep him stronger. Dr. Balfour Mount, from the Palliative Center, came to our home to make sure our premises would be adequate for Stavros' well being. They were. He said a woman doctor would visit Father once a week and report to him. I was grateful that he went along with my plan of keeping silent about the cancer – after also trying to dissuade me. Dr. Mount was an impressive man, tall, slim, with grey hair, handsome. He was kind, chatted to Father, and was supportive. When Father asked him when he would be completely cured, the doctor squeezed his hand and said: "We don't know. It will depend on your body. You are not very young, you know, and your lungs are not very strong. We will take it one day at a time. Just try to eat well, take your medicine, and rest." I found him humane.

That was three weeks ago. I resigned my position as treasurer and executive secretary of my husband's engineering office, found a good secretary to replace me, and dedicated all my efforts to my father's happiness.

We took him with us whenever we went out, arranged a decoder for deaf persons on our TV, and I cooked all the dishes he liked. Our youngest daughter, Kathy, was kind and cheerful with him. Our eldest one, Gabriella, sent him little notes and postcards from Toronto where she was working in a dream position with City Bank – recruited as soon as she graduated from the University of Western Ontario.

That Sunday, we went to the afternoon dance of the Greeks Association from Constantinople (Istanbul).

"Please, let us have the best table so that my father can enjoy the Greek dances and see everyone. He has cancer and only a few months to live. I don't know if we can even make it to the next gathering," I said to Stavros Torossis, the Association president.

He looked at me with pain in his eyes, squeezed my arm, and disappeared.

Within a few minutes, the best table in front of the dance floor was arranged and everybody began to come over, pouring love and joy over my father:

"Stavros! How nice to see you! You look great!"

I went to the washroom to hide and cry with mixed feelings of despair and gratitude. When I managed to compose myself and return to the dance hall, I saw my father laughing heartily, his eyes sparkling with pleasure. I saw him clap with enthusiasm at the Greek dances. And I saw him in a deep political discussion with Anghelos Kyriou and his wife Nenna, active members of our Association. Later, Anghelos approached me with his project: he wanted to create an archive of the memories of all the Greeks from Istanbul. Could I help? Could I gather mementos, call members? Could I note down and record their reminiscences? I said I would think about it.

Once home, I thought how this project could help my father by keeping him immersed in his memories instead of living his day by day deterioration. So I jumped ahead and presented the project to my Father as a direct request from Anghelos.

"Anghelos says that you are a living encyclopedia of the *Romiossini* – of the Greeks of Constantinople," – I told him. I explained that Anghelos wanted him to record his memoirs of Istanbul for the Association's archives, for our children, and as one of a series of research articles to be published in our newsletter. Besides, the articles would be precious for our family, I added. Stavros agreed to do it.

II – Stavros' Parents & His Youth

"*H*is gaze was riveted on her, mesmerized. Small, thin, fragile like a porcelain doll, skin all white and pink, she was leading the dance. They were all young, festive in their elaborate white national Albanian costume – traditional *foustanella* kilt for men, and long dark skirts with white embroidered aprons and blouses for women, worn for the Easter Feast. Unable to control his urge, Anghelis stepped in, breaking the line just beside her. She barely reached his shoulder. She flashed him a wide smile and handed him her kerchief. He held it tight as she twisted and whirled, jumped and stamped her feet in the frenetic steps. She was flying and Anghelis was flying with her, his steady hand supporting her with the now twisted kerchief. Her long golden braid running down to her waist followed the sway of her body. When the flute, the mandolin-like *lahuta*, the violin and the drum stopped playing, Anghelis bowed to her:

'My name is Anghelis', he said.

'Neranzo!' Bitter Lemon, she replied laconically.

Her blue eyes were smiling, but her sensual lips remained mute as she examined him seriously.

His Macedonian-Thracian outfit of shalvar trousers, vest and boots, all black except for his white shirt, identified Anghelis as an outsider. He did not wear the traditional black head-gear and his wavy black hair adorned his stern oval face. His skin was sun-darkened from working in the fields and orchards; his black eyes were tender. A curly moustache covered his thin lips.

He followed her through the church plaza to some long side-tables set for the Easter *Aghapi* lunch. The smell of roasting lamb and *maghiritsa* soup filled the air amid shouts of *'Hristos Anesti! Alithos Anesti!'* (Christ is risen! Truthfully resurrected!). The villagers knocked red-dyed eggs together, to see whose egg would not crack – and be the lucky one.

Neranzo gestured to him to join the table, but Anghelis, realizing that he did not speak Arvanitika, the Greek-Albanian dialect, and that she obviously did not speak Greek, bowed again and moved away. He sat at the head table, beside his uncle, the Bishop of Ilioupolis who had been invited by the local priests to celebrate the Easter Sunday Mass and had asked Anghelis to accompany him.

'I want this girl,' he announced to his uncle.

'Her name is Neranzo. You must ask her hand from her father for me.'

The Bishop looked at Anghelis, flabbergasted.

'Are you crazy, or what? You've just met her. I don't even know who her father is.'

'Well, find out. You are the Bishop!'

'And do you expect her father to agree to give his daughter away, just like that?'

'He should feel honoured, if the Bishop asks him to. I just want her, no dowry or anything. I have a good orchard. You know how hard I work. I am a good man. I will make her happy.'

The Bishop shook his head in doubt. 'It's not so simple. And we don't even know if she wants you!'

'I am sure she does!'

'Well, we'll see. I will try.'

She did. And her father agreed. The Bishop betrothed them the same afternoon. Two days later Neranzo left Altintash, her Greek-Albanian village where her parents and friends had immigrated from Albania years and years ago, and followed her groom across the border to Eastern Macedonia-and-Thrace, to close-by Maltepe and Keshan, her new homeland, her new town. She brought with her only a *bohtcha*, a clothes' bundle, and the golden coin necklace that she had been wearing at the dance."

Stavros was smiling mischievously, happy, lost in the memory of his father recounting with pride how he had married Neranzo in two days.

I looked at him, content. I did not want to break the spell…

After a while I asked. "Well, how did they communicate? They didn't speak each other's language or dialect."

"Love doesn't need a language. Doesn't need words, my child!"

"How old were they?"

"My father must have been in his mid-thirties. And my mother about in her mid-twenties. She was not very beautiful, but she was striking."

***

Yes, Neranzo must have been striking in her youth. And she must have been respected too. I was about five when Father used to bring me to visit her on weekends at Skoutari, modern Üsküdar, on the Asiatic Coast of Istanbul.

I was impressed by how everybody loved her and was striving to help her. She no longer used her Arvanitika dialect. She spoke only Greek in a mainly Turkish-speaking neighbourhood. Anghelis had passed away by then – a faint shadow to me – and Neranzo was wearing her widow's black from head to toe. Her long braid was coiled in a crown around her head, emerging like glistening yellow corn silk through her black *fakioli* tied in a knot on top. Her piercing blue eyes still knew how to smile.

She lived in a ground floor room in a grey wooden Turkish-style house, just across from the great forest that covered the hill of Skoutari sloping down to Kouzgoundjouk. There was a marble floor on the mezzanine. The kitchen at the back led to a small courtyard where the Armenian landlady kept two goats. Beside the kitchen was a typical Turkish toilet with a hole in the floor, high wooden sandals on each side, a small tap for washing and towelettes on a nail. An intricately carved balcony extended around the second floor with wooden-grilled narrow windows.

Neranzo's small room had two cots separated by a handmade black and white *kilim* that she had knitted, a rough walnut dresser with a closed cupboard on top, where she kept a few dishes, mugs, cutlery, sugar and coffee. On the dresser lay a small mirror, a pewter pot and a *djezveh*, the small brass Turkish coffee pot with a long handle. A small brazier, a *manghal*, that she

moved outside every night (covered with a bronze round *tabla* whenever lit with coals), an oil lamp and a bronze candle holder both arranged on the window sill and a single wooden chair completed her furniture. An open wire-meshed *fanari* hung outside her room in the dark corridor. It held butter, white cheese, and smelly treasures like salami and *pastourma*. We both loved these dark, thin dry meat slivers spiced with garlic and red pepper in a buttered toast sandwich. Her neighbours must have done her shopping as there were no shops in sight for a very, very long distance.

Her room smelled of fresh ground coffee, and spices like cumin, cinnamon, mahlep and clove powder. Every morning she would grind her own coffee from the roasted coffee beans kept in a wooden box that was impregnated with their aroma, and would make coffee for two. She would pour a small demitasse of coffee – a delicacy that Mother forbade me to touch – into a large bowl of hot fresh goat's milk for me while I was toasting two slices of bread skewed on knives over the red coals of the brazier. We would then spread fresh butter on each toast, mine sprinkled with sugar, and eat it with creamy white cheese. At night, I loved to undo her braids and comb her thin hair with a square ivory comb, feeling its silkiness in my small palms, as she sang to me old ballads about Albanian heroes and heroines. In the afternoons, she would often put her chair by the porch and knit or spin wool. Neighbours, especially Muslims, provided a steady supply of sheep wool and Neranzo was always busy knitting or spinning. I tried my hand at both. I was not good at spinning uniformly but I learned how to knit a scarf at a very young age.

I loved my visits with my Yaya Neranzo. I was lonely and bored in our two-room Istanbul apartment; my mother was too protective of me and did not allow me to play on the street with the neighbouring Greek and Turkish children. I wonder now how she would have felt if she had known the freedom Neranzo used to grant me.

For starters I played outside all day, around the tall oak tree, on the chamomile grass. I played with Arminé, the landlady's ten year-old daughter. Arminé taught me how to catch ladybugs and silk worms in the mulberry trees and keep them in a glass jar, its metal-cover pierced with a nail and filled with mulberry leaves. I would watch them through the glass. She also taught me how to tie a thread to a golden beetle, keep "him" in a jar or in a pierced matchbox, and take "him" out at will to make "him" fly buzzing around us. When Neranzo saw the matchbox with the beetle inside she exploded. How could I be so cruel? The "animal" would die in there. It had holes to breathe through? Nonsense! What about the thread around its body? How would I feel if they tied a rope beneath my armpits and whirled me in the air for amusement? And then threw me in a tight prison! Hein? With tears in my eyes I held out my matchbox to her. She cut the beetle's thread with her nail scissors and we let the "animal" fly free. So much for my first domesticated "animal".

On some sunny days, Neranzo would send me to the forest with an extra-large napkin, its four coins tied in each corner to form a basket, to gather pine cones for her laundry fire. "No farther than two lengths of goats," she would admonish, because wolves roamed deeper in the forest. They were afraid to come closer because of the men, but if I were to advance further… "I don't want you to become their lunch!" she would say, frowning, shaking her index finger.

I would go into the forest, a few meters beyond the allowed boundary, my heart pounding. Often the silence and calm would alleviate my fear and I would sit on the soft pine needles below an umbrella-pine tree, slowly eating the soft pungent pine seeds from the fallen cones around me, putting the dry cones in my "basket" while studying the magic life of the forest. The small birds flitting around me: brown, grey, yellow and the ones that had a red or red-and-black chest. Listening to their songs and their duets. Gathering wild daisies. Smelling the resin of the pines and the balsam of strange trees. Playing with the ladybugs so soft on my skin. Never able to catch the yellow and white and orange butterflies in their dance. Nor the squirrels in their frantic plays.

Once I dared advance further, attracted by the shimmer of the Bosphorus Sea beyond the trees and the faint sounds of busy Kouzgoundjouk, the city lying downhill. I got lost! Could not trace my steps back. I must have fallen asleep. I woke up in the strong arms of Gregory, the neighbour's son, who put me gently on Yaya's bed, under the lighted oil lamp. Neranzo did not scold me. But that was the end of my errands in the forest.

"What a couple they must have made!"

Father's voice brought me back to the present. "Albanian and Thracian! Both bold, both opinionated, strong, tireless and courageous. Albanians descend from the Illyrians, you know, in the Balkans: Epirotes. They say that Constantine the Great and Justinian I were both Illyrians. Albanians were fearless. They were recruited as mercenaries by the Ottomans (some vizirs were Albanian, like Köprülü) and they fought in the Greek resistance of 1821."

"Mother Theresa is Albanian too," I said.

"Who? Well… As for my father, he was originally from Uzunköprü, part of Adrianopolis – city of Adrien – modern day Edirne. It was close to Didimoticho in Eastern Macedonia and Thrace. Thracians too were brave warriors. They took part in the Trojan War. Their emblem was a dragon. They also fought beside Alexander the Great, you know, and fought as mercenaries with Romans and Gauls as well. They say that Byzas – the founder of the city of Byzantium on which Constantine built his empire – was also a Thracian."

Cough… Stavros got excited every time he talked "history".

"So, where were we?"

"At your grandpa."

"Ah, yes. My Papou Antonis was from Uzunköprü. He had nine children, all boys. Barba Ilias, my uncle, was the eldest and the closest to us. He was illiterate. Didn't go to school. But he was imbued with love for people. By now they were established more towards the south, to Keshan, where the land was more fertile. We had a large orchard there..."

Stopped again. He took long pauses to calm his coughing and his breathing. And a few sips of the now cold tea... I respected these breaks and watched, with delight, his eyes sparkle in spite of his physical discomfort.

"When did you move from Eastern Thrace to Istanbul?" I wrote on my pad, after a while.

He took the pen from my hands and scribbled on my pad:

"Maltepé, the village where I was born, is situated on a hill on the road that we called Susa. Susa links Keshan to Uzunköprü, the borough to which we legally belonged and which had a railway station. I was born August 18, 1904, and left for Istanbul with my mother in 1909. My father was already in Istanbul, in Skoutari, working as a market gardener at Bahtchivan Niko. He only came to Uzunköprü during the summers, to spend a couple of months with us...

"So... I was playing on our threshing-floor one day, when my cousin Hristos arrived from Karadjahali... In fifteen minutes we were in the horse carriage and on the road to Karadjahali. At midnight, in a rough *araba* horse-carriage and with another youngster, Luluri, we went through Thimiki (?) and we arrived at Kalivia where we stopped. There is ... the Kaliviotissa (a song)... and on the top of the hill there is the church of St. George. The famous Kalivia feast was on. During the whole night there was music and dancing. Hristos led the street dance... I still remember the tune ..."

Stavros hums it...

"In the morning, Hristos borrowed for us the covered payton from the Bishop of Iraklias who was staying at Kalivia for the feast. And towards night we arrived at Rekdeköy [unreadable]. My uncle Ilias, had given me a *pipinghi*, a whistle, during another Thracian feast from Loutza. Now I had also a harmonica from Kalivia..."

Father handed me back my pad. Then he cleared his throat and narrated:

"We boarded a ferry boat. I had never seen the sea before. At first, I thought it was a large river or lake until I realized its vastness... I was overwhelmed. And when we arrived at the Port of Istanbul I was stunned by all the buildings, the skyline with the tall minarets, Süleymaniye, Haghia Sophia... I was in awe. Bewitched... We transferred to another boat and crossed over to Skoutari, to the Asiatic coast."

Stavros said he was born in 1904. [His Turkish birth certificate stated 1910.

He had told me once that they had declared a later birthday to the authorities to avoid his being recruited for military service]. So they arrived in Istanbul in 1909, a couple of years before the first Balkan Wars of 1912-1913.

"Where did you stay at Skoutari? Do you remember?"

"At Fistik-Aghatchi which means Pine Tree, and Bülbül Yuvasi (Nightingale Nest), near Dar Hamam, in a wooden house."

"When and where did you go to school?"

"I arrived at Skoutari, in 1909. My cousin George was very literate. He taught me how to read and write. So when I went to school at Skoutari Primary, in 1910, I skipped from grade one right to grade two. I stayed there until grade seven. So, then, I went to the National Gymnasium of Hadji-Hristou in the City of Istanbul – which later became the Tarsis Varidou school that you attended. I could not afford to buy books, so I would borrow them from my classmates just before exams and study them till the wee hours of the night under the light of the oil lamp, or even by the heat of the oven at the bakery whose books I kept. And I was getting the highest marks. I met all my friends there… My best friend Iosiph Polychronidis and his brother Nikos… I met them in 1910 at the school. As soon as I arrived…"

He coughs. Pauses, then goes on.

"We remained friends till I left Istanbul for Canada. Their wooden house was close to the Jewish cemetery. Iosiph played the mandolin then (later he played the violin) and his brother Nikos had a striking baritone voice. Nikos worked at first at Nikolopoulos, then he continued his studies at the Saint-Joseph French School… Iosiph went to the French Business School of Galata, called the Arab's School. There was also Iraklis Katsinopoulos. His sister Eleni had a beautiful voice, she sang in the *Tetraphonia* (Quartor Choir). And also Stefos Papadopoulos – Julia Inglesis' father (Julia, Kathy's godmother). After the Skoutari school, Stefos continued to the Megali tou Genous Sholi. He was three grades ahead of me... I was in grade three, he was in grade six. There was also Ilias Orfanidis. A genius! He went to the Language School. [Hadji-Hristou?] However, I did not finish the Gymnasium. I still had one year to finish it… "

"Why?"

"Why? Because I had broken my leg and could not travel from Skoutari to Poli (City, for Constantinople) every day. I also needed to work… My father could not work any more…"

Stavros took a long pause to control his wheezing. I gave him a cough drop. He kept it in his mouth. When he could control his breathing better he started talking again in a softer voice.

"There was this great fire in 1920. We were living in a two-story wooden house. It had a well. The house caught on fire and my mother saved it by going up to the roof and pouring water that she drew from the well over the fire ... It was a blessed well. Around the orchard we used to have a wall but the Italians had taken it down as they were going to build street-car tracks up to Tchamlidja (Çamlica) hill. So my father used to sleep down there so that thieves would be discouraged from entering the orchard.

"Then, one night he hears... a voice: 'Angheli! Angheli!' Second night the same. Third night again... He asks: 'Who are you?' The voice answers, 'I am St. John' and a hand points to the well.

"My father describes the dream to the Bishop of Chalkidonos. The bishop advises him to put an icon of St. John and a votive candle by the well... You see, our well was linked, underground, with the well of St. John of Passalimani. So then, the night of the fire, the Aliens' Fleet was in the Bosphorus. And they even got out and tried to help put the fire out..."

"How did the fire start?"

"How did it start? An Armenian woman was frying eggplants. Her wooden house caught on fire. Then the wind pushed the flames down to Dar Hamam. From Dar Hamam the fire spread to the Police Station, then to Havra (Synagogue), then to the grocery shop and to the beautiful Jewish houses. They all burned down. My mother invited all the Jews to come and sleep in our orchard – it was very large – while the fire spread towards Selamsiz. It was stopped by the high walls of Surp-Agop, the Armenian Church. Otherwise all Yeni Mahallé would have burned because of the strong wind... I was working as a secretary at Zahariadis then – I had quit school in 1919. So when I saw the flames leaping in the sky, I said: Hey! What's happening? But I knew the orchard would withstand... It was very big. But anyway I went to see with my own eyes before being reassured... So, Neranzo had offered a very helping hand..."

"So you quit school in 1919. What about the Sorbonne Scholarship?"

"That's another thing. It came later, when I had left school and was working as a secretary at a bakery, at Dimitri Nikolaïdis. I was also doing literary works and translations on the side. After I had done a critical analysis of the writings of St. John Chrysostome, an archimandrite from Makrohori, now Bakirköy, offered me Homer's *Iliad and Odyssey* as a gift, and I translated it into French. The principal of the Military High School appreciated my efforts and offered me the Sorbonne scholarship in 1924."

"Oh, Hadji-Hristou was also a Military School?"

"Yes. Partly."

"Was it linked to Greece's Sholi Evelpidon? The School of Military Recruits?"

"Yes, if you wanted to go there… It was not obligatory. But here (at Hadji-Hristou) they favoured those willing to go to Athens, to Sholi Evelpidon. They were preparing officers for the Greek Army. Polyris, the chief of the Greek army, and Tsigantides, were at my school. As well as George Iordanidis, the Chief of Military Staff. When he visited Istanbul as a Military Attaché, he went back to our school, visited his classroom and looked at his desk where he had carved in Greek, 'George Iordanidis'…"

"Really?"

"Sure! But the Greek (lessons) of Hadji-Hristou were much superior to those of the Megali tou Genous Sholi, the High School of the Nation. Because ours was a private school, expensive, and had better teachers. Since they got paid better… It was my godfather, Ilioupoleos, the Bishop, who had enrolled me there and was overseeing my studies. So, to cut it short, the principal of the Military School Branch of the Hadji-Hristou Gymnasium, Alexandros Papadopoulos, was a former classmate and friend of President Romeo Point-carré of France. That's how he came to offer me the scholarship."

"What happened, then?"

"What did you expect to happen? My father could not work any more. Both my parents spoke only Greek. When, all proud, I announced the scholarship to my father, he stayed silent. Then he bent his head. 'Where are you going to leave us, Stavri?' he asked, as he used to call me. 'What will happen to us?' he whispered. So I had to turn it down. It was the only right thing to do…"

A pity! I wondered what would have become of him if he had gone to the Sorbonne…

I wanted to clarify one more thing: "Let me understand this. The National Gymnasium of Hadji-Hristou was a kind of college with a Military School and a Language School as well, right?"

"Right."

"And it was the same building housing Tarsis Varidou, the private Greek school that I attended?"

"Right."

"What a coincidence…"

Stavros started to cough bad again. He spat some phlegm on a tissue paper that he folded and refolded into a small square…

"You are tired, Father. Let's continue tomorrow... I'll go and cook supper now..."

He nodded. Patted my hand as if to thank me. Then rested his head on the neck-cushion and squinted at the pink glowing sundown through the garden trees... But his mind was traveling back to his youth...

III- KATINA

We have just enjoyed a perfect weekend.

Gaby's college sweetheart, Chris, drove from Toronto to Montreal to see his parents and she came with him. They arrived late Saturday night. Gaby ran to her Papou and Chris had a long chat with him about their life in Toronto. Stavros has always been excited about cities and places new to him. He likes changes and challenges.

Sunday we went to the psarotaverna *Molivos* for lunch. Gaby had missed good Montreal Greek food. It was a gorgeous, crisp, sunny day. We convinced Father to join us, for Gaby's sake.

Gaby and Kathy helped him up the restaurant stairs. Once inside, he sat with pleasure at the head of the table, beside the window. The blue and white checkered table cloths, the white-washed walls, the green plants, the Greek village artifacts and the silver-covered St. Nicholas icon by a lighted votive lamp evoked for him cherished childhood memories. He hardly touched the grilled squid but he enjoyed the boned grilled sea-bass, the *tarama* fish-egg salad and a bite of *lukumathes*, the honey fried small dumplings. After a sip of straight ouzo, he added some ice cubes to it, for the first time in his life…

"Welcome to my club!" I said jokingly, clinking my narrow glass with his now milky one. He waved his hand and made a funny grimace… He looked happy, content. For Gaby, he wore his hearing aid. So when the Greek owner, who was from Imvroz island – now belonging to Turkey – put on some recorded Turkish songs, especially for us the Polites, (modern Constantinopolitans), Stavros smiled, amused. We had a wonderful time.

Sunday evening the house was filled with Gaby's friends: Monique, Karen and Tracey, her high school classmates, and Paule and Rachel, the next door neighbours she grew up with. It was all lively talk, bright laughter and friendly noise. And everybody went to say "Hi" to Papou. Like the good old times…

Chris came to pick up Gaby next morning.

Now, in the early afternoon, the house was silent again. The sun was hidden behind low grey clouds. Stavros was gloomy, watching the monotonous, drizzling rain. "The fun is finished," he said, with regret. "It was good as long as it lasted…"

"You miss Gaby…"

"Yes… With this job in Toronto and Chris there too, she will never come back to Montreal."

"She will. She will come to visit. And she will be here for New Year's Eve. We always celebrate it all together."

"Christmas! New Year's Eve! … Chris is a nice guy. Clean, sincere. I like him. When are they getting engaged?"

"Oh, they're still young. Just out of university and starting promising jobs. They're not ready to get married… Give them some time."

Stavros sighed. He adored his granddaughters. When they were small, he took them to preschool, then to primary school across the park, and picked them up every single day. Even when he worked for Peter's, the owner of the neighbourhood eatery by Steinberg, in the small mall. He would open the restaurant at 7 in the morning, then walk home to take the girls to school at 8:30, and afterwards walk back to the restaurant. And when they grew up a little and were embarrassed by his watchful presence, – "We're not babies any more!" – he would let them walk ten meters ahead of him. He had never let them out of his sight. He spoiled them every month with generous handfuls of pocket money – in spite of my protests. And now I've started doing the same thing with my grandchildren! He even wrote a touching article in our Association's newsletter (of the Greeks from Constantinople) about them: "*Which of the two*?" In it he wondered whether he preferred the strong and independent "blacky one", Gaby, with her thick straight black hair, or the sweet "golden chestnut one", Kathy, who then had curly chestnut locks with golden sun streaks… He concluded that he loved them both the same…

Stavros coughs hard. "This syrup of yours is for the birds! It's doing nothing."

The sentence is like a leitmotif for him. He uses it often when a fit of coughing hits him...

"Do you want a Spider?" I ask, trying to cheer him up. *Give him anything he wants… Spoil him. Let him enjoy every moment he has.*

"A Spider?"

"Yes!" I write for him, "You still like it, don't you?"

His eyes light up. "Sure. But… Do you have vodka?"

"*Smirnoff*! Your favourite."

"But, you don't have Crème-de-menthe—"

"I think I do. Let me check."

"If you do, two shots of vodka, one of Crème-de-menthe."

"On the dot!"

I prepared his beloved Spider cocktail. He used to have it every evening on his way home, at the *Degustation* bar in the Flower Passage of Pera, Istanbul's main street. And he had taught the barman of *Top-of-the-Mast*, in Fort Myers Beach, how to prepare it. Tony, the barman, used to call the concoction "Spider".

"Here!" I say, putting the cocktail glass in his hand and placing a small bowl of ice cubes with a pair of ice tongs on the side table.

"Thanks. It's still dark grey and raining harder," he says glancing at the garden. The sound of the heavy rain drops is amplified by the metal fire-place hood. Stavros takes a small sip of the cocktail and smacks his lips, savouring its sweet burning taste. Without a word, he picks up the tongs and adds two ice cubes to his glass.

I put my arms around his neck. He pats my hand.

"Let's bring the sunshine in," I write, sitting beside him with my tape recorder and my note pad. "Let's talk about Mama. When and how you met her," I add, as I hand him his hearing-aid. He puts it on, without protesting.

"Katina? You never asked me that, before, my child…" He laughs. "I met her in 1925... I was going out with a girl then, a fisherman's daughter, Angheliki. She loved me and wanted to have me around... She did not want to get serious, wanted no betrothal. But me... I have an old-fashioned head. When I want a girl, I don't want her to... I mean, I have to marry her first. But she kept telling me: 'Why bother? What do we need betrothal and marriage for?' Anyway..."

He taps the armrest of his chair with three fingers and squints his eyes...

"One day we were partying with my friends, Joseph Kolassis – a great violin! He was the uncle of George Iordannidis, from Samsun – and, say what was his name? my friend Yannis Koukkidis, myself and another guy, Savvas Iliadis. It was the end of a hot day... don't remember the month... On Prinkipo Island. We were partying at the open air *Christos Café*, you know, the one by the clearing in the pine forest at the foot of the mountain that has the St. George monastery at the top... Suddenly, we hear this divine voice, coming from above, from far away... from the top of the mountain... So, then... we all decided to find out to whom this voice belonged... Because, you see, we were all musicians... We breathed with music... I played the violin then... So we walked up the steep gravel road...

"It was pleasant, you know, the uphill pathway road... as you walk, you brush past vigorous fragrant bushes, mountain tea... pine resin... and *karabas*, and a kind of musk. As you climb up you get a bird's eye view of the sea on your right, with the islands spread out below... It was sundown... The sea was changing colour, foaming at the shores. The sky was getting darker... The air was misty, hazy... as if clad in a purple veil... And there, near *Krimnos* – the Precipice – we came to the open air café, by the monastery... And the Voice soared in the plaintive notes of a sad song. So then, I approached ... There were three girls. Evghenoula, her sister Marika and your Mama.

"'Who is this girl singing' I asked the taller woman of the group.

"'O *Akidés*!' – The Candy – answered Marika with a smile.

"The girl was really sweet like candy. Katina was her name. Dark hair, dark eyes. She was small... In fact everything about her was small..."

I see Katina in the steamy Galatasaray *hamam* during our weekly visit to this Turkish bath. Seated on a wooden stool, she leans forward to wash my hair, with a lavender-lemon square of pure oil soap. *Komili.* I am sitting on the raised hot marble floor, beside the marble basin in the wall niche, breathing in the heavy soap-smelling air and listening to the sounds echoing around the white marble walls. Shafts of light pour in from the hamam dome's small polygonal windows... Mama pours a *tas*, a large bronze sauce-cup, of hot water on my hair, rubs it with soap and lathers it.

Indeed, as Father said, everything about Katina is small. Smaller in height than the other naked women around us, small feet, small fairy hands, small erect breasts, small ears, small mouth with wavy lips, small perfect teeth flashing a luminous smile, small arched eyebrows that look pencilled – though they are not… But her fiery, black, almond shaped eyes are huge. She has straight jet-black hair that she puts in clips every night to make it wavy, sculpted arms and legs, a narrow waist, pink-pearl smooth skin, *balik eti* – or fish-flesh as they call it in Turkish – not skinny, not fat, just right.

Later, I move beside her onto the large octagonal marble massage slab. The *hamamdji*, the bath attendant, a plump middle-aged smiling woman, her black hair pulled back, her full breasts bare, her belly and thighs covered in a multi-coloured sarong, helps my mother lie on her stomach. I wonder at the black noodles coming out of her skin under the *hamamdji*'s vigorous scrubbing with a *kessé*, a horse-hair glove. Mama had just washed herself with soap! Now the attendant washes her again in a foamy lather and rinses her with hot water from a *tas*. I also get a *kessé* on my thin legs and arms and I feel embarrassed, especially because of the gaze of the little boys – Friday mornings are for women only (evenings are for men) but boys below ten or twelve can accompany their mother.

I feel grown up as I put on my small high wooden sandals, rented for the day to protect our feet from the scorching heat coming from the marble floors. Then I follow Katina in the tepid room where she spreads a turquoise hair remover cream, called *hala*, on her legs and armpits. She still has her pubic hair. Turkish women put *hala* all over their bodies, including their private parts… After about fifteen minutes and a wash, we are back at the steamy center room for a final soap wash and rinse.

Wrapped in our thick red-orange-white striped *peshtemals* (bathrobes) and teetering on our high wooden sandals, we walk out to the cool marble hall. Another attendant, also in a multicoloured sarong, breasts naked, hair hidden in a turban, comes to open our wooden cabin with her long iron key. We sit on the narrow black leather *minder* and Mama dries me and gives me a vigorous massage with *Pereja* lemon cologne, 'to close the pores'. We nibble at sweet sesame sticks and drink *Gazoz*, a kind of *Seven-Up*, to replenish the loss of liquids during the hot steam of the baths. Then we change into fresh sun-smelling clothes.

Once outside, all pink and invigorated, we stop for lunch at a *malébidji*, a pudding restaurant – I never understood why it was called "pudding" since *malébidjis* also used to serve chicken. We have chicken-noodle soup with wedges of lemon, followed by shredded chicken on rice, and for dessert vanilla and blueberry ice cream for me – I like the small square or triangular spoons it is served with – and for Mama *dondurmali tavuk-gögsu*, a pudding made with shredded chicken and milk and served with vanilla ice-cream… Delicious! How I cherished my Friday outings with my mother! …

"And her voice! What a voice! Divine! Difficult to describe it… Crystal clear and so unusual… A mezzo soprano, yet a mixture of Martha Eghert and Ima Sumah. She was reaching both very high Mi and very low notes… And so moving…" says Stavros. He seems to be dreaming backwards.

Moving, yes. I remember my mother singing when I was young. The crystals stirred in the chandeliers and the window panes shrieked… And I watched people cry listening to her. It reminds me now of Nana Moushouri. Katina reached a higher pitch but her voice was as touching…

"Really moving…" continues Stavros, his eyes closed, the tapping on the arm-rest continuing. "She was hurting… She was wounded… Tears glistened in her eyes… I found out she had just broken up with her fiancé, Zacharias. This guy… was a dance teacher in the dance-parlour Katina attended. Evghenoula, her best friend, Genny as she was called, told me later that Zach was ten years older than your Mama. An elegant and smooth talking dandy. He attracted women like honey. He knew he couldn't get this fierce and spirited young girl so he proposed to her… with a diamond ring and all… So, dazzled and naïve, Katina accepted. She believed in his pledge of eternal love and faithfulness. But some 'good willing' friends reported to her that he had been seen with another woman. Your Mama could not accept disloyalty. So, with the help of Genny, she set a trap for him, arranging a meeting between him and Genny in front of the Post-Office… At Galata Saray… So, then, at the specified day and time, as Zach was slipping his arm around Genny's waist, Katina jumped from a street car in front of them. She slapped him in the face, spat on him, and threw her engagement ring at him… She was very hurt… She would never forgive this second betrayal by a person she loved and trusted… "

"Why second betrayal? When was the first?"

"The first? It was by her own mother. When she was a little girl. Her mother took her out of school and put her to work so that her small income would help educate her half-brothers in Italy… "

It came back to me now. Katina only half-talked about it when I was young.

She would only say that she was pulled out of primary school and thrown into work: "That's why I want you to complete your education. Education is everything in life." It was in Katina's character to lick her wounds, bury her secrets and not to say a word about those who hurt her…

It was a few years before she died that Katina talked about it again. She had just received a letter from an elderly cousin, Eleni Paleologou, now living in Athens. This letter opened old wounds, the troubling event resurfaced for her and she told me the whole story. "My sister, Katina. I will have to reveal to you a secret about your birth before I leave this world…" said the letter. But Eleni died of a heart attack before revealing the secret. Her daughter, Eleni Marouli, did not know anything about it, but had sent the letter figuring it would be important for Katina… Now Katina was putting together pieces of the puzzle, beginning to understand. She was only nine, at the head of her class and the pride of her teachers, when one day, as she returned home from school, she found her mother, Frasie, crouched in a chair, her face covered with tears. After her first husband, Leo, died, Frasie had married a widower, Anghelis. She had two sons from Leo, Mario and Bruno, who were kept in Italy, by her dead-husband's family and were raised in Florence, while Frasie kept the younger Katina with her. The relatives were poor, so they asked Frasie (now called Frosso) to contribute towards the boys' education, as if the fact that she had remarried had made her rich.

"Your brothers in Italy need money to go to school. You know, boys need an education to survive in life. Girls can do without it. Especially you. You are bright enough to make it without schooling," she had tried to explain, to Katina, tears ravaging her face.

So, Katina's meagre pay was to help for the education of these far away "brothers", Mario and Bruno, whom she had never met and never would… Katina had always wandered why Frosso did not take Irini, her older sister from school and send her to work instead of her. Irini was in grade six and a good average student. She would finish primary school in just a few months. So why choose Katina?

From that day onward Katina had difficulty trusting anyone who claimed to love her. She learned to be self-sufficient and resilient and count only on herself for both her physical and spiritual needs. Now the puzzle started to take shape. She was the only black-haired, black-eyed person in the family… Her mother adored her and used to exclaim to her "You are my best child, my darling, you will always have my blessing. May everything you touch turn to gold…" There was an aunt. Mati. Frosso's sister? Eleni Paleologou was Mati's "daughter".

Everyone had died now, even her own sister Irini, and Katina would never get answers to her questions. But she figured out that, as was the custom at the beginning of the century, children of widowed women or men were adopted by family members to lessen the burden for the widowed partner of raising them alone. So, Katina must have been kept by Frosso and Eleni could have been her elder sister adopted by Mati (or was she Anghelis' daughter?). Irini, Katina's older sister, must have been a half-sister, joining them as the daughter of Frosso's second husband Angheli, a shoemaker, who was also widowed. And Marika, her younger sister, must have been her real half sister, born to Frosso and Angheli. Naturally Frosso could not ask Irini, Angheli's daughter, to quit school and go to work to educate boys not related to them... That would also explain Irini's sometimes strange behaviour towards Katina and especially towards their mother... Katina cried, sobbing, seated on the porch stairs, making the letter wet with her tears... She was crying for the bitterness she had felt toward her mother and her fate, for the inexplicable, at times, behaviour of Irini and for Eleni, the sister she never really knew...

"Strange that all three of us had to interrupt our studies and not complete our education to our potential. Mama, at a young tender age, you as a youth and giving up the Sorbonne and me at seventeen, out of sickness, obliged to forfeit my Robert College bursary..."

"But you avenged us, my child. The day I saw you get your degree, *cum laude*, from Concordia University, was the happiest day of my life," said Stavros with pride.

I remember his eyes sparkling with tears as he hugged me after the graduation ceremony. "You made my dream come true! It was as if I received this degree myself... I am so proud of you!" he had said.

It is true that I did it for both my father and my mother. When Katina died, I stayed home for a while to take care of my daughters whom she had been "raising". Then, encouraged by Tito, my extraordinary husband, I went to university. Part time, at the beginning, when the children were at school. Full time later. And I also joined Tito's engineering company, Sysgraph Inc. I juggled office work, home, parenting and schooling. I was realizing not only my own dream but the dreams of my parents too.

"Do you remember the tune of the song Mama was singing on the mountain? The words?"

Stavros nods. "It was the *Kamini*, from the Street Woman of Sakelaridis...

Olympia Kampioti (Kandioti?) made it famous…"

He hums the song, in his now cracked voice:

Whoever has felt the heart bleeding in this liar life
And is suffering in silence,
Let him come and live with me, two coupled,
And let the two sorrows become one…

Tears come to my eyes. The song brings my mother vividly back to life. I have listened to this song many times. I know it. I join Father in a low voice:

A heart, orphaned by love, is like a wilted spring flower,
Like a nightingale that lost its voice,
Like a heavy, heavy clouded sky…
A heart, orphaned by love, is like a deserted, spider-webbed church,
Like a dark night…
And every hope for her is forever lost…

"And this other one", continues Stavros, '*Don't talk to me about him…*' It finishes with '*But… Talk to me about him, now.*'"

He stays silent for a few moments… Recollecting… Savours a sip from his Spider. The rain drops tick… The recorder hisses…

"That night, Yannis asked Marika out, although he was going out with Polykseni… the scoundrel…" – he laughs – "and Evghenoula agreed to go out with Savvas, so I, in spite of myself, had to ask Katina out…"

Yannis a scoundrel? What about you, Father? What about Angheliki?

"So we agreed to go out as three couples and to meet across the Tünnel, the underground... Now, I liked that girl. She was so sweet… I wanted to help her mend her broken heart. Because it seemed that she was still very much in love with Zach… That's how it started… In the meantime, Angheliki's mother investigated me, to find out how much I was earning. I was an oil broker then at the *Ladoskala*, the Oil Market. She asked Dimitros Kondopoulos, another oil-broker – a type! – about me. He told her I could hardly sell an oil barrel a week. So, she doubted that would be enough to guarantee a good living to her daughter."

"When did you start to work as an oil broker in the Oil Market?"

"In 1920. I started at Saïd Isketcheli. I was a broker by 1922 and already an independent broker by 1924. And I remained an oil broker. Saïd wanted me to work for him, to sell his oils. He was ready to top what I was earning. But I refused, I couldn't do it. Because an honest broker cannot offer just any oil to his clients, he has to be choosy. Offer the one that the client likes. Offer the best for the price… Yilmaz also got mad at me because he could not make me work for him. Ktenet the same… But, by now, other oil merchants trusted me. Like Ahmet Güre, Sapoundjighil, Komili… They said, 'Stavros is an international oil broker, he can't cheat.' Even Zarpli, who tried everything to make me a partner or give me a higher commission, which I refused, had to respect me…

"Now then, where were we? When Angheliki came to tell me all that her mother had found out, I cut her out. Tak! Like a knife! What the heck! I never asked her what she did or how she lived! ... So, when I met your Mama, I liked her really a lot… Evghenoula (Genny) later met Dimitro Parlakidis and wed him…"

"I thought you heard Mama's voice for the first time at the foot of Skoutari, at Koushoundjouk, and you walked up through the forest to her…"

"Oooh! That was later, when we were engaged. Then whenever your Mama sang at our forest outings, people would clap their hands down at Koushoundjouk and walk all the way up to us, at Skoutari, to meet her… Our choir master was so impressed by her that he proposed to make her an opera diva if she let him train her…"

"Who? Mazlenikoff?"

"No, Mazlenikoff was the first choir master. The choir started in 1926 and lasted three to four years. We had two masses, you see; a Byzantine one and a Greco-Russian, four-voice one. With many Russian worshippers. The second choir master was Razimovsky. He was the choir master of the Imperial Russian Quator… He was the one who proposed… But your Mama declined. She didn't want all the training and the difficulties and the limelight and the fuss… She was only singing for her own pleasure… Like a nightingale…"

"When did you get engaged?"

"In 1926, October 29th." Stavros laughs. "Funny! I was often wearing the *fez* – the Muslim red cap with the black tassel – in the Oil Market, at Eminönü. You see, we were only two Greek brokers among a Turkish milieu, and the Turks still wore the *fez* in spite of Atatürk's abolition. We didn't want to look different; our livelihood depended on being trusted and accepted as members of the group, so we were also wearing the fez. So when Aghissilaos, Irini's husband, saw me with Katina, he ran to tell her parents that Katina was going out with a Muslim Turk!"

Cough… He laughs again…

"Imagine the turmoil of Frosso and Angheli, your grandparents! They were convinced I was Greek when they met me, but Aghissilaos had doubts that I was not… *veros*, a real Greek. He thought that I would bring for the engagement, a priest from the Papa Eftim Turkish-Greek-Christian sect. So, when he saw me arrive with Papa Georgis, the priest of the nearby St. Constantin Greek Orthodox Church, he was astonished… We had a traditional betrothal with blessings and exchanging of the rings and all… "

He finishes his Spider. Licks his lips to get the last drops. Places the empty glass on the side table.

"It took place at Evghenoula's house. Your Yaya had rented rooms at Evghenoula's mother's, at Tarlabashi, Yeniyol, not far from the church… Evghenoula, Anna and Marika, the three sisters, were daughters of Dimitros and Eleni Hadjiantoniou. Dimitros, their father, had passed away then…"

"My mother's surname was Kalafatidou?"

"Yes. Angheli's parents must have come from Kalafat, though they were originally from the Trabzon seaport on the Black Sea. Your Papou had three sisters. Areti, who had adopted Konstantinia; Frosso, who lived on the outskirts of a *virané* – hill – near our home in Emin Djami. Your aunt Frosso had a daughter, Anna, wed to George Vassiliadis. Anna was the mother of Kostas Vassiliadis, your second cousin, the ping pong champion. The third sister was Terpsi (short for Terpsihori), mother of Iakovos, who lived up the hill, close to the Mosque.

"Your Yaya Frasie, had a sister (?), Mati, mother of Eleni Paleologos. Frosso – as Frasie was known now – was the daughter of Yacumi (or Giacumi or Jacumi, you can't be certain with the Turkish alphabet translation). She was called the Contessa… I don't know why. Her ex-husband was Italian, from the Florentine community in Istanbul. So, Katina, your Mama, had two sisters, Irini, the eldest, and Marika, the youngest. Irini and Marika were both blond but not Katina. Irini later followed her printer husband, Aghissilaos Djallas, to Athens. Your Yaya was very fond of Katina, she was her preferred one. She adored her."

Father falls into silence for a while…

I remember Papou Angheli at his windowless shoemaker shack, up a hill. He was rather short, with sandy blond hair, very blue eyes, a wrinkled round face. Wearing a tan black-stained leather apron, toiling with sharp scalpels on iron shoe moulds, a small portable Singer sewing machine behind him, repaired ordinary shoes resting on a small chest on his right and women's fine laced leather boots lined up on a small shelf on his left. The same dainty boots Mama wore in her childhood photos. He must have made them for her… I loved the smell of fresh leather and shoe wax…And the rhythmical sound of a hammer beating on leather soles clinking against the iron mould. He worked with the door open during the summer, under a naked light bulb in winter.

As for Yaya Frosso, my recollection of her is very vague. I see myself seated beside her on the red-flowered quilt of a large iron bed. Her wavy chestnut hair is spread out on a white lace-bordered pillow, her oval face pale, her lips opened in a faint smile and her right hand making the sign of the cross on my forehead. Katina used to tell me that her mother never kissed her children on the cheek, always on the forehead. And she used to bless them with the sign of the cross. I heard that she was very beautiful. My aunt Marika had told me that I had Frosso's wavy chestnut hair and green eyes…

Stavros bends forward. He smiles…

"We were happy… Despite your Mama's dance escapades… She loved to dance so much that at the end of her work day, at the Haute Couture Atelier, she would return to the dance parlour just for the sheer pleasure of dancing. I admit that I was a bit jealous of Zacharias. I did not want her to see him again. She knew it. So, she tried to hide her escapades. But her red cheeks betrayed her. And I would check her armpits and they were wet from the sweat… So, she couldn't deny it." He laughs, "But she couldn't help herself. Dancing was her passion."

(She passed this love of dance to me and to my daughters… And now to my grand-daughter Caroline, who is studying classical ballet and jazz-ballet.)

"Why didn't you go with her?"

"I couldn't. Impossible timing. Besides, I could never learn... She taught me the Tango and the Slow, but the other ones? No…"

Yes, I was the lucky one. Dancing with my father the Tango and the Slow, at the tea-dance parties or the café-restaurants with a live band or at the "evenings" we were attending, while my mother was swirling on the dance floor with the husbands, the brothers and the fiancés of her friends who knew her passion and obliged because she was such a good dancer... And my father smiling at her with pride and indulgence…

"I was still living in Skoutari… at Baglarbachi, close to Yanni Koukkidis' house and across the Malébathes. I was usually catching the last boat liner to the Bosphorus, at midnight… Hmm… One winter night, I arrive at Köprü, the Galata Bridge, and see no boat. Zilch! And it was raining, and the sea was rough, foaming, with high waves… Now? What do I do? I could walk back to your Mama's house but… my parents… we had no telephone or anything… And on such a night… they would think I drowned or something… They would freak out from panic... So ... I see an old *kayiktchi* near a large row boat. 'Ten liras to take me across,' I offer him. 'You must be mad *oglum*,' he says. 'Twenty liras!' I double. That was a lot, a lot of money, back then... 'Are you a good swimmer, my son?' he asks, studying my face. 'An excellent one,' I reassure him. So... We enter the boat... He was an old sea-wolf... an expert rower. He manages to mount the waves avoiding getting hit on the side... But we are both wet by the waves splashing... The thirty minute crossing takes us a whole two hours... When we finally reach the Asiatic shore, 'You are not going back!' I admonish him. He laughs. 'Not tonight! You bet!'..."

Father eyes are glistening. He plays with his wedding ring...

"My parents were frantic when I arrived home, cold, dead tired and wet. My father gave me two shots of Raki; it is stronger than ouzo, you know. My mother insisted to give me a massage with alcohol and apply six *ventouzes* on my back, to prevent pneumonia, as she said... I hated those sucking-cups with the flaming cotton balls tossed inside! But they worked...

"When I explained my ordeal to Katina the next day, she made me swear that I would not attempt it again, that I would spend the night in their apartment instead and I that should warn my parents not to expect me home on stormy nights... "

Stavros stops for a while, as if searching his memories. His eyes gleam as he resumes:

"Later Iosiph moved to Idjadiyé and we moved also to the house where you were born."

"Across the forest?"

"Yes. It was there that I got the typhus. And my father and my mother got it too. It started a Holy Friday. In 1930. And it lasted forty days for each one of us. Your Mama had to move in with us and nurse all of us... What an ordeal!"

"You were not married yet?"

"No."

"When did you get married?"

"In 1932. The 27th May of 1932, the day the Turks had entered Constantinople. We got the *Nikâh*, the Civil Marriage... I am hungry. Get me something to eat!"

"A snack? *Cheez Whiz*?"

"*Hongroise*!" he corrects me.

I run upstairs, to the kitchen, to make him an open grilled-cheese sandwich with Bulgarian Cheddar, sprinkled with paprika, and a glass of tea sweetened with five spoons of sugar, as he likes it. Hongroise used to be our favourite beer appetizer around the Istanbul's café-bistros – like *Lala*, *Degustation*, or at the Bosphorus, by the sea, with a hot-tea steaming samovar. The smell of the grilled melting cheddar makes my mouth water too...

Stavros savours the sandwich…

"When did you have the religious marriage?" I ask, impatient.

He waves his hand. "Hey! Let me eat first! …"

He finally resumes:

"We got married on the 27th of October, or something, in 1932."

(I checked later on their marriage certificate; it was the 7th of October).

"Why did you have to wait for so long? From your engagement of 1926? Six whole years…"

"We could not afford to get married earlier. We were both working but not making much. Katina was saving for our household and I—"

"You, were rather the spender, weren't you? You loved to spend whatever you earned. I remember when I was young you would blow a month's earnings in one weekend! ..."

Stavros laughs, his eyes sparkle.

"Well, what is life without some pleasure! Especially when you don't indulge often. So some flowers, some sweets, some little luxury for Mama, some books, a trip in the country… you know…"

I know… How many Fridays Father would come home with not one but two huge bunches of flowers, enormous white chrysanthemums or Calla lilies for Mama and daisies or pink carnations for me, *Madeleine* pure dark chocolates and pastries for both of us: triangles of colourful layers of cake enrobed in chocolate for me, chocolate-filled éclairs or mille-feuilles filled with English pastry cream and sprinkled with powdered sugar for Mama.

Whenever Father came into some money he would spoil us with reservations for a threesome weekend at Splendid Palace or the Akasya Hotel in Prinkipo or a boat trip to Shile, by the Black Sea, or an excursion to Florya, with its pink beaches. And he would always bring home a pile of books: Greek mythology for me, Arsène Lupin, or Le Saint, or Agatha Christie stories for him, Greek novels for all – I cherished Stratis Myrivillis; loved his *The Teacher with the Golden Eyes*, tried to emulate his lyrical modern Greek style in my school compositions – Max de Vezit (?) and Delly romances translated in Greek, *Thysavros* and other magazines, for Mama. There were music sheets for his violin, a new silk tie for him, some silk stockings or something for Katina. Not forgetting the lottery tickets. He would not fail to buy lottery tickets till the end of his days, hoping to win the jackpot and offer a dream life to all of us, as he would say as an excuse. It was like Christmas every month.

'Stavro, darling, you shouldn't! We still have the rent to pay and we owe money to the grocery shop…' Mama would protest.

'Next week, I am expecting a big sale and a large commission… You will see. Now, let us enjoy ourselves!'

But the big sale would not materialize and Katina would have to work overtime to pay our debts…

We loved to picnic at Prinkipo with Evghenoula and Anna and their husbands at Hristos or at Saint-George's open-air café-restaurant. Both had only thatch-seat chairs and the men used to arrange two or three chairs in a row for me to have a short nap, or turn a chair upside down to make a back support for stretching out on the pine needles.

Clockwise: Dimitros Parlakidis, Kostas Marinakis, Katina, Evghenoula, Anna, Erato, Stavros.

Stavros, an only child, born late to elderly parents, brought up in poverty and spoiled by his adoring uneducated farmer parents who considered him a godsent gift. Stavros, who was never scolded nor disciplined, was used to getting instant gratification for all his wishes. He was an extreme optimist and romantic, a poet at heart and a fatalist. He believed all his dreams would come true some day even if he did not labour for them. He had no patience. He wanted to live now, enjoy life to the fullest today…

"Anyway… We got married at the Panaghia Church of Pera.

"Your Mama was worried," he continues. 'Well, my Stavro, the church expenses? ...'

"Now, my friend Iosiph was to be the Koumbaros. He was my best friend and he felt he owed me; I was the middle-man and had arranged his marriage to Afro, the sister of Ferit, daughter of Iskender Bey…"

I can see Afro playing the piano for my mother. I enjoyed the music and was mesmerized by the flight of Afro's fingers on the keyboard. I dreamed of being able to play like her some day... I can also see the snail-infested walled courtyard of her parents' wooden house at Bakirköy, when Mama was sewing for the day for the Iskender Bey's household. Inevitably snails were the main course for lunch…

"But at the last minute, Iosiph couldn't come. So he gave fifty liras for me to Kotso Antoniadis, our mutual friend, apologizing and asking me to find another sponsor. I don't hold any grudge, make no fuss. I go and print the invitations. Then I go to work at George Djambazoglou. He tells me, 'Stavro, if you have no sponsor, I would like to be your Koumbaros…' Rich man… 'Thanks', I say, 'but Katina's sister will be the sponsor.' He adds, 'I know you are short of work these days and you'll have expenses. Take these fifty liras, as a gift.'… And so, most of our friends (laugh) also offered money. Very few sent gifts. Your aunt Marika was the Koumbara. The Bishop of Irinoupoleos crowned us."

He must have had an array of bishops in his family!

"There were Evghenoula with her husband, some friends…"

What about Katina's parents?

"My father and my mother were there also…" adds Stavros. "Imagine, Father wanted to light a cigarette, and had no matches. So he went to light his cigarette at the church candles! 'The bastard! It didn't light!' he complained."

Stavros laughs.

"Well, I put them both on the ferry boat for Skoutari and then we went, with your Mama, to celebrate at *Lala*'s. Our friends were all casually dressed. 'Well now,' I say, 'you see Katina? We got married and also had our wedding reception at our favourite restaurant. You worried for nothing.' Then we went to sleep at Evghenoula's where your Yaya (Frosso), Anghelis, Marika and Katina were renting a room. Evghenoula and her husband Dimitro went to sleep downstairs and they gave us their bed for the night. Just like that... Your Mama was expecting you then..."

I frown...

Father is startled by my reaction. "What? You are a married woman now, you understand... Besides, we were officially married already... We had our civil marriage..."

Katina must have really loved him a lot to put up with the shame of being pregnant before being married in the Church – considered the greatest dishonour back in the 1930s. It must have been devastating for her and her family. And to put up with a "borrowed" bed in lieu of a honeymoon!

Afterwards they went to Idjadiyé, Skoutari, at Stavros' parents' rented loft, to start their married life.

IV - Married Life: Katina and Stavros

"So, where was I born?"

"At Idjadiyé. With the help of Gülyan Hanoum, the Armenian land-owner, who was a midwife. Your aunt Marika was there also. Marika and Katina were very close. You were born on the 24th of March, 1933, a Saturday, at four in the morning. It was the Eve of *Evanghelismou*, the Feast of the Annunciation. That's why your Christian name is Evanghelia, which means "Good News". You were baptised at the St. Panteleïmon Church of Koushoundjouk in August, the same year. Your aunt Marika was your *Nouna*, and we named you Evanghelia-Maria Erato. Maria' was added by the priest by mistake. It was your godmother's name – from Marika. And Erato was my choice, the name of the Muse of Love songs... You were the child of a love song..."

Stavros' gaze is veiled... Lost in his memories...

Gülyan Hanoum used to call me *K'z'm,* my daughter – a traditional Turkish appellation for a young girl – when I was visiting Yaya Neranzo. She also called me Totoula, the short form of Eratoula, little Erato, a nickname that stayed with me. I wonder if I called myself Totoula when I was a toddler, unable to pronounce Eratoula. And Father, an admirer of Russian literature and culture, called me Eratoushka at times, and called my mother Katoushka when he was particularly tender with her.

Gülyan Hanoum, as I remember her, was a small woman in her late sixties or early seventies, her curly salt-and-pepper hair in a bun. She wore loose, long, gathered brown skirts, always covered with a white apron, and long-sleeved blouses. I visited her house often to pump water from her well for Yaya Neranzo, or to get fresh eggs from her henhouse at the back of her open courtyard. She had a turkey, a black-and-red rooster, and brown and white chickens. I favoured a white one. I used to slip my little hand underneath the brooding hen and gather the warm eggs, under the approving supervision of

Gülyan Hanoum. I had to always leave at least one egg for the hen to brood over.

The midwife lived alone. In the daytime she used the mezzanine room to the right of the huge kitchen-dining room. All the floors were made of large red terra-cotta tiles. This kitchen impressed me; it had an enormous black iron hood and a charcoal oven, large cupboards all around, a large round earthenware container for fresh water that she dispensed with a pewter mug. Jars of jam and pickles lined the glass shelves on the tall windows. A huge dark wooden table and wooden chairs occupied the middle of the dining room and a red velvet covered *minder* ran underneath the windows.

She often asked me to join her on the upper floor. She had explained once that it was there that I was born. It was an open loft. Two red cut-velvet *minders*, adorned with golden tassel trim and covered with white lacy runners, formed a corner by the angled large windows which had wooden shutters outside and sheer white, crocheted curtains inside. A huge bronze brazier in the middle of the room, a large brass double bed with a crocheted white cover against the back wall and a low pearl-inlaid side table completed the furnishings. I suppose she must have lived on the first floor when my parents lived here.

I wondered when Yaya Neranzo had moved into the small room, two houses left, down the road. Maybe when her husband Angheli had passed away? Or when my parents moved to Istanbul? Between the two houses, was the large white house of the Papageorghious, the Malébathés as they were nicknamed because they had a dairy business.

"Were the Papageorgious related to our dear friend Rozita Melkonian's parents?" I ask Stavros.

"To whom?"

"To Rozita. Panaghiotis Papagheorgiou's daughter? We were related to them through my aunt Irini's husband. Rozita's mother, Ourania, was a Djallas too."

"Oh, you mean Papagheorgiou, the one who had the music store by Tünnel?" he answers. "No. Not related. Kyria Elissavet lived there with her children Loula, Kitsa and Gregory (the guy who had rescued me from my forest escapade). They were friends of Despina, the daughter of Avraam and Anastassia Nikolaïdis who later changed his name to Angheloglu. We were very good friends with Avraam. What a small world to meet Despina again in Montreal, at our Association and married to Apostolos Ayanoglu!"

I remember Loula and her beautiful voice. She loved to sing in the house, in the forest, on the hill. For the joy of it. A happy smile always adorned her face. She looked and sounded like Deanna Durbin. I dreamed of looking and singing like her one day... (I knew I could never match Katina!) And her brother Gregory played the guitar divinely. With Katina and Stavros they formed a neighbourhood group, gathering often at the forest to sing under the stars.

I liked visiting with the Malébathés. Their white wooden house had a large marble entrance, like an interior courtyard, with a tall marble fountain-basin in the middle, a tall potted palm, raised rooms at the sides and a double staircase leading to the bedrooms upstairs. It looked like a typical rich Turkish *Konak* house. I was mesmerized by the echoing sound of the rushing water of the fountain, the only continuing sound in the silence, something so different from all the houses I knew. Someday I would like to have a house just like that...

"When did you move to Istanbul?" I ask Father.

"We moved in 1934. To Hamalbashi, close to Emin Djami mosque. At Samandji Ferhat Sokak, number 4/1. The first floor. The owner was Ibrahim Bey. Ibrahim Samanoglu... His wife was Ismet Hanoum. They were from Crete (Girit), moved to Istanbul with the 1923 Lausanne Pact's People Exchange – which lasted seven years, so many were the 'exchangeables'– and the whole family spoke Greek all the time... Now, according to the Lausanne Pact, all those established in Istanbul were considered *établis*, established local residents. However the Turks changed the clause around, ruling that *établis* were considered to be only those registered by 1910 in the Police archives. One and a half million Turks came from Greece and two million Greeks left Turkey for Greece. Now this number has been increased. Today (1973) about four million Turks on the coasts of Ayvalik, Edremit, Izmir and Istanbul, are considered as speaking (and writing) Greek; and about three to four million Greeks – around Izmir, Thrace, Istanbul, the Black Sea – speak Turkish. This is very important."

"You have a point, Father. Almost all of Izmir Turks speak Greek. Our friend Dr. Egeli also speaks Greek. His father used to speak Greek. And Dr. Kafadar, the cardiologist, also understands Greek."

Father nods, leans forward. "Now, people consider Venizelos (the prime minister of Greece in 1923) to be a great man. For me he was nothing. Had no value! He is the cause of the English-French struggle in Salonica and of the Balkan War. If Venizelos had not agreed, the problem would have been solved..."

"How? I don't understand."

"Well, that's a long story, my child, impossible to recall in a short time. A long political imbroglio. I will explain it another time..."

Stavros taps his fingers on the armrest. Takes a deep breath.

"Anyway," he continues, "the Samanoglus lived on the second floor. Nice people. We became good friends... Do you know that Plutarch's *Parallel Lives* was translated into Turkish? Anyway, the volume in ancient Greek that we have was presented to me by Ibrahim Bey... Just to show you how good his Greek was... The third floor was rented to a young Turkish couple with a daughter. Günay? Ours was a small apartment, by the entrance... Lots of Greeks around, in the neighbourhood..."

It was a small apartment indeed... One irregular bedroom, almost triangular in shape; two windows with iron bars, facing a *virané*, a slope running down to Kasimpasha, a farther port town. Then there was a narrow windowed corridor with a mesh food cupboard – where we kept meat, white cheese, cheddar cheese, jams, milk, yogurt and bread – and a walnut chest of drawers with a large mirror reflecting the outside view. Next, a Turkish toilet with a "hole" and an overhead chain for flushing water, and a small water faucet that was useless – we had to fetch water from the basement. Across from this was the wooden apartment entrance door, and to its left a small square dining room with a large iron-barred window facing the pebbled road and a tall four-storey apartment building. We had to go out through the main entrance hall and turn right down the stairs to get to the basement and to a half-lit underground kitchen with a tiny window: a square dark cubicle.

The basement was also used as a common laundry room and a storage area for the whole building. I was not allowed to go down alone, because of the huge sewer rats running around. Even Ibrahim Bey's red cat, Mourgo, was afraid of them! How did Katina manage to cook all those delicious meals in that scary, dilapidated tiny space? The rare times I accompanied my mother, when she was cooking on a charcoal range, was to fetch water with a pewter mug from the cylindrical terracotta *küp* – an earthen water cask covered with cloth and a wooden lid – or to help her carry up the dishes she had prepared, like fried zucchini or eggplant, cheese pies, fish, or grilled hamburgers and French fries... To bake food, like cake, lamb and potatoes or stuffed peppers and tomatoes, we had to use the bakery oven close by, down the hill...

We kept all our dried food in this basement kitchen: rice, beans, lentils, flour (I often had to clean portions of them from insects or mice excretions), sugar, tins of *Komili* olive oil, squares of lemon scented *Komili* soap. We also kept some charcoal there and, in an alcove, the wood for our stove.

In our upstairs main apartment, there was a white French porcelain stove in the bigger triangular room which was the bedroom and the sitting-room at the same time. The stove's thick silver painted pipes meandered throughout the ceilings of the apartment. This precious stove had a cover that we could lift to reveal a round grill that served, for almost nine months of the year, as a heating plate for boiling milk, tea or coffee. We used its grilled iron front opening to toast bread skewered on a knife. Every morning, from September to May, it was Father's chore to fetch the wood from the basement, stuff the stove and light it, even during spring because it was humid – except for the hot summers. We would wake up to the sound of the crackling fire, to the smell of the painted tin pipes mixed with that of the burning wood, and to the heat that filled the air.

I slept in a narrow cot by a window. My parent's brass day-bed was in the wall corner. A tall walnut wardrobe, a small walnut round table with carved lion paws, some built-in shelves and a portable Singer sewing machine, usually out of its case and on the table, completed the furnishing.

Although I was 8 years old, I was not in school yet and I was bored. I loved to sit by the window sill, beside the jars of Mama's home-made sherry liquor left to sweeten in the sun and the earthen carafe wrapped in a wet cloth to keep the water cool... My feet were dangled down, in the air, as I watched the Gipsy and Jewish kids playing in the *virané,* as we called the slope. They skipped ropes, kicked a tin can, played "Jump over the Sheep", ran and hit each other and danced in a circle singing old songs. Mama did not allow me to play outside. Was it because the Gipsy vendors would steal me and sell me for profit, or the Jewish rag collectors would use my blood (horror!) in their *hamursuz*, unleavened bread? 'No, silly! Those tales are told by parents to frighten small children and keep them inside. Not true. Simply put, you become whom you befriend.' And she did not want me to befriend street children and become a street girl...

Street girl? Just by playing outside?

Sometimes neighbourhood couples stopped below our window, to flirt, whisper sweet words or hug, and whenever Katina caught me looking at them, she would get me inside in a hurry and close the sliding window with a bang! Early every morning, I would sit again by the window and watch the Marines, from the Kasimpasha Marine Academy, march up the hill across to *Ok Meydan* – the Arrow Field – to the martial rhythm of their military band... Like a moving white snake. Often they sang. I could not make out the words, but I liked the marching tune. Once up on the large fields they would carry out their military exercises – now only white dots in the distance. By noon I would try to be at my "lookout" for their return.

I cherished seeing my mother sew. She sang non-stop, her voice covering the Singer's rattling, pausing only to cut the thread with her small, sharp, teeth. She was like a fairy, creating little miracles, sewing mostly by hand. Simple dresses that could hide every imperfection. "A little gathering at both sides of the belly, and it won't show …" "Vertical stripes will make you look slimmer and taller…" "A gathering at the shoulders will make your bust look fuller…" "An A-line dress-coat is all your thick waist and full body needs to look great…" "A bias cut is always flattering…" She would let the material flow across bias over her shoulder or drape it, hand over her stomach, to demonstrate her point.

She sewed elaborate gowns with silver thread embroidery, or flowers worked in sequins or crystal beads. She would decorate blouses, underwear and nightgowns with festoon and *à-jour* stitches… Of course she made her own patterns. She could copy anything from a photograph – she would draw a rough sketch as a suggestion for a client. She was talented and so much sought after that she had to refuse clients. She would often prepare a whole *trousseau* for a bride-to-be, including the bridal gown, suits and winter coats, lingerie, and work till the small hours… She would combine remnants refused by clients – using two or three at a time, plain, dotted, striped, flowered – to make the most original, exquisite dresses for herself and for me. We both were the best dressed people I knew, the envy of all, especially me whom she spoiled with delight.

I was allowed to "clean" the semi-finished garments by cutting and tearing the basting threads. To clean-cut the paper patterns she would design. To iron the folded and uncut material some clients brought over, with a warm iron that she would double-check herself with a damp index finger. And on rare occasions, when she was in a great hurry, she would allow me to *surfiler*, overcast, some hidden seams of a garment, hidden because my stitches were not as uniform as they should be. Nothing else! She refused to let me sew. She wished that I could have all my clothes made by the best seamstresses or buy haute-couture dresses! ... But never sew my own! ... So, I indulged myself in embroidery and became very good at it.

Whenever she was at home for a day, if she did not have a rush order, Katina would care for neighbours' toddlers, babies really. She adored babies. They were like dolls to me. I was glad to have company and I tried to look after them. I remember Günay, our third floor tenants' baby girl, and Aysen, our next door neighbour's little daughter, who both loved Mama so much they used to call her "Mamaka", mimicking me.

When Katina was working at a client's house, she would take me with her. I liked that. It was entertaining to visit different homes: some had flower gardens – like the Sisters by Bellevue – and would offer us arms-full of heavenly smelling honeysuckle, lilacs and lilies. Some had luxurious living rooms, others had domestic servants and a few had small children of my age to play with. I liked visiting Nadji Bey's house, a country estate at Bakirköy, where I was free to roam in their large garden, especially during sunny winter days when fresh snow glistened on the bushes. They used to gather this pure snow and offer it as a dessert sprinkled with hot molasses. A treat…

Later, when I was a bit older, Mama used to entrust me to Aunt Frosso who lived down the hill, or to Ismet Hanoum, our landlady. Ismet Hanoum had a daughter, Tomris, older than me, who let me play with her brass toy kitchen battery. I also liked Halidé, their adopted mulatto girl, sweet like chocolate and very affectionate towards me, and Shahsiné Hanoum, their live-in aunt, who was a professional knitter. I loved watching her create intricate red-and-white ski pullovers, hats and mittens, and crocheted lace-like *liseuses* and table runners. I learned a lot from her.

I am drawn out of my reverie by Father's cough… I give him a tissue paper. He spits in it, folds it and leaves it by the side table.

"It wasn't the best dwelling for you," he says. "It was humid and the kitchen in the basement was full of rats. Do you remember the thief-rat? The huge rat coming down from the rooftop terrace and hopping the wooden stairs at night with a piece of bone in his front feet? We all thought it was a thief and tried to catch him!"

He laughs heartily. I smile.

I remember. Ibrahim Bey in a knee-length *entari* (night-gown) swinging a pair of fire tongs and Father in long white underwear brandishing a handful of black-pepper to throw on the thief's eyes and me opening the heavy iron front door to let the "thief" run out without harming us…

"I wrote a composition about this thief-rat at Ismet Hanoum's at Ste. Pulchérie and got an award for it," I tell Father.

He nods, his eyes glinting. Plays with his wedding ring. Resumes his narrative.

"After a few years, we were doing better financially and when the third floor tenant moved out we rented it. Now, that was a large sunny four-room apartment with a proper kitchen and all. You had your own room and my mother joined us."

I recall this apartment well. I lost my window sill but gained my own room, the middle one, with a large window, a dresser and, at the right corner, an *iconostase* shelf holding an open dark wooden box crowned by a cross. In it we had arranged icons of saints with a votive lamp in front. To my left was a large living room with tall windows, four on one side and two on the other, all adorned with orange-red cut velvet drapes and white blinds. A large new couch, pale green, stood in front of the four windows, two new cane armchairs on either side. The old chest of drawers with the mirror fitted the blank wall, and in the middle was the round table. In a corner, a brand new Singer sewing machine, this one with a foot pedal... Yaya Neranzo occupied the room next to mine. The small but sunny kitchen with a red tiled floor was in the middle of the apartment, facing the entrance door. It had a tall window, a large hood, a charcoal grill, a double sink and a small Coleman oil stove. Our mesh food cupboard hung from the ceiling, fitted with fly-catching glue-paper spirals. Now we had a proper marble Turkish toilet – the type you had to crouch over – with a running water tab and its own small window. Finally on the left of the entrance there was a large sunny dining-room with a big rectangular table, chairs and a buffet. All new. Such luxury!

But the most important thing was that I finally got to attend a proper school, Tarsis Varidou, successor to the International Language College that Father had attended, now a private primary school. Who took me to school on the first day? Katina or Stavros? All I remember was *Mam'zelle* Lukia, the fortyish dark-haired principal, taking my hand and presenting me to *Mam'zelle* Martha, in a huge many-windowed sunlit classroom with maps and anatomy posters on the side walls and a huge blackboard covering the whole front wall. I sat in the fifth row at a wooden-desk – I was tall.

What a difference from the windowless basement class with long benches at *Despinis* Aspassia's neighbourhood preschool where we had learned to read and write on small slates with a *kondyli*, a hard round writing chalk stylus. Now I had a proper, divinely smelling leather schoolbag with crisp new books and lined exercise books and a wooden *cassetina* with a sliding top where I kept real pencils and an eraser.

It was here, in this classroom, that I met Tito Sahapoglu, a chubby, dark-haired boy with huge black eyes, who was to become the man of my life; and Sofoula Papadimitraki, a blond tall girl – our neighbour as I found out – who was to become my best friend.

And the fairytale part of the school adventure were the two huge wisteria trees on the upper playgound area, their grapes of flowers perfuming the air and spreading the earth with pink and yellow confetti. For me, longing for familiar forest trees in our barren small street, this was a real miracle.

Strange though, that Katina left school at age nine and I enrolled in school at almost the same age. Why did my parents keep me home for so long? Was it because the better Greek schools were all private, with steep fees we could not afford? Were we too proud to consider the free Greek-community schools? Never mind! This was the best school in town, with French lessons introduced in Grade One, the only subject that remained as a reminder of the old International Language College of Stavros' time.

Well, the good life, finally! Katina was happy. She sang all day and night: *My Sweet Rezeda, Violetera, O Kitara Romana, Santa Lucia, Two Black Eyes, When I Drink Wine,* Sophia Vembo's hit *Athina and Again Athina,* and the one I liked best, *I Will Make You a Baroness…* Its lyrics rang like a fairy tale:

I will make you a Baroness,
Rich and noble,
I will deposit my crown
Just for one kiss from you…

All happy songs…

Katina loved to cook in her new kitchen and to entertain after years of restraint. Our relatives and friends were often invited over. I remember Papou Anghelis (Mama's father), and my aunt Marika, her husband Kosta, his sister Smaro, my cousins Mihalis, Stratos, Frossoula, Yorgos the baby… And Evghenoula with her husband Dimitros. Katina's laughter cascaded now, reverberating in the large rooms.

Our most frequent visitors were Katina's client ladies and some neighbours, mostly the young woman from the apartment across the way – Marianthi, daughter of Kyria Loksandra and sister of Doctor Kyriacos and of the Archimandrite. Marianthi was a beautiful young woman. I thought she looked like the Italian film star Sylvana Mangano. Marianthi was betrothed to Mihali Kondorouha, an exquisite cabinet maker. She would come over for company, with her knitting or her needlework – she was embroidering her *trousseau* – and she would ask Katina for advice about her small domestic problems with her brothers or her fiancé. At such moments Katina would ask me to change the oil or the wick in the votive lamp, or to fetch some fresh water, or to go and buy some sugar from Kyr' Diamantis – our grocer in the next street. Anything she could think of to make me leave the room. Their whispers would change to normal tones when I reappeared. Katina knew how to listen. Secrets were sacred and she gave advice like an old philosopher. People loved her and entrusted their confidences to her.

We even had a house helper now, Kyria Sophia, a hunch-backed middle-aged woman who came every Friday. Katina treated her as one of the family and, while the smell of the floor wax filled the room, she prepared Sophia's favourite food, *bizelia araka,* green peas stewed with lamb.

"I remember the blackouts with dark blue paper glued on the windows. And the long queues for ration coupons for bread and dry food. White bread was a sheer luxury… It must have been around 1939-1940?" I ask Stavros.

"Yeah! We had it easy! Turkey didn't get into the war."

"You put up a huge map of Europe on the wall and listened to the news on our small brown bakelite radio. You followed all the movements of the Allied Forces and marked their advances with small flags pinned to the map… You talked with passion about it…I remember names like Hitler, Rommel, Göring, Dunkerque, Maréchal Pétain, Général de Gaulle, Luftwaffe, Churchill, Lord Eden, Mussolini, Montgomery, El-Alamein…"

Stavros raises his eyebrows. He can't believe that I have remembered all this. "Well, my child—"

"And you criticized the generals' moves," I interrupt, "shouting, 'That was a stupid move!'"

Stavros smiles. He nods. "It must have been my military college education. I guess I always wanted to be a general or something…" he says with pride.

God! He enjoys this! He doesn't seem to be bothered by the tragedy of the war. He seems to have fun with the different strategies. Like a game! Will I never know you, Father?

Disturbed, and angry at being so, I change the subject.

"You used to play the violin to lull me to sleep… What tunes did you most loved to play?" I ask.

"*Cavalaria Rusticana*!"

"And *Kol Nidre* also! The Jewish *Yom Kippur* hymn?"

"How could you remember? You were so young—"

"You used to whistle it to me later, when I was older. When you didn't play the violin any longer. Why did you stop playing?"

"A large barrel fell on my left hand. Cut it. Crushed my left fingers… See the mark?" Stavros bents to show me a white deep scar in the middle of his palm, at the base of his fingers. "Couldn't play anymore!"

"What a pity! You played so well. Violin has been my favourite musical instrument ever since… When did you learn to play?"

"I started to play in 1921. My first teacher was an Armenian, Papazyan. Then a friend of mine, who played very well, recommended me to his teacher; Reinhart. He was really good…"

I see myself opening the treasure chest in the old attic, by the fourth floor rooftop terrace – before we moved to our second home in the same area, in Istanbul. I was nineteen then. I wanted to take with me to our new home the violin and whatever other "treasures" I would find in the chest. A spray of golden dust mixed with the smell of mould filled the air as I opened the lid. Inside, shreds of papers, Russian rupees, pieces of Greek newspapers, a faded newspaper page entitled "*Pateras*"– Father –, half a page of *APOGEVMATINI*, where Stavros used to write sometime under the headline *The Quill*; pieces of newspaper columns of a serial novel "*Ston vomo tis aghapis*: *Matomenos Vrahos*" – On Love's Altar: Bloodied Rock – by Stavros Evangelidis. All eaten up by mice or vermin… The violin in pieces… because of the dried glue and humidity… holes in its body… Only the bow still intact but with the strings falling apart…

"You don't have any copies of your articles in *APOGEVMATINI?*"

"What? … No…"

"What were you writing about?"

Stavros closes his eyes, grins.

"It all started with a badmouthing article about Olympia Fengara, Evghenoula's boss,"he says. "The best haute couture designer in Istanbul. Evghenoula asked me to do something about it. I avenged her in *The Quill*. It created a stir. The guy who wrote the offending article had to present a written apology to Fengara. Afterwards I continued, now and then, as a satirical columnist. Anonymous…"

"What about your novel, "*Ston Vomo tis Aghapis*" subtitled "*Matomenos Vrahos*?" Was it ever published in book form?"

Stavros startles at my recollection. His eyes brighten. "You know about it?"

"I found some shredded pieces in the old attic chest. Nothing was salvageable, neither the violin, nor the novel. You don't have a copy?"

Stavros sighs and shakes his head "No."

"Not a manuscript?"

"What did you expect? We didn't have typewriters or anything. I was writing on sheets of paper, handing them over to Cavaliero Marquizos, the newspaper publisher, who was my friend, and he published them. The manuscripts were never kept..."

"Could we write to *APOGEVMATINI* and ask for a copy from their archives?" I persist, mad at myself that I hadn't done so at the time.

"What for?" Stavros sweeps the air with his hand. "What is done is done... We should not dwell on the past..."

"Why such a dramatic title? What was the story about?"

"It was a love story. About a Greek girl who lost her lover and committed suicide by jumping off a cliff to the sea. Her body hit a large rock and her splattered blood stained it..."

"Gory! Why did you choose to write such a tragic novel?"

"It was a true story. In the news. It made a deep impression on me. Disturbed me. I felt I had to write about it..."

"Did you write any other novels?"

"Short stories."

"There was also another page, a novel I guess, signed by you.

O *Pateras.* – The Father. Remember?"

Stavros nods, a happy smile playing on his lips.

"Was it a novel?"

"You could say that. Or a long short story."

"About?"

"About a father's strife and his sacrifices..."

"Where else did you write?"

"At *METARRYTHMISIS*... Since 1925. Mainly articles..."

"No other novels?"

"No, only articles."

"Why not?"

Stavros shrugs his shoulders. "I had no time for novels..."

He had no time for many things... Neither did Mama... What would their life have been like if they had had more free time to indulge themselves? ... If money had been a bit easier for them?

Stavros beats the armrest with his fingers. Changes the subject:

"You know, I was rather naughty in my youth and women usually took a shine to me."

His voice brought me back from my daydream.

"And the ones I did not respond to attacked me to your Mama. Katina told me that the tenant across the apartment, eyed me like a Frankish Holy Host... 'Don't worry', I reassured her, 'she is not my type!' She believed me.

Yet, when you were a baby, whenever she went out for a whole day to sew, she locked my good clothes away!" He laughs heartily. "Hey! What days! ..."

Why was he telling me this? Was it true? Or was he trying to compensate for his weakened manhood because the tape recorder offered him a ready audience?

Then I remembered the Taksim incident: "Good friends" had reported to my mother that Stavros had been seen at Taksim with his arm around a young woman's waist.

'A shame, I tell you! She was very young! Could have been his daughter!'

'When did you see them?' asked Katina.

'Sunday, strolling in full daylight!'

'What was she wearing?'

'A multicoloured jacket. And white skirt. And she had long chestnut hair.'

'Well, that was Erato, our daughter! Stavros takes her to church every Sunday and then they stroll together at Taksim Square before coming home,' Katina answered calmly.

How badly intentioned could they be? I must have been eleven or twelve then but at 1.66 m tall I could have passed for older. However my hair was long and I wore short white socks. And that Sunday I had been wearing the green-white-and yellow chequered jacket that I had knitted... How could they have mistaken me for a "young woman"?

Then, the Fort Myers incident came to my mind.

It was a few years after Katina had passed away. Father, as usual, had accompanied us on our yearly Florida vacation.

That night we were at our favourite seaside restaurant in Fort Myers Beach, the *Top of the Mast,* that featured dance with a live band. Our table – by a glass wall – faced the ocean. The golden sun glided slowly into the sea leaving a lilac-rose haze over the beach and a special glow on Father's sun-kissed face as he enjoyed his Spider cocktail, in small sips, his right hand holding the glass and his lighted cigarette.

I looked tenderly at my father. Although he was over seventy now, he looked younger. Tall, slim, with slightly grey hair, hazel-green eyes with a penetrating gaze and a boisterous laugh he attracted attention easily.

The live music had a good beat. It was loud and enticing. My husband had already been led to the dance floor by our teenage daughters and he was rock-and-rolling with them à la Travolta. All eyes were on them. Stavros and I watched with pride. Tito was a great dancer, almost a professional. I recalled how, only a few years before, whenever we danced in public, people formed a circle and clapped or even sat down to watch us.

The trio returned panting to the table, quenching their thirst with the cold drinks that Stavros had ordered: pina-coladas without alcohol for the girls, margarita for Tito and strawberry daiquiri for me. I beamed at my husband, not hiding my happiness. When the music switched to a *slow,* I took Father's arm. He smiled, balanced his lighted cigarette on the ashtray – it would be a sacrilege to extinguish it – placed his drink on the table and, taking my hand, followed me to the dance floor.

Even after so many years of dancing Father was still stepping on my toes, paying no attention to the music but looking with interest at the young people around us. I was pleased to see him relaxed and content for the first time in a long while. He gave Jim, the bartender, a captain's salute – two fingers touching his forehead.

When the music changed to a *cha-cha,* we returned to our table. Father lit a new cigarette from the butt of the old one.

"You know, Dad," I remarked with a smile, "I noticed you were a hit with the ladies over there. One of them, that good looking blonde, was watching you all the time."

Stavros only grunted.

Dinner was served and the orchestra took a break. We had ordered grilled grouper and fried calamari, ouzo for the adults and iced-tea for the girls.

When the orchestra returned and began to play an upbeat *rumba,* the blonde woman that I had noticed staring at my father came to the table and invited Stavros to dance. She was pleasant looking, fairly well preserved, and clad in a black *fourreau* sleeveless dress.

"I regret, my dear lady, I don't know how to dance to this music," Stavros replied.

"I'll be pleased to teach you," she responded, and pressed her hand on his arm.

Embarrassed, Stavros looked into my eyes, his eyebrows raised in a question mark. Was he asking me what he should do or was he seeking my permission? I was startled. I nodded, amused and amazed at the woman's boldness as she led Stavros to the dance floor.

Tito must have noticed my troubled look.

"Relax! She's harmless," he reassured me.

"He doesn't realize that some women who seem nice really aren't. She could be… He's so naïve in that respect—"

"Naïve? At his age? Come on! He is healthy, spry and still attractive. He bites into life. And he can take care of himself! He's lonely, Erato. Let him live!"

I shook my head.

Next day, at sundown, as I was preparing some fish for dinner, I heard Father's stentorian voice from the beach: "Erato! E-ra-too! Hello! He-l-looo!"

I ran to the balcony, fingers white with flour, wondering what was wrong.

Father was standing below on the sand, shoeless, chest bared, wearing only khaki shorts, holding a lighted cigarette. Yesterday's blonde, wearing a colourful one-piece bathing suit, was clinging affectionately to his left arm.

"She is my daughter!" Stavros explained to the woman and began to speak to me in Greek.

"*Mou kollissé apo to Public Beach. Then m'afini.* (She met me at the Public Beach and has been hanging on to me ever since. Can't get rid of her.) *Ti na tin kano?*"

What to do with her? Why is he asking for my permission again, I wondered.

"*Eména rotass? Kané o,ti théliss,*" (You're asking me? Do whatever you want), I answered, irritated.

"*K'i mama sou?*"

My Mama? God! She is still alive for him! He still adores her!

How to tell him Katina wouldn't object? I looked down and I noticed the white heron on the beach, the white heron that had kept a vigil across from our balcony ever since Mama had died. It suddenly opened its wings and flew towards the open sea. Was this my answer? An omen for Stavros to be relieved of the past?

"Wherever she is, she wouldn't mind. Have a good time," I shouted back in Greek to Father.

He stood there for a minute, silent, thoughtful. The woman sensed his hesitation and put her head on his shoulder… Then Stavros gave me his captain's salute, and walked away with her.

Let him live, Tito had said, and he was right. Humming, I returned to the kitchen …

After a short while, I heard the key turning in the condo door.

Father walked in.

"Finally, I got rid of her!" he announced triumphantly, beaming.

I stared at him. *He could not betray Katina!*

Back to the present. I nod and, with a smile, touch his now almost translucent hand. From old photos I can see how attractive he was when he was young. Katina must have had a rough time trusting in his love and trying not to be jealous. These happy recollections were a way for him to deny his present physical condition…

He felt young and virile and attractive still. And most of all, still loyal, still faithful…

V- The Beginning of Decline

"*Y*our father is expected for a nuclear bone cat-scan, next Wednesday..." ordered Dr. Plante.

"Why? You said nothing else could be done for him! You did the lung biopsy... And if I remember correctly, you also checked his bones. Three months have passed... Why put him through another time-wasting ordeal?" I protested.

"Listen, Dr. Egeli asked me to take good care of your father. We have to find out whether the cancer has advanced to the bones. If so, it will cause excruciating pain. We must know, in order to help him. If nothing else, prescribe him some morphine. The scan is a long procedure but it doesn't hurt. You don't want him to suffer unnecessarily, do you?"

No, I didn't. Besides, I trusted our neighbour, Dr. Egeli, the Muslim Turk obstetrician from Istanbul who saved Kathy's life and mine during an extremely difficult childbirth. He was the chief surgeon of the hospital and his word had clout. He loved my father...

I convinced Stavros that he had to have a bone density test so that, if necessary, the doctors could prescribe a medicine to prevent old age bone weakening... For his own good...

He protested, as usual...

It was cold and shivery, this early December Wednesday. The roadsides were white with snow. The hospital waiting room was full. In spite of our appointment, we had to wait. It took a very long time. Stavros became restless. So I tried to distract him.

"Do you remember the words of the other song Mama was singing when you heard her for this first time? The one starting *Don't talk to me about him*?" I wrote for him in my note pad.

"*Don't talk to me*... It's a Russian tune... It goes like this..."

He started to hum the song off key:

Why did you remind me about him?
The wound is still hot.
It is his fault that I don't laugh,
that my body hurts and wilts…
It is his fault,
but if he ever returned to me
I would tell him
that my wounded heart
has forgotten everything.
Talk to me about him now.
Talk to me only about him from now on…

People were staring at us, some amused, some curious, some annoyed. I didn't care. It was as if nothing and nobody existed except my father and my determination to calm him and make him forget why we were there. I loved this song. It was one that Mama used to sing on request, when I was little. I knew the tune and most of the words…

"And this other one," said Father, and started to sing:

Forget if I loved you,
if I cried bitterly over you.
Forget if I desired you.
Go to find joy elsewhere,
Give me the last kiss,
Don't deny it to me, my light…

"You were not jealous?" I asked.

"Why?"

"Because those songs might have reminded her of Zach. They reflected her pain for him, no?"

"No… We were deeply in love…"

Father's name is called. "You come with me, inside!" he says, matter-of-factly.

"I will try," I reply.

"No. You don't try. You come with me!"

Since the day he went for some X-rays at another hospital and the attendants had broken his ribs trying to turn him over – because he could not hear their commands – he would not go into an examining room without me by his side… The attendants, here, were sympathetic to my explanations and allowed me to go in with him…

"They will just take pictures of your bones, many pictures. It will take a long time. Here, take some lozenges for your cough. Try to sleep. I will stay with you, just beside you," I reassured him.

"Sleep? On this narrow, cold metal cot?"

He closed his eyes. In spite of the small flat pillow behind his neck, being on his back brought on coughing spells… He spat in a Kleenex tissue that he kept in his palm, then put the cough drop I had given him in his mouth. He sighed and tried to relax again after a glance at me.

I wondered what he could feel. Fear? Not likely. Apprehension? How much did he guess and tried to deny or to hide? My heart sank. I tried not to think… I had to stop thinking…

"The cancer had not attacked his bones, thanks God", explained the doctor afterwards. But I should be prepared for his physical deterioration that was imminent now… He should eat protein to keep some muscles… The CLSC visits should become more frequent.

Noella, the CLSC liaison nurse between Verdun and the Royal Victoria Hospitals, was a gorgeous blond. In her mid-thirties, she looked like Raquel Welch and had a contagious warm smile. She won my father's trust immediately. I was amazed that he made the effort to meet her upstairs, in the living-room. His face lit up at her presence. Often, he also put his hearing aid on. For her. If not, Noella communicated with him with a note pad. I was grateful that she was going along with my strategy. One day, she took me aside:

"Your father is deteriorating physically, but mentally he is great. How do you manage?"

"By keeping him busy and interested. I am trying not to let him think too much about his condition. And he is optimistic by nature. He must be doing his best to erase anxious thoughts from his mind."

"Congratulations. Keep it up."

* * *

Now a young student, Robert, came every second day to help Father with his bath. Peter helped him into the bathtub, and onto a non-slipping stool, while he bathed him. Then he would help Stavros out of the bathtub, dry him and give him a vigorous massage with a special lotion. Father felt good afterwards. He enjoyed this attention.

"How much do you pay him?" he asked one day. "It must cost a lot."

"It costs nothing. The government office, the CLSC, sends Robert for free.

I am only giving him a tip for his good work. This is our famous Canadian health care," I reassured him. "We all contributed to it with our pay cheques, you included...You deserve it."

"And Noella, and Dr. Mount's visits too?"

"Yes."

"Well, with my old age pension and now the health care, for the first time I am glad I came to Canada. We couldn't afford one hundredth of such care in Istanbul... I am thankful..."

It was the first time Stavros admitted being thankful to Canada.

A few years earlier, after we had arrived, he had almost given me a nervous breakdown by declaring his move to Canada was the biggest mistake of his life. "I was someone in Istanbul, loved and respected, and I became one of the living-dead here," he had exclaimed with bitterness when he was left jobless.

Indeed Father was someone in Istanbul. He had become a respected international oil broker. Eminent merchants called him *Istavri Efendi* (Sir Stavros). And Patriarch Athenagoras, just before we left Istanbul, had offered him the position and title of *Archon Myropios*, Master Ointment Maker of the Patriarchate, for the Holy Thursday ceremony when the ointment for healing and the last rites is prepared and distributed to all the churches. The choice of pure oil was important to this ceremony, and Father had advised the Patriarchate about it for years. And he had to turn this honour down because we were leaving...

"I didn't force you to come..." I had protested then, with pain.

"Your Mama gave me no choice. When you announced you would emigrate and offered to take us along, she said 'I'm going, whether you come or not. Erato is our only child and I will not live an ocean away from her and our granddaughter risking to see them only once every few years...'

"What could I do? I accepted losing my roots, my pride, my job, my friends, for you and your Mama... I worshipped her and I adored you..."

"How did you feel leaving Istanbul?"

"Sad. Very sad."

He sighs, squints his eyes... frowns... Then he resumes, his gaze fixing a distant image in his mind:

"Yet, also hopeful for a new life. And glad to finally be able to visit Athens. We were to stay there for a week. Irini, your Mama's sister had insisted that we stop there for a while before sailing to the New World."

Katina, Erato, Gaby, Stavros, leaving Istanbul, 1964

"'I probably won't see you again,' she had pleaded. Since we would have to change ships anyway, Tito accepted. Greece, Athens... It was a lifelong dream... Gavril, Amélie and Marion were tearful at the docks. Tito promised to start procedures for them to emigrate too as soon as we were established in Montreal... As the ship pulled away and the port offered a magnificent panoramic vista, my first arrival at this port decades ago filled my memory. I didn't know if I would ever see it again... My heart sank... The ship's name, if I remember, was *Akdeniz.* A Turkish boat. It was in October of 1964, and the seas were very high, so the trip to Piraeus was not an easy one."

He laughs now, stirred by a special memory. "Only you and I – who for decades was used to high waves due to my almost daily crossing to Eminönü by rowboat – were moving about with the crew and some rare passengers on deck. Everybody else was sick in bed." (I had taken pills against sea-sickness but Tito, Father and Mama had refused to take them...).

Stavros stops to cough... Stays silent for a while, his fingers drum the armchair. Then he continues:

"Piraeus appeared to me disappointingly flat and plain after Istanbul... But it was sunny and warm. Yanni Gavrielidis, Tito's great uncle, was waiting for us. He was working for Athens Travel and had made all the travel arrangements for us. He was extremely helpful. He checked our main suitcases in storage until they were to be transferred to the transatlantic ship. He had booked a very nice suite for us at a quaint hotel in Athens. Amalia it was called. Very central, by Stadiou Avenue."

I recall the hotel. Entering the lobby from the warm street I was impressed by its coolness thanks to its terrazzo floors. It was all white with pale blue wall borders and painted wooden shutters. It had a restaurant downstairs which was very practical as there would be no need to bother about food or going out to eat in the neighbourhood. The suite was bright and large, also in white and blue, with a queen size bed and a cot, and a nice sitting room with couch, cupboard, *bahut,* round table and chairs. Both rooms had tall windows, with shutters, and were facing the avenue. Clean, nice and comfortable.

"Tito took us out that first night, inviting all your relatives to a nice *taverna* at Plaka. Your aunt Irini and your first cousins Stamo and Dimitri, their wives, and Yanni, and his sister Olga, were all there. Tito was ordering rounds and rounds of *Mavrodaphni*, a very heavy sweet red wine. We probably all got drunk but it was nice to hear live bouzouki and all those Greek songs. We had a great time."

I remember that good time. Tito kept shouting popular song titles to the musicians, but often the orchestra's spokesman would shout back: "This one is travelling!" or "It's gone sight-seeing!" It was the time when composer Mikis Theodorakis was exiled and his songs black listed…

"Next day you were to leave for a week's tour of Europe. Your aunt Irini came to our hotel early in the morning," continues Stavros, "and invited your Mama to spend the whole week with her at her house. 'Who knows if we will ever see each other in the future!' she cried. Now, Irini lived alone in a very small house and it would not be easy for all of us to share the dwelling. Furthermore, the house was far away, at Pangrati, and you had to take two buses to get downtown, which was difficult for Irini to do; and even more so for us, with Gaby. Yet, your Mama accepted, against all our warnings. 'She's my sister, I may not see her again,' she claimed.

"So, you helped us settle in with Irini and Tito gave us enough money to get by for a week. He also asked Stamo, your cousin, whom he saw that day – I believe Dimitri was at work – to look after us and help us if needed. Then you left for your trip to Europe. You would join us a week later at Napoli when our ship stopped there."

Oh yes, it was a wonderful trip. Tito and I first took the train to Belgrade, where Nadia, Tito's cousin, and Aunt Lena, his mother's sister, were waiting for us at the station and we spent a few precious hours together. After a short stop at Salzburg, we arrived at the unforgettable town of Innsbruck with its colourful ski chalets and flowered window sills, and a cable car up to the mountain offering breathtaking views.

Next we stopped for two days and one night in Münich where we met Fred, Tito's brother. We stayed at a charming hotel, with light down-duvets (new to me) and hearty breakfasts. It was a beautiful city, with picturesque streets and arty wrought-iron shop signs. And mainly old neoclassical and baroque buildings, many with conical roofs. The city had an impressive plaza, and jolly beer gardens offering up-beat music and frothing steins of beer. Often a patron conducted the orchestra in a classical concert. While listening I would switch my typical but bloody *Münchener* dish for Tito's appetizing Austrian Schnitzel! We continued to Heidelberg where Tito had worked one summer as a university exchange student.

Then we were on the train to Italy. First Milan. *La Scala*. *La Galleria Vittorio Emanuele II* with its glass roof and trendy fashion shops and restaurants. The cathedral known as *Il Duomo*. After Milan we stopped at Verona to see the alleged house of Juliet and its famous balcony (more romantic than I dreamed about). Then Padua and finally fairytale Venice. The lace-like Doge palaces and the Piazza San Marco with its outdoor cafés and hundreds and hundreds of grey pigeons. The *Bibliotheca*, the bridges, the long, smooth gondolas and the singing *gondolieri*... The Lagoon and the Lido... The *vaporetti*. We visited Murano Island and its glass factories, spacious, noisy, clean. We bought there some wonderful souvenirs, including a large navy blue vase and a turquoise love-bird set that we still have. In Venice we also bought two walking life-size dolls for Gaby, a blond one and a brunette. Then on to Bologna where we met some Italian friends, an architect and his wife whom we had met at Istanbul. They took us to a rustic restaurant where we had delicious ravioli Bolognese and good red wine. Then we continued to Ravenna, to beautiful Florence, with the awesome statue of *David* and the tower of Pisa nearby. Next stop was Rome. We did not see the Pope, but we did visit the Vatican: I remember being more impressed by Michelangelo's *Moise* and his *Pieta* than by his *Last Judgment* in the Sistine Chapel, maybe because it had not been restored yet and seemed very dark and murky.

We reached Naples around the 6th of November, 1964. Here we tasted, for the first time, real Neapolitan pizza. Scenes run like a movie in front of my eyes, scenes that I had forgotten but kept alive in the small black and white photographs of Tito and me… And then, my Mama's tearful face…

"Mama burst into sobs when we joined you in Naples…" I said to Father.

"Yes. She was relieved to see you. Because, against all her expectations, our sojourn in Athens was an ordeal for her. You see, your aunt Irini left us on the second or third day of our arrival at her house – I don't recall when exactly – to help Poppy, Stamo's wife, who was having her baby. I don't know if it was the excitement of the birth of the baby or what, but nobody cared about us, none of our relatives came to see us. Irini had no phone. I didn't know my way around and as I told you, you could only go downtown with two long bus rides. I thought of returning to the Amalia Hotel. I checked. But it was fully booked by now and we couldn't find a room in any other hotel around there. Besides, Katina kept hoping that any day Irini would come back. But Irini didn't… Not even to say goodbye as we left…"

Stavros stops to clear his throat and recollect.

"Tito's uncle Yanni helped us a lot. What an exceptional guy! He visited us every day; he took me to the market and showed me around. Took me to Pendeli Mountain, to Acropolis that I so longed to visit... And his sister Olga liked Katina and Gaby very much. She also came almost every day, always bringing something with her. A casserole, a cake, sweets, fruits..."

Such a sweet, kind lady, Aunt Olga. She and Yanni were Papa Gavril's first cousins and we called them Aunt and Uncle. Olga embroidered divinely. She gave Mama an evening-bag in the finest *gobelin* that she had embroidered. It was a Watteau forest picnic scene in a medallion on a burgundy background. You would think it had been stamped out and not hand-stitched…

Father's voice drags me away from my reverie:

"I asked Katina whether she had quarrelled or anything with Irini. 'Not at all!' she protested, puzzled. As I told you, no phones to communicate with anyone. Your Mama couldn't understand… Myself neither. Katina took it to heart and became very sad. She felt abandoned and betrayed yet again by all those she had cherished for so long. It was for them, her sister and her nephews and their families that we had stopped in Athens. It was to be with Irini that Katina agreed to leave the cosy hotel we had settled in. And now she was left all alone, imprisoned in a tiny, jail-like house. She refused to accompany me on my outings. … I don't want to think what would have happened to us without the money Tito had left us and without the vital help of Yanni and Olga. So, you see, that dreamed visit to Athens turned into an ordeal."

A coughing bout stops Stavros. He resumes after a while:

"Yanni insisted that we all take pills, *Dramamine*, against sea-sickness, because he knew the Atlantic crossing could be harsh at this time of the year. He also upgraded us into a beautiful, sunny, luxury deck suite on the *S/S Olympia*. Two communicating bedrooms! He was of such great help, Yanni! I will never forget the kindness of this man!"

Father delves into his memory treasure for a while, gaze far away. Then he continues:

"The voyage was smooth and pleasant. We were impressed to be invited to dine at the captain's table. A Greek captain. He was a perfect host. We had our pictures taken with him. On the ship we met the Vlahopoulos'. His wife Irini, whom he called Nounou, was pregnant. Once settled in Toronto they asked you to baptise their first born, Nikos junior, you remember?

"Vlahopoulos had a beautiful tenor voice. At the amateur night, he was a hit singing *Granada* and *Viva Espagna* in Spanish. Then, you teamed up with him and Nounou, and on the talent-show night you sang as a foursome the *Kaïmos* (the Pain) by Mikis Theodorakis. What a success!"

We both sink into our memories… I appreciate Father's sharp memory and the pleasure I see him experience as he reminisces.

"Our ship, the S/S *Olympia*, arrived at Halifax about a week later, on the 14th of November, 1964. A plain port, but it looked like heaven to us. We had to go through Canadian immigration. Pier 41, was it? Katina was impressed by the Greek signs, *Kalos ilthaté ston Kanadha,* welcoming us to Canada. We arranged to ship all our baggage to Montreal. But before that we had to open every suitcase because Tito had declared as liquor the *Ouzo* and *Metaxa* given to us by Yanni, as well as the Italian wine you had bought in Italy, and he did not remember in which suitcases he had put them! Finally, we were issued our Canadian Immigrant cards and we returned to our ship to continue our trip to New York, as planned. Again, this was Yanni's suggestion, as it would cost not a penny more… I felt something at the sight of the Statue of Liberty and the sky scrapers filling the clear sky… Such a different sight from Istanbul's minarets… In New York we stayed with Gaby, with Evghenoula's sister Anna and her husband Kosta Marinakis, in their flat. They were happy to see us. And you and Tito went to visit your friends… Remember?"

"Yes, I do remember."

Tito had leased a brand new 1965 Chevrolet Impala, yellow exterior, black interior. Slick, awesome car! A first impossible dream come true! For it would have really been impossible even to dream of owning or renting such a car back in Turkey at that time! ...

We visited his best friend from Istanbul, Yakup Paker, just married to Ruth. He was teaching at Columbia University.

Then we met our good friends Tassoula and Yanni Sirimdjioglou, a travel agent colleague of mine from Istanbul who had changed his last name to Sirimson.

And finally my classmate Wallis, from Ste-Pulchérie, and her husband Laszlo Urmenyhazi, Tito's friend from his youth. They were living in a small flat with their daughter Christel – born in Istanbul, almost the same age as Gaby - and their newborn, Marianne. We were really glad to see our closest Istanbul friends in America. We felt as if we had never parted.

Then with my parents and Gaby we drove to Boston to visit Aunt Smaro's family, (my aunt Marika's husband's sister), her husband Kosta Duci, their kids Christina, Stan and Sandra. They owned a beautiful, white, two-storey wooden house and were happy to welcome us and baby Gabriella. We left my parents and Gaby in their care and off we went to tour the surrounding area. The Ducis treated Gaby like a doll and gave her an adorable pink winter outfit with a brimmed hat and leggings. What a generous person Aunt Smaro is! She has such a great heart! Orphaned at a young age, she always worked hard. In America more than ever. With her husband they provided a university education for all their children and later she offered a dream marriage to Sandra. I love them all very much and I respect her tremendously.

When we left Boston to finally drive to Canada, the weather was still nice and mild.

It was sunny and bright when we arrived to Montreal. Minus 17 degrees flashed on a high pole up on Decarie Boulevard. Tito, wearing only a jacket, stopped the car at a stop sign and got out to experience this "minus 17". After a few seconds he felt a crack in his nostrils. They were frozen... Welcome to Montreal!

"We settled temporarily in an old second floor loft on Hutchison Street close to Park Avenue," Father's voice rang in my ears. "It was dark, dry and smelly but the rent was very reasonable. It would do for a few weeks, we considered, before getting into something better. We discovered ready-to-cook food, like Kraft macaroni and cheese. We left Gaby with Katina and then, we three, Tito, you and I, launched into job hunting. The apartment was overheated and very dry, and Gaby came down with a nasty cough. It was the second or third day of our arrival and when we returned home one afternoon with Tito we saw that Gaby was having difficulty breathing. Tito took her in his arms and hailed a taxi. 'To the nearest hospital,' he said to the driver. The guy took a look at Gaby and drove straight to Ste-Justine Hospital.

When Tito came back, he didn't have Gaby. 'Where is Gaby?' asked Katina anxiously. 'They kept her in the hospital. They said it was serious. They put her in an oxygen tent,' explained Tito."

I remember I had been frantic that night when I got home from my job search. Tito took me to the hospital…

What a frightening ordeal!

The worst part of it was that we were not allowed to see our baby during her hospital stay. "To avoid making her scream and cry which would worsen her condition and delay her healing," the doctors explained to us. "But she only speaks Greek! She will be lost! Feel abandoned! Traumatized!" I protested. "Don't worry, she will be in good hands," they tried to reassure me. So, I had to observe her while I was hiding behind doors and columns… I saw her being fed by a smiling young nurse in a humidified glass toy room... She looked all right. But when, after seven days, we took her home, Gaby wouldn't talk to us for two weeks! ... We were scared and anxious, but thanks God her trauma was not permanent; she bounced back to normal. And to our relief the hospital agreed that we could pay our bill in instalments. At that time, as landed immigrants, we were not yet fully covered by healthcare provided by the government.

After a week of rejections such as "You are over qualified!" and "You're going to leave us for a better position at the first opportunity." "So, sorry, but no thanks…" or "You don't have any Canadian experience," I finally found a job as a secretary with Mr. Silverman, owner-president of a zipper manufacturing firm on Notre Dame East, in Old Montreal. He was sympathetic to my plea: "Yes, I know I don't have a Canadian experience, but how am I going to get it if nobody gives me a chance? You must have been a landed immigrant once yourself, or your parents. Did you or did they have any Canadian experience then? Please give me a chance, I am a fast learner." He looked at me seriously, then, "You're hired," he answered, his hand outstreched to shake mine…

Two weeks later, Tito got a position with Shawinigan Engineering as a simple draftsman (he is an engineer with a Master's degree), but Stavros was still looking.

The moment Tito got a regular job, we moved to a nice "home" at 5500 De Salaberry, Apt. 105, near Gouin Boulevard, across from the Sacré Coeur Hospital and within a walking distance of the Cartierville train station. Modern, grey-white three story apartment buildings or triplexes, the basements used for indoor parking. Our friends from Istanbul, Julia and Stratos Inglessis, (Tito's classmate from Zografion), Julia's parents Zoe and Stavros Papadopoulos (he, Father's friend from yesteryear), were also in the same building. Talk about luck! It was a sunny 4 ½. The building had an underground garage, an outdoor pool and a small playground with swings for children. A dream! We got some basic furniture at Woodward's with our last dimes…

As the days and weeks passed we were amazed by the layout and the new products at the supermarkets, the great shops, the donuts (Mr. Donut), and Kentucky Fried Chicken, the streets lit with Christmas decorations and the many Santa Clauses. I took the train, every morning, from Cartierville to Place Ville-Marie downtown and then walked down to Notre Dame East. But Tito had to go further and he hated waiting for a bus in sub-zero temperatures, so his first pay went to a down payment on a new car. With an easy-to-get car loan – unheard of back in Turkey – he bought a brand new 1965 Chevrolet Belair; turquoise exterior, black interior… We were able to roam around and discover our new city.

We soon adjusted to the Canadian winter; it was cold but dry, sunny, clean and beautiful, in contrast to the humid, bone-biting and brown winters in Istanbul. The apartment was always warm (central controllable heating) and we had the company of good old friends for ourselves and our parents. We also met Anna and Michel Alibranti and their grown-up children Beba and Alex. They were also from Istanbul. It was not long before we met other expatriates too.

We visited downtown Montreal, picturesque Old Montreal and Notre-Dame Cathedral, St-Joseph Oratory and its Christmas *crèches*, Place-Jacques Cartier with its plunging view to the Old Port and the summer shows with clowns and bands and fire eaters. We visited the huge malls, the churches and the restaurants with their new-to-us cuisine… We drove up to the Laurentians, or, thirsty for water views, along the Lachine Canal up to Ste-Anne de Bellevue, and around the Richelieu River region. We would often go to Vermont, crossing the U.S. border just for fun, and then drive along Lake Champlain. The lakes and rivers had to make up for Istanbul's seas that we missed... Istanbul, surrounded by two seas, the Black Sea, and the Marmara

Sea, the Bosphorus strait uniting the two and the Haliç (Golden Horn) inlet…

Soon after we upgraded our furniture to Kay-Van's… Life was promising and beautiful.

I remember how my mother cried when she first saw the lighted cross on the top of Mount Royal. And how she cried even more that first spring when the police stopped all traffic on Côte Ste-Catherine for our church's (St. George Cathedral) street procession of Christ's symbolic body on Good Friday night…

Father's voice brings me back to the present..

"The Immigration Officer (in Istanbul) didn't warn me about the difficulties of finding employment here… It was only once we got to Montreal that I found out that my accounting experience was useless here. I needed to learn Canadian accounting methods. So, I learned English at the YMCA, then went to Sir George Williams and got an accountancy diploma, at my age, helping even the younger students. And when I brandished my diploma at the Employment Bureau, as a proof of my competence, the answer was 'You're over fifty! The market is full of young graduates. It will be very difficult to find a position at your age.' And my experience? Thirty years of experience that I adapted to local accounting procedures? It didn't count…"

He sweeps the air with his hand… "I was not afraid of work. I didn't want to depend on welfare. I would never accept money from Tito or you for my cigarettes or personal expenses. And both your Mama and I wanted to contribute to the household expenses… Yes, I know," he adds emphatically noting my expression of protest, "your Mama was looking after Gaby, and later Kathy, and cooking for you… and both you and Tito thought this was a big help. But Katina and I felt it was not enough for our shelter and livelihood in this new country where you both worked so hard, you with late hours in overtime and Tito with two jobs (moonlighting as real estate agent) So I accepted work as a bus boy and floor-sweeper at London Clothing Manufacturing. You should never be ashamed of any job that brings you honest wages, my child… The only bad thing about it was that it did cost me my hearing. Thirty *Singer* sewing machines running all day long…

"Later I was glad to work at the counter and as cashier for Peter, at our neighbourhood restaurant… I was treated well at Peter's. Everybody called me *Barba* Stavro. Peter and Antonia, his wife, treated me like family. The waitresses saw a confident and father figure in me, and Peter made me a Spider vodka-cocktail every night. I was the one to close the shop and open it in the mornings… It felt good…"

I see Father and Mama with Gaby, enjoying for the first time the ski slopes during our day excursions to the Lawrentians or to the Kahnawage Indian resort. Then I see Father brave our first harsh Canadian winters in his thin grey wool coat, wearing his new faux-astrakhan hat (that soon replaced his Istanbul Republica one) drawn deep down to his eyebrows with ear-muffs protecting his ears from the biting cold, and a grey mohair scarf that I had knitted covering his neck; the lighted cigarette dangling from his lips, walking on the icy roadsides while steadying himself on his metal-pointed cane…

He had to wait in the sub-zero temperatures, shivering, morning and evening, to take two buses and the Metro to and from London Manufacturing.

Oh, he had tried everything before accepting this job. But he soon realized that French was not enough in this bilingual city, so he started teaching himself English. First, with a *Linguaphone* course. Then he went to the YMCA and later to Sir George Williams' English and Accounting Classes, as he just recalled to me. He must have considered these English lessons quite an achievement because he kept all his exercise books and test sheets, not surprisingly marked '*Excellent, as usual.*' He also kept two composition tests:

> '*A small* [sic] *Arabian Story*'
> *A thousand years ago the Halif Omar was reigning in Bagdad. One*

day he announced that he was giving a gold bowl to whom would be able to tell him a real lie, otherwise he looses his head. With the hope to take the gold bowl many people were coming to the Halif Omar.

But he would always answer "this is possible." It couldn't count as a lie. Someone said that a camel was flying and answered again "that is possible, God willing". At last came a young man who said:

"Your Majesty, my grandfather lent your grandfather a barrel full of gold pounds.

Now give me either the gold bowl or the barrel full of gold pounds."

In Turkish: YA TOPU, YA KÜPÜ

And,

'A majestic ceremony' (Expo 67):

HOME WORK.

NAME: STAVROS EVANGELIDIS. Tuesday November 7th, 1967.

A majestic ceremony.

I saw all the ceremony where expo 67 was closed last Sunday. I heard the speach their excellencies Messrs general governor, Pearson Johnson and finaly the splendid speach of the Mayor of Montreal Mr. Jean Drapeau, who is to say the truth the real hero of expo 67.

Now we haven't expo any longer, but all Canadians we have it in our memory, and we hope to see another EXPO in the same place next year.

I used to go and visit everyday: Man and his world.

I would like to summarize our expo in the following true-story: An American asked a Canadian what is the difference between Montreal's expo and New York's Fair.

The Canadian answered:

THE SCORE IS: MONTREAL = 67
NEW YORK = NOTHING!

St. Evangelidis

After his Accounting Diploma from Sir George Williams, Stavros, ignoring the Employment Officer's warning, applied for an accountant position on his own. He had kept religiously the *GAZETTE* and *LA PRESSE* ads for accounting jobs even though he couldn't get one. He opened his own imports company and tried to introduce the Greek, French and English communities to imported goods from Turkey, like olive oil, soap, *Rakı* (the national Turkish drink) and canned cooked meals. He even approached established food companies to act as a representative or broker for them in return for a small commission. It did not work. It was too early for such a market then. Montrealers were not ready to try these new foods and products. Ironically, Turkish food and products abound now in specialty shops.

Then Stavros set up a small business with Paula and Amway pyramid goods that, even with door-to-door canvassing and home demonstrations, brought very little profit (all the while he kept copies of his letters and receipts – I wish he had done so in the past, for his writing...).

Finally, discouraged, he accepted this job at London Manufacturing. At least he had a small but steady income and could contribute to our new life. He was content, Katina was happy.

Tito's sister Marion joined us after a while and we all enjoyed our new life.

Gaby, Katina, Marion, Stavros, Erato (crouching).

Now, after years of feeling guilty about my father's hardships in our adopted country, his new attitude about his coming to Canada was a heartening balm to me.

* * *

The garden is all white this morning. The naked trees are clothed in iridescent glistening crystal gowns. Sunny but cold... Not a single bird in the garden... Stavros sips his sweet hot tea in silence, his gaze empty. How may I bring some cheer to him?

"You know that Yaya Neranzo used to sing in Arvanitika to me? In

Albanian?" I write in my pad.

He stares at me, interested. I've got him!

"Yeah," I continue, pressing the button of my recorder, "this one for instance":

Kokoriku koundesh
Misguli zonia bishtin.
Bishtin ku?
Vat'i perdru.
Perdru ku?
E hingir zogazit.
Zogazit ku?
Vat'im biolio meli..."

Stavros laughs heartily. At my false pronunciation or at the memory?

"What did it mean?" I ask.

"It's a children's song; about a rooster who chases a hen that went to gather honey..."

"And she used to tease me with a silly tale," I continue:

There was a rooster, with a leather slip...
Get up so that I start from the beginning.

"When I would get up she would repeat it, ending with, 'Sit down so that I start over.' And I was getting up and sitting down a zillion times in a row before realizing that there was no beginning; she was teasing me!"

Stavros laughs, happy. His eyes shine. She probably had played the same tricks on him when he was a small child...

"You know," he says smiling, "your Mama didn't know any of the songs of Neranzo. Those were rebel songs, thieves' songs... Famous during the Greek Revolution when Greek Albanians fought to liberate Greece from the Ottoman rule. There is this one:

Fierce Albanians,
where is Ali Pasha?
Oré, he is inside, sleeping,
and fears no one...

"Ali Pasha was an Albanian Janitchar himself, a Christian youngster raised by the Sultans as a Muslim Ottoman soldier. He was appointed by the Ottomans as a Controller of Albania. He was in love with Vassiliki, a Greek-Albanian girl... And that other one, *Lingo's* song."

Stavros' eyes are sparkling now. A wide smile crosses his lips…

"This Lingos, will become a hero. Many songs have been written about him, like that *Dhiavene Lingom'…* (Walk my Lingo…) and *O Lingos o Leventis* (Lingos the Brave). The French wrote about him calling him *Le Roi des Montagnes*. He was the most honest, the most ethical guy. Queen Amalia, the wife of Greek King Othon, fell in love with him. It was said that Amalia was a virgin when she died… Because Othon was… And Lingos fell surely in love with Amalia, but she was the Queen… So at the end I think that he left Greece and went to Turkey, because Turkey was the den of the 'goat-thieves' as they were called…"

Stavros stops, to clear his throat and regain his breath. He continues: "Then there is the song of the 'brave thief' Kitsos; *Kitso's mother's* lament:

Kitso's mother was lamenting on her walk;
'My Kitso, where are your weapons?
Where are your fighting clothes?'

And Kitso's answer:

'Crazy Mother, hero-strangler Mother,
You don't cry over my youth,
You don't cry over my bravery,
…But you cry over my damn weapons,
…over my damn fighting clothes…'

"They beheaded him.

"But Kitsos was brave [and generous]. When he went to Athens, to drink a coffee, he left a gold coin (as a tip). "

"Was this during 1821?" I ask.

"No, this was not during the Greek Revolution. It was during 1750 to 1800… The Resistance was going on before that… Then… [songs about] Dalis, Lavazanis… Also a song about brave girls, *Ta Koritsopoula*; another one about young heroes, *The Eaglet*, and so on… It's the whole history of the Greek rebel fighters. I had read all about them by some luminaries, Aristidis and Iakovos. Beautiful pens."

He slides back on his reclining chair, rests his head …

"I also remember the *Bridge of Arta…*" I write.

"Now the Bridge, my child… There was the Bridge of Devré and a Turkish-Albanian song about Devreli Hasan, about his crossing the Devré Bridge at night—"

"No. I mean another one, a Greek one that Yaya used to sing."

"Oh, *that* Bridge... When its architect finished it, he said, 'I will sacrifice the first woman who crosses it.' And she was his wife! ... It all started when Sultan Selim had built the Selimiyé Mosque at Adrinople (Edirné)... Its four minarets were so strategically placed that they could be seen from everywhere and seemed to swirl... After that, the Sultan ordered a bridge built, past Uzunköprü. The Bridge of *Arta*. When the Germans went over it during the First World War they were so impressed by it that they claimed: 'We cannot make such a strong bridge. Even if you bomb it or cross it with tanks, it will stand firm.'"

Stavros' gaze is fixed on the garden... When his gaze is lost like this I know that he withdraws to the Greek Revolution and Resistance. He straightens up in his chair, body leaning forward, hands grabbing the armrests. He says in a high pitched voice: "Kapodistrias was a hero vice-regent. But he was against the English. And the English put George Mavromihalis in to kill him. Then Miaoulis, with one cannon, burned the Admiralty of the Greek fleet."

"Why?"

"Because the English wanted to control it... And till today we (Greeks) are expecting justice from God! Americans and the West were trying to put Greece on their side to fight against the Russians! How on earth could Greece fight against Russia? Greece saw only good from Russia. What did the Americans do? They wanted to get to Athens, and immediately the Tsar came. 'Tak! Stop!' and he opened war. In 1898! ... Then, Serbia. Because Austria threatened them, he declared war on Austria."

"Who, the Tsar? Russia?" I ask.

"Yeah. There was the Orthodox Alliance. Now even if they have a Church again and a Patriarch, it is not the Old Russia. Although, Russians are descendants of Old Russians. Many Russians with Greek names like Ignatios, are Greek-Russians."

"Was Athanassios Diakos (the Resistance hero) also Russian?"

Stavros becomes animated. He gesticulates with his hands, his voice rises.

"No, Mother! Only Theodoros Orlof, the Great Katherine's lover, was for the Greeks. Ypsilantis, and all his gang, were Greeks. Russians did not fight against the Turks. Greeks did. Athanassios Diakos was a deacon. They were fighting (against the Turks) with Memvrionis and Lingiotakis with about two thousand warriors. Then in the middle of the fight... a cry: 'Who is Diakos?' – He was famous –. 'I am Diakos!'... So they capture him; handsome, brave... The Turkish commander asks him: '*Oré Biro*? Do you become a

Turk?' Answers Diakos: 'I am born Grekos, I will die Grekos!' So the Turkish Bey takes him and skews him. Alive! And Diakos sings: *'Look at the time that Death came to take me...* ' – this was made into a song. An Albanian passes nearby and sees that Diakos was to suffer another ten hours before dying. *'Oré Ghiaouri!'* he cries, takes his pistol and 'Tak!' he kills him so that he (Diakos) finds peace..."

Cough... Stavros regains his breath, sweeps the air with his hand, and resumes:

"When Androutsos learned of the killing of Diakos, who was his best friend... He gathered all his braves and attacked (battle of Syravlis?). He forced the Bey out...

"Then it was the turn of Thodoros Kolokotronis (named after Theodore Orlof). Kolokotronis was illiterate but brave. Whereas ancient Spartans' logo was: *I tan I epi tas*, either with my shield (alive) or on my shield (dead), Kolocotronis' logo was: *Eleftheria i Thanatos*, Freedom or Death! The tragedy is that he did not succeed... because most of the braves were Albanians and spoke Arvanitika... And when Dramalis fell, it was tragic..."

I don't follow all of this well, not having studied the Greek Resistance. But I don't want to cut the thread of his thoughts.

Stavros takes a sip of tea. He stares at the sky, through the ice-embroidered patio door. He appears lost in thought.

"The Sultans had no army" he says, animated. "They sent Enver Shanli from Serbia. Markos Botcharis cut him into pieces! Finally Hünyit Pasha, who was in charge, became prisoner. And when the Turks saw the impasse, they sank the Egyptian and the Moroccan navies so that they would win over the Greeks... And for what? The Janitchars, about twenty thousand, were mostly Greeks. But dangerous! They had the power to elect whoever Sultan they wanted. So when they gathered at Ok Meydani at Istanbul, the reigning Sultan cannoned them all down," gesticulates Stavros, "Taka, Taka! ... That was back in 1815. So, during the 1821 Revolution, the Turks had no fighting force. Because the Janitchars, wherever they went, slaughtered and pillaged, whereas the other Turks were lenient, soft. The fall of (Ottoman) Turkey was due to the absence of Janitchars. And also to the absence of the Albanians and the Kurds. So very few Turks able to fight had remained..."

We did not feel the hours pass as we both plunged into the realm of Resistance heroes, their heroism and their dens...

* * *

Today, December 21st, 1985, Father hands me a letter.

The two-page letter continues in five points, with Dr. Plante's correct diagnosis and explanations for pneumonia, and sums it up with "Now, all symptoms are gone, except difficulty in breathing and some dry cough; and the doctor should change or supplement his prescription with Tylenol and some new drugs and vitamins for complete healing and the lung specialist (he meant Dr. Mount) should be advised and consulted also." Dated and initialized...

I remind him that he breathes better on the reclining chair and that it would be better for him to sleep there during the night also. I explain to him, on my note pad, that all drugs have side effects and react differently for each individual. Difficulty in breathing is probably one of them. Even if the doctor prescribes another medicine it could still have the same side effects... I remind him of my own sick days in the past with my side effects. And the effects drugs have on Tito who takes medicine for high-blood pressure, and on Gaby, who cannot accept even Tylenol because it gives her arrhythmia. And that *Ensure* is the extra liquid vitamins his doctor prescribed him but that he refuses to take. Maybe it is time to try it? In the meantime I would talk to the doctors.

From that day on, Stavros sleeps in the reclining chair...

* * *

Christmas! Gaby is home...

For the next few days the house is filled with holiday preparations, Christmas tree decorating, cooking, get-together parties for both girls and their friends, and the traditional New Year's Eve family gathering.

Tito's sister Marion and her daughter Roxane, his cousin Eleni with her husband Yanni Riga and our friends M. and L. come too.

The girls asked that I make my *salamato* chocolate-biscuit cake. Tito arranged for a Turkish buffet through an Armenian caterer so that I would not have to cook all day. Artin and his wife did a great job. They prepared *yalandji dolma* stuffed vine-leaves, rolled *sigara* cheese böreks, *arnavut djiğeri* – Albanian fried liver – for my father, creamy eggplant salad, spicy *kefté* meatballs, cold fish with Russian salad dressing, rice-stuffed mussels and tuna, *tarama* fish-egg salad and *kokoretch* – grilled rolled intestines.

Father made an effort to stay in the living room and to savour some of the Turkish food, mainly the soft creamy dishes that he watered down with a milky glass of *Arak* (an Egyptian substitute for *Rakı*).

As we were nibbling, the girls ran a funny gift exchange with improvised lottery-draws where every guest, upon the drawing of his name, could "steal" a gift from anyone else, till all the names had been drawn.

Tito, Gaby, Stavros, New Years's Eve 1985

Kathy played her favourite Pachelbel on the piano, then she was joined by Tito for a four-hand improvised rendition of Hadjis' *Give me a sea-shell from the Aegean Sea.* Finally Tito treated us to a whole repertoire of Greek songs that we sang in chorus, in low voices, including New Year's Carols "*Aghios Vassilis erhetai*" (St. Basil is coming) and *"Oi Zografiotés irthané/Na sas poun ta Kalanda..." (*Zoghrafiotés came to sing you the carols*)*. This was the special song the students of Zografion College used to sing when they were going around to the rich houses in Istanbul, performing for donations to their school fund-raising campaign to help poor students - Tito played the accordion, then.

Father was a good sport throughout the evening. He kissed the girls tenderly as he thanked them for their beautiful gift, a soft beige cashmere cardigan. But he looked tired (or sad?) He tried to keep smiling, but around eleven asked to be excused and went to lie down on his reclining chair, in front of the TV.

I had a lump in my throat through the whole evening, glad to have all my loved ones around me but filled with heartache as I realized that there would not be another New Year's Eve celebration for my Father, no other spring probably, no other summer for sure, no autumn, no winter…

Stavros with Kathy, New Year's Eve, 1985.

I retreated to the bathroom for a good cry, then washed my face, redid my make up and came out trying not to spoil the evening.

At midnight, Tito poured champagne in the prepared glasses to welcome the New Year. We hugged and kissed each other, our eyes wet with emotion. Then he cut the *Vassilopita,* the traditional New Year's Eve cake, in honour of St. Basil, the bishop of Caesarea, who used to distribute cakes to poor families and would hide a gold coin inside, towards a dowry for the family's daughter or daughters. Tito divided the cake into equal pieces for each of us, plus one for the house, and instructed us not to say a word until we all had tasted and examined our piece of cake.

I ran down with some cake and a glass of champagne for Stavros, but he was asleep in his chair, a quiet beatitude on his face. I did not wake him. Gaby got our *bronze* lucky-coin – a penny. She will be the lucky one for the New Year.

VI - The Struggle

A week later, Madame Asbeth calls to let us know about next Sunday's New Year tea party given by our Constantinopolitan Association. Would we attend? And should she reserve a table for us? I promise to let her know. I remember how good Father felt a few months ago at this Association gathering. Why not try it again now? It could really be the last time…

I ask Father if he would like to go. He is not sure he can, but he says we should go. I tell him we would not go if he didn't come. It would only be from 3 to 7. We could go at 3 and leave earlier if he felt tired. It would only be a few steps to our car and then a smooth ride to the hotel entrance. And we could see all our old friends from Istanbul.

Well, if he is all right, he will make the effort, he says.

I call and make the reservations.

As if the heavens agreed with us, it is a sunny, balmy winter day. Stavros is dressed warmly. I chose to wear my light blue chiffon dress with the flowing skirt, to look my best both for Stavros and for Tito. Before we leave, I throw my recorder into my handbag.

The Hall is full. I seat Stavros on a very comfortable chair facing the music, the dance floor, and the podium. People, who know now of Father's illness, flock to our table to greet him with joy. Stavros is wearing his hearing-aid tonight. I press the button of the recorder.

"Happy New Year, Stavré! Are you OK? Great to see you!"

"Kyrios Hadjis! Our judge. I admire you! You are our pride! Our ever-young Hadjis!" answers Stavros with enthusiasm, shaking the judge's hand vigorously.

As I move around, I hear snatches of Father's high-pitched conversation with our friends: "You went back to Istanbul? After eighteen years? It must have changed a lot… Stayed at Prinkipo? Yes, it's normal that Andonis –

owner of a famous sea-side restaurant in Istanbul - does well in Athens. Because he knows his trade well and he is a hard worker... Stratos? Yes, expected. You see he is an accountant... so many accountants in Athens ... He should do something else."

Tito, Kathy, Stavros, Erato

Father Halkias conducts a prayer for the New Year and then blesses the *Vassilopités.* He has studied in the Theological School of Halki Island, in Istanbul, and shares a real kinship with us. He is present at each of our gatherings since the founding of our Association.

Tito is seated at the piano, rolled-in especially for him once it was known that we would attend, and we all sing the Zografiotes' New Year carols about St. Basil coming to town with "pen and paper" ...

Applause.

"Bravo Tito!" shouts his cousin, Eleni Riga.

Back at our table, handshakes continue: "Anghelos? (Kyriou)..."

"I saw you coming in, Stavré, and—"

After a while Anghelos approaches me and asks whether I have started interviewing Stavros about his memoirs. I tell him that I am recording him, and that actually a tape is running tonight. He is delighted and he expresses his eagerness to listen to the tapes.

The ladies distribute the *Vassilopités* to the tables. The large one is made by the Atlas Pastry Shop, on Bernard street (where we find all the delicacies from Istanbul), and the smaller ones are made by the ladies' committee. Other cakes and biscuits are also served, with tea and coffee.

Mary Kalipolitis is at the podium: "Ladies and gentlemen we are waiting to see who are the *Vassilopita* coin winners. We have two winners tonight! ... Oh, the lucky winner of the Atlas cake is Kyria Vavarikou. Give her a warm applause! We wish her success during the whole year."

Stavros's voice is close to me: "Nice gathering. A real group of Istanbul … And there is something I noticed here – and I have visited many places – that the happiest and most civilized people are the Canadians…"

"The second lucky-coin winner tonight (from our *Vassilopita*) is Mr. Kalipolitis," announces Mary.

Tito, always a joker, shouts laughing, "He knew it!"

Mary smiles and exonerates her husband: "He did not choose the piece of cake, they gave it to him. He didn't put the coin inside it. Others cut the cake…"

At our table, Stavros continues: "… And again before I left … I have here my daughter, my grandchildren…"

People come to greet me: "My Eratoula!" This is Elisso Fokaefs, the daughter of Kyrios Diamantis, our kind grocery store owner in Istanbul, who had become a good friend of my mother's here. And Yolanda Frangulaki-Pantzopoulou, another schoolmate of mine, from Ste.Pulchérie. Amazing how so many friends from Istanbul are gathered in this hall tonight.

"Do you see how much people love you, how they all come to greet you?" I remark to Father.

"My child", he answers, "a Greek spreads always his warmth…"

Tito plays oldies at the piano. A group gathers around him and sings. I join in: "*Return to me. I am waiting for you…*"

Stavros' stentorian voice startles me: "*Return to me. I am waiting for you…*"

Is it the enthusiasm of the moment? Or is he thinking of Katina?

Tito plays the whole repertory of Greek songs we used to sing in Istanbul, and now everybody joins in.

"*I will adore you*"; "*A friend that came from the past*"; "*Lies, Lies, I taught you only lies*"; "*Please, waves, do not wake her*"; "*Dreams that last only one night*"; "*We were going by tram and others with carts*"; "*I wish the sea were wine*"; "*One more glass of wine"*; and finally the lullaby "*Yélékaki*" that Mama used to sing to me when I was little:

To yelekaki pou foris…
…
(The vest that you are wearing,
it's me that I sewed for you.
I lined it with sorrow and tears…)

Stavros joins in again at the leitmotiv:

Aïdeh to mallono ké to vrizo,
Aïdeh tin karthoula tou rayizo.
(Aïdeh, I scold him and I swear at him,
Aïdeh, I break his little heart…)

I can't believe my eyes and my ears. Stavros is beaming, gesticulates, sings high, with full lungs, his eyes sparkling, his hands beating the tempo! He becomes animated and shouts: *"Ali Dayı! Kır belini Ali Dayı, Kır belini, Hay, Hay,"* – a Turkish folk song – and starts singing it without waiting for Tito to play. Tito obliges. They applaud Stavros. He continues with another Black Sea Turkish folk dance:

Hamsi koydum tavaya da bashladim oynamaya…
(I put a small fish in the fry pan, and I started to dance…)

More applause. .

"I Voskopoula," (the little Shepherdess), shouts Stavros again.

Tito is playing another tune, but Father starts singing,

"Mia Voskopoula aghapissa…"
(… I fell in love with a little shepherdess…
I was a ten-year old lad…)

He is overexcited, sings off key, shouts too much, but the whole audience joins in and sings with him as Tito continues to play … I am in awe. So much support, so much empathy, so much love from these people for Stavros… A warm wave embraces me and I feel part of the group as never before, proud to belong to such a wonderful community… A miracle is taking place in front of my eyes! Father forgets he is ill. He doesn't even cough! The power of mind over body? Except for dipping his cake into his cup of tea, he enjoys life with all his might! Is he really that happy or is he forcing himself, sensing this is the last magnificent sparkle before the sunset?

When Tito tired, finally stops playing, the DJ puts on Greek dances. Tito gets up and joins in a *Syrtaki* with a couple. Stavros stops his animated political discussion with friends, puts two fingers to his mouth and whistles. I join the dance, the lively *Kalamatiano* now, with a glance at Stavros. I want to offer this sight to him. As I expect, he interrupts his heated debate. He is looking at us beaming and clapping his hands noisily in tempo... We repay him, with a frenetic fast-stepping *Hassapo-Serviko*. People join Stavros in whistling with enthusiasm.

Surprise! Father wins at the gift lotteries! Yorgos Musmulis, the vice-president, helps him get to the podium where he exchanges his ticket number for the prize, a bottle of Greek *Metaxa* brandy.

"Buy a ticket for me," Stavros says to Tito, giving him some change. "My luck has turned. I should win the lottery, now."

We leave after an elderly and joyous St. Basil, impersonated by Kyrios Vafiadis, arrives and distributes gifts to the children.

Once home, as I help tackle Stavros into his reclining chair, I lean over, hug him and kiss him on the cheek. "You made me very happy, tonight, Father," I say. He smiles and pats my shoulder without a word.

During the next days Stavros slips back into his old fragile self. Not only does he not join us for dinner, he also doesn't touch the tray that I bring to him. He claims he has difficulty swallowing, although I make sure to prepare smooth purées and soft eggs.

It is almost eleven when I wake up this Saturday morning – I'd stayed up late to watch a good TV program.

Stavros is awake, dressed and shaven. He must have managed his morning toilet on his own. He did not call me (or did I not hear him?).

"Sorry, I'm late, Father. What would you like for breakfast, or rather brunch?"

"*Papara!*"

"Coming. Do you want *THE GAZETTE?*"

He shakes his head. "No!"

Pretty laconic this morning! Is he crossed at me, or something?

As I prepare his favourite soft meal, small pieces of white bread in a bowl of hot milk with lots and lots of sugar, I empty a can of Vanilla flavoured *Ensure* into the mixture.

"What are you doing?" asks the angry voice of Kathy as she stands in front of me at the kitchen counter. I did not hear her coming.

"What do you mean? I'm preparing Father's breakfast."

She reaches for the *Ensure* and shakes it in front of my eyes:

"You are cheating him! You know he doesn't like this!" she scorns me.

"But he doesn't eat enough varied food. I have to fortify his body, his muscles," I defend myself at her unexpected attack.

"You are so selfish, Mother!" she exclaims, raising her voice.

"Selfish?" I look at her, astonished at her anger. An immense pain fogs her eyes.

"Yes, selfish!" she cries. "Who do you thing you're kidding, Mother? Him or you? You know there is no cure, you know he is going to die. Fortify his body, for what? For prolonging his agony? The best thing that could still happen to him would be to die today, now, immediately! While he still has all his faculties, all his dignity! While he can still stand up and walk! While he is still without pain! He knows, probably consciously, but maybe subconsciously, what to do. To stop eating, to end it sooner. But no! You have to fortify his body! Against his will! You don't want to let him go. For you, not for him! You want to keep him alive for you! If you want to help him, let him go, Mother! This is the only help you can offer him."

She is trembling.

I am trembling. Her words sting me like slaps in the face and enter my heart like a knife. She is only sixteen. She has never spoken to me like this. We both have tears in our eyes. She turns and leaves the kitchen and shuts herself in her room.

I sit down, my knees too weak to support me. I know she adores her Papou. Could she be right? Did I have the wrong approach from the beginning? *Let him go! Now! The only help that I can offer him is that? To help him die?* He was so well, so full of life, full of joy, a week ago… I bury my head in my hands and start to sob. Tito is still asleep. He has not interfered all these months, he's let me do what I wanted to do, going along with me, trusting that I was doing the best I could. What now? ...

I go and kneel in front of my Virgin Mary icon, at our iconostase. "*God, Christ, Virgin Mary, help me, guide me…*"

I know that my initial prayer has been answered. The cancer has not spread to his bones, Father has NO PAIN. What should I do now? How can I help him die? With dignity ... "*In your hands, my God…*" I whisper. God will decide the "moment". In the meantime, even if Kathy has a valid point, I feel I will have to fortify Father's body for the same reason she feels I shouldn't: to help him keep his dignity. It is this dignity that helped him enjoy the feisty afternoon a few days ago, and the love of people around him. Yes, the lack of dignity might be imminent. But for the moment I can help him preserve it. I side with the doctors. *Fortify his body, his muscles, so that he can still stand up.* Yes, this is the only way to help him keep his dignity. For as long as I can. The love, our love, he will have it to the end. The rest, the "moment", I leave it up to God. I will do nothing else to stop it coming...

Stavros eats his *Papara* smacking his lips. "It has a strange taste," he says, "what did you add to it?"

Astounded that his taste buds are intact this morning, "A vanilla bean," I lie. "Do you like it?"

"Mmm... Not really. Don't add any next time."

I acquiesce, promising myself, without any remorse, to buy a natural brand of *Ensure*, without any flavour additive.

"Feel like talking?" I ask him, when he finishes.

"What do you want to talk about?"

"Yozgat! Yalvatch! The forced 'military' – or rather concentration – camp for non-Muslim Turks. When and how it happened?"

Stavros sits back, his head on the headrest... His fingers tap on the armrest. His gaze turns inward, in recollection... I press my recorder button. A hiss...

"It was in 1941..." he starts, "end of April or something..." *Close. First of May, as I double-checked.* "They gathered twenty classes."

"Why?"

"After Greece lost the war... (Cough) ... When the Germans entered Athens... Because there was a fear that the Germans would march through Turkey. You see, when the Germans entered Thessaloniki, its Armenian residents, ignoring the fact that they were Greek citizens themselves, rioted against Greeks and attacked and vandalized Greek shops."

"Who? The Armenians?"

"Yes. And the Mayor of Athens, Kostas Holiatis (?), when he visited Istanbul, declared that the Armenians had forgotten that they were 'guests' ... Whereas Greece protected its minorities. It is known that the Greeks protected all the Jews of Thessaloniki. This is marked in the Golden Bible... Anyway... So, there was the fear that the Germans would enter Turkey, to gain strategic advantage (against Greece). But the Armenian incident in Greece was known. And there were one hundred thousand Armenians in Istanbul, all pro-German. So there was a probability that the Armenians – long-time enemies of the Turks since the Armenian genocide under the Ottomans – would collaborate with the Germans and create a problem. The plan was to gather twenty classes, Greeks, Armenians and Jews, and intern them in Anatolia."

"The rumour was," Stavros continues," that the 'conscription' plan was mainly against the Armenians. But they could not take away just the Armenians. How? In secret? Risky. Politically then. So, Inönü, decided to evacuate all non-Muslim Turkish citizens from the city. There was the triumvirate of Atatürk, Fevzi Çakmak and Ismet Inönü. Atatürk, the founder of the Turkish Republic, was dead, Inönü was president and Fevzi Çakmak [pr. Tchakmak] was in command of the army. If we were sent to Anatolia in civilian clothes, we would be massacred. So Marshall Fevzi Çakmak said: 'If we take them, we must clothe them in military uniforms.' So we all wore military uniforms. That saved our lives..."

Stavros stops, clears his throat, spits in a tissue paper. Then resumes:

"We were separated into three groups. Armenians, Greeks and Jews. And we were assigned to Givgionia (?), to Afyon-Karahisar and to Kütahya... Under the control of the gendarmes. They took us to Karaköy in trucks and then they loaded us into small boats to send us to Tuzla. Your poor Mama was running along the quay with the other women..."

I remember the day Stavros was taken. It was sudden. A taxi had stopped in front of the house – I don't recall the time of day. A small fat man stepped out, asked for Katina and explained that he was sent by Yusuf Yilmaz, Stavros' friend from *Ladoskala*. Yusuf wanted her to know that Stavros, along with others from the Oil Market, was taken "soldier", that Yusuf Bey had sent him to take her to the quay where they were gathered, and that Stavros needed some underwear – Yaya Neranzo was not home at the time, she must have been at the church.

Katina called our neighbour Marianthi across the open window and asked her to come and stay with me. Then she prepared Stavros' underwear.

"Everything is going to be OK," she reassured me, and followed the man to the taxi.

It was night when she came back. Troubled, pale, long-faced, exhausted, but composed.

"Where is Father? What is happening?" I asked.

"Where is Stavris?" (as she used to call him) asked Neranzo, startled that Father was not home yet.

"He is OK," answered Katina, "he will be away for a while. He will be OK. Now go and get some butter and eggs from Kyr' Diamantis," she said to me.

This is it. She wants to speak alone with Marianthi and Neranzo. It must be serious, I thought. I ran as fast as I could to the grocery shop and back. I caught bits of sentences as I entered the apartment:

"In trucks… Then to… in cattle wagons… Like animals… No windows, nothing… Don't know… Everybody says they just cannot kill them… International incident… They will have to protect them… Don't know …"

Neranzo was leaning against the door, her gaze lost, biting her lips.

"What is really happening?" I asked, putting the paper bag on the table.

"Well, Father has been taken soldier. There is a war going on, you know… But Turkey is not in the war. They are sending them to the middle of Anatolia. It's a secure zone, away from every battle. So, he will be OK," Mama tried to reassure me again in a voice that struggled to appear calm.

"When is he coming back?"

"We don't know…"

My hands trembling, my heart pounding, I went to light the votive candle in the iconostase and pray to God to keep Father alive and well. Neranzo watched me expressionless, without a word or a sign, then she retreated to her room.

Katina did not cry. In fact she never cried in front of me after that, even though the rumours were that we would never see our "soldiers" again… She just lost her smile and her zest for life… But she was strong and courageous. She took immediate steps to face our new life. She dedicated all her efforts to me and to our survival without Stavros.

First, she sold all the new furniture, keeping only the old essentials and the new *Singer* sewing machine, and moved back to the first floor, vacated by a tenant who did not pay his rent.

Second, she enrolled me in Tarsis Varidou as a *demi-pensionnaire,* that's eating at the school's kitchen at lunch-time. That left Mama free to be away for a full day.

Then she started to work daily at Evghenoula's haute couture atelier, *Genny's,* at Sakiz Agadji. She also managed to keep the best of her old clients by working at home on nights and weekends, till dawn.

For the first few weeks she brought me to school herself and came to take me home at 4. The girl next to me in class was Sofoula Papadimitraki, who lived up the hill, on the same street as us, close to the mosque. Her brother George was in a higher class at the same school. After a few weeks, I joined them and we traveled to school and back home together – later, we made the trip just the two of us, Sofoula and I. On foot. Forty-five minutes each way.

Now Yaya was spending all her mornings and afternoons at the nearby Sts. Constantine and Helen church. – *Why? Did she have a need to pray for Stavros?* 'I found some friends of my age, we talk together…' she had explained.

So Katina entrusted me to Ismet Hanoum, our landlady, until she came home – some days as late as 7 p.m.

I actually enjoyed staying with the Samanoglus. I loved to share a snack of toast, butter, sour-black-cherry jam and cheese with Tomris, their only daughter, and watch her draw in black Chinese ink and then pencil-colour maps and animals and parts of anatomy for her geography or her physics homework; or do her writing or math exercises. She would let me use her small wooden number-game where little numbered square-pegs had to add up to the same total vertically and horizontally.

I loved the glow of their exquisite red-and-gold Venetian glass oil lamp on the large rectangular table, loved to listen to the Children's Hour on the Turkish radio broadcast, hum the songs with the children's chorus. I loved to watch Shahsiné-Hanoum's (Ismet Hanoum's sister) flying fingers knit or crochet colourful ski jackets and lacy blouses. Loved to fondle Mourgo, their fat, old orange-striped cat. Loved to listen to the family's Cretan Greek chat – '*kouzoulath'ken afti,* she got crazy, that one'; '*tché na soo po*, and I will tell you'– and I loved to share their early supper of patties filled with meat or spinach, accompanied by boiled dandelion salad dressed in bitter lemon.

The moment Katina got home, she used to rush to the basement kitchen to prepare a quick dinner for the three of us – always forbidding me to go down to the basement, except with her, to help her bring some plate upstairs, maybe because I was very thin and sickly or because of the rats – then wash the dishes, clean the table, check my homework, do some laundry, and retreat to her spot at the corner of the brass day-bed to finish a garment, mostly by hand.

I wanted to help. I longed to help. I was allowed to iron for instance. Starting with handkerchiefs, napkins, tablecloths, sheets, pillow cases and face clothes and towels – all square things. Then I "graduated" to ironing pyjamas and nightgowns. Finally I could touch blouses and shirts. Our own only, though. Mama would patiently show me how: starting at the back first, then the two front laps – the buttons face down over a thick towel – then the *empiècements*, followed by the sleeves. Cuffs would be next and the collar the very last. Those I had to sprinkle with starch water and start ironing on the wrong side first and finish on the right side. Finally I would put the garment on a wooden hanger and hang it on the back of a chair. After I passed all those "tests" with flying colours, Mama would allow me to iron some sewing material, first to take the wrinkles out, then opening up some seams and finally ironing some large skirts. Always with a protective cheese-cloth so as not to risk scorching the garment. Yet she would only allow me very elementary tasks for sewing chores. Like taking out the white basting threads or, more rarely, making an overcast on the side seams, which, naturally, was never to her satisfaction. It was not only that she didn't trust me. She didn't want me to learn this trade that she had been forced into and that she hated. Sometimes I busied myself making simple sleeveless or kimono dresses for my tiny finger-size plastic doll.

Katina often worked till the wee hours. She was up again before daybreak to light the woodstove, prepare breakfast and kiss me goodbye with a sign of the cross on my forehead: "God be with you." How did she manage to keep such strength and stamina? She never shed a tear in front of me. Never uttered a complaint. She just stopped singing altogether… Mama, who sang all day long… Who sang while bathing, sewing, cooking, cleaning... For her singing was like breathing. Now it was as if she stopped breathing...

The next time I heard her sing I was eighteen, during our first trip to Greece, after the end of the war, to finally visit our relatives and friends who had escaped the atrocities of German occupation and the aftermath… It was when visiting my father's old friend Heracles and his wife Anna. They begged Katina to join them for a song. "To remember the good old times." She did, her voice not faltering, the tears glistening on her cheeks… And the other time was about twelve years later, in our home in Montreal, during the engagement party for Tito's sister when Marion asked her to please sing a song since her own mother, Amélie, was not there to sing for her. 'I cannot, I forgot how,' Katina protested at first, but then she gave in to our begging and sang, in a low voice, accompanied at the piano by Tito… This time it was Stavros whose cheeks glistened with tears… and ours too… But Mama did not sing again…

Father's voice brings me back to the present.

"We got off at Tuzla… We stayed there three or four days. Then a few freight trains with cattle cars, no windows nor… They herded us into these cattle cars, closed us in. And only when we had a need to… they would open the wagons, at certain points in the wilderness, to let us out to do our … job…. When we arrived at the capital, Ankara, the Jewish women were waiting in cars to have a look at their husbands who were in these freight cars.

"We stopped at some station, then we were transferred to trucks and we left for Yozgat. During the trip, some trucks overturned and people got lost. How many, we don't know. When we arrived at Yozgat, some people stoned us… And there were some Cretans who pitied us...

"Anyway, they took us up on the mountain… The workers were down the hill and we were up the hill. In tents."

Stavros is interrupted by a bout of coughing. When he breathes freely again, his hand makes a sweep in the air.

"We stayed there approximately a month and a half. A few letters arrived from home, distributed by the gendarmes. They were eager to get money from us. The chief of gendarmes called some of us "Bad Blood". That was meant for the Armenians (whom they distrusted). There were about six thousand Bulgarians as well, with us. They all had Turkish citizenship but spoke Greek. Bulgaria, to help them, took two hundred thousand Turks captive in the mountains and declared that if a single nose of those Bulgarians (in Yozgat) bled, the Turks in Bulgaria would be eliminated. Yeah … Bulgaria played a great role at that time. Russia also, as protective of the Armenians…"

"After the battles of El-Alamein and Stalingrad," continues Stavros, "the army replaced the local gendarmes – because the gendarmes were accepting bribes… There, they separated us. Some of us went to Fats (?) and Yannina, others I don't know where. But our group was to go to Sparta (Isparta), to Yalvatch."

Cough again… Stavros slows down, drums the armrest for a while. Resumes.

"It is then that Atlamazoglou got sick and needed aspirin and quinine. So I went down to the city, with a friend, to buy some for him. On our way back, a gendarme tried to hit me with his rifle. I grabbed the rifle and gave him one. "Pat!" Took him down. Night! Raining strong too. He could not find me ... When we reached our mountain camp, Atlamazoglou, who didn't know me well then, told Petros Papadopoulo: 'Get Stavros' address in Istanbul.'

"After a while your Mama told me in a letter that Atlamazoglou had sent her two cans of olive oil, one can of *Urfa* butter and I don't know how many pounds of pasta, beans and legumes…"

Yes, people were constantly helping us during these difficult times. Especially Father's Turkish friends and clients. Yusuf Yilmaz sent a large check to Mama claiming this was a commission Stavros had earned from selling olive oil and had asked him to keep it for "Erato's education" and that there was more to come from other clients who would remit the money to him now so that he could forward it to her… Nadji Bey (whose wife and daughters were also Mama's clients), sent us wood for heating – difficult to get in those war years – claiming that Stavros had ordered and paid for it. When Father's good friend Neshet Akol also sent a truck load of wood and kitchen coal, Mama protested that Stavros had already sent us some through Nadji Bey. Neshet Bey maintained that Stavros had ordered some through him also, to make sure we would have enough for the long winter. Ibrahim Bey, our landlord, assured Mama she would not have to pay any rent till Father returned.

And Kyrios Diamantis Kavadias, the Greek owner of the small neighbourhood grocery store, told Mama not to worry; he would keep an account open for her till Stavros returned and would get his payment then – although it was doubtful whether Stavros would ever return. Kyr' Diamantis' own son, Yanni, had left as a volunteer to join the battle for Greece. Yanni never came back… It is indeed a very small world, as Kyr' Diamantis, after his wife Hariklia passed away, emigrated to Montreal with his daughter Elisso and her husband Yorgo Fokaefs whom we met through our Association. Elisso, now mother of Magda and Kosta, maintained a close friendship with Mama here.

Stavros continues his tale, looking at me. "I became good friends with the Turkish colonel, named Nuri Bey if I remember right. So, when they prepared the transfer lists, some Jews changed them and substituted their friends' names for some of ours. Whereas we should have been together with Atlamazoglou, Oreopoulos, etc… 'Stavro, they are separating us!' warned our friends. I went to Nuri Bey and protested that some Greeks had been substituted. Nuri Bey was startled. 'You make the list!' he said to me. And I did. So we were together again, Anestis Yenidounyas, Atlamazoglou, Petros Papadopoulos, Oreopoulos and others. We took the train to Ankara and then to Eskishehir… One of our friends was playing cards and losing a lot. Not only his own, but also the little money I had and that he had asked me to lend him to help to pay his debts. Atlamazoglou saw that I was not smoking, not eating, not drinking. He took me aside and asked me what was happening. When I explained, he gave me some money. 'You can help your friend', he told me, 'but give him no money. Give him a pack of cigarettes, offer him a glass of tea, but not a cent. Deal?' 'Deal,' I reassured him. What days…"

Stavros's grey-green eyes turn inward, in retrospection.

Those were indeed difficult times for all of us. Especially the first weeks without any news from Father.

First, I remember, Mama trying very hard to be brave and not to succumb to depression. Very soon after Stavros' departure, she realized she was pregnant. She could not afford to bring a child into her life at this time, so she had to abort this baby. She never forgave herself. From that day on she considered herself a "murderess"... In her whispering conversations with Marianthi I had overheard sentences like, the doctor had said 'What a pity! You have a constitution to bring many healthy children to this world.' And he had advised her to go to the top of a deserted mountain, at Skoutari Forest, or Tchamlidja (Çamlica) or elsewhere, and scream with all her might and let all this rage and pain out of her system and then cry or sob for hours if she had to. To take away the bitterness that was poisoning her ...

Those first weeks were hard for Neranzo also. She was gone to church all day, and started to coming home later every afternoon. Till one day, some "good friends" reported to Mama that Neranzo was badmouthing her. 'He was a genius her Stavri. Could have married a rich woman with a large dowry and live like a king. But, no, he had to choose this penniless girl...'

Katina faced her mother-in-law directly. 'Is it true what I heard? Did you say those things about Stavros and me?' she asked her.

Neranzo did not excuse herself. She looked Katina straight in the eye. 'Yes, I did,' she admitted, 'not because you are bad for him or anything – on the contrary – but because I believe that if he had had a rich wife he would not be gone. She would have paid bribes, found a way to save him.'

Katina looked at her in disbelief. Then in disgust. At that point in her life, she could not accept another betrayal. She had treated this woman with love and respect, she had nursed her back in Skoutari when they were all sick with typhus, she had looked after her, sewed all her dresses, coats and underwear, she did not let her do any housework and... Mama did not even defend herself. As was in her habit, she did not utter a word, just turned around and retreated to her room. But from that day on she did not address a single word to Neranzo. She continued to take care of her, even continued to sew for her, but she would only clean her room when Neranzo was away or prepare a basin for a bath and ask me to help my Yaya.

Things did not get better when Father's reassuring first letters arrived after a long delay. If Neranzo asked for news about Stavros, I was to communicate it to her. And Yaya refused to join us at the dinner table, even though she was welcome. I had to bring her food on a tray to her room. I was full of hurt, because I adored my mother and I loved my Yaya deeply. I could not understand why Mama could not forgive this woman who had no one else in the world and who lived for her only son who, according to all predictions during the first weeks, would never return. And I could not understand why Neranzo was not apologizing to this woman who respected her and took such good care of her, who was hurting as much as she was herself, if not more, and was struggling to secure a decent life for all three of us. I promised myself not to be like either of them when I grew up, but instead to be forgiving, non-judgemental and humble.

I look at Father. "You broke your arm there," I remind him.

"Yes, my elbow. They first took me to the Officers' Hospital, Djebedji (Cebeci), in Ankara, to fix it. Murat Hodja was the best surgeon there at the time. I must admit that they treated us well, like Turkish soldiers. Then I was sent to Sparta, to recover."

"It was the right arm? Yes? That's why you couldn't write and Mama got anxious because of your long silence, and came to Sparta, by train, to visit you?"

Stavros smiles, happy. He plays with his wedding ring.

"What a crazy woman!

"Although I had sent her a telegram explaining I was well and I would write soon… She didn't listen. She thought I was wounded more seriously or something. To travel alone in the middle of Anatolia!

"You know, some lecherous man tried to bother her on the train, but a very polite Turkish Army officer, a *zabit*, saved her and offered her his protection during the whole ride.

"She was a beautiful woman your Mama. And once she arrived in Sparta, the Turkish officers offered us a private room, and they enjoyed the diversion. A Turkish wife would never do such a thing… at the time…

"They talked for days about Katina's visit..."

I remember the commotion that Father's telegram – "I'm OK. Broke my arm. Healing at Sparta," – caused after his many weeks of silence.

"I don't believe he only broke his arm," Mama explained to Marianthi. "Something is wrong with him. I have to go and see him with my own eyes. I cannot live like this!" So she entrusted me again to Ismet Hanoum, asked Marianthi to keep an eye on us, that is on Yaya and me, "only for a few days", and off she went, in a most exquisite multi-coloured flowered silk dress, "to cheer up Stavros..."

"You returned in August of 1942, if I recall correctly, almost after a year and a half," I say to Father, "with a stiff arm. And although you praised the care you got at Djebedji, you went for help to Niko, the *Kavassis*, the chiropractor *portier* at the British Embassy. It was Niko who finally fixed your arm."

Stavros laughs. "Yes, the bones had grown the wrong way. So Nikos had to break my arm again, put the bones back in place correctly – without any painkiller or anything, just a shot of whisky, but he was good and fast. Thanks to him my arm healed properly and found its lost mobility."

He rests his head on the pillow.

"Tired?" I ask.

"Not really..."

"Want a cup of tea? A cigarette?"

"A cigarette? It's such a long time since... Where are you going to find any?"

"I can't find your favourite *Export Plain*. But there's Tito's *Benson & Hedges*. Filtered. He left a package on the counter."

"I can try... And a coffee, please, with lots of milk and sugar. Six spoonfuls."

I bring him the coffee and light his cigarette. He takes a deep puff... and coughs. He waits to recover his breath then takes a second puff... Coughs again... "Neah!" he exclaims as he extinguishes the cigarette in the ashtray I hand him. "Filtered cigarettes are not for me." He takes a sip of his coffee.

"When did you start to smoke?" I ask him, to distract him.

"When I met your Mama. True!" he explains, as I raise my eyebrows. "She told me she liked the smell of tobacco on my breath... Half a pack led to one, then over the years, to four packs a day ... But I never inhaled. I do not inhale. So there is no harm done to my lungs..."

Right! I think bitterly. He became a ferocious chain smoker, striking only one match in the morning and lighting one cigarette on the previous one till he went to sleep. He even swam with a lit cigarette in his mouth!

"But it is a bad habit. And especially bad for women – your Mama never smoked. So when you turned twenty I offered you your first cigarette, remember? I told you it was addictive like hashish and asked you to look at me and use the cigarette accordingly."

I remember, indeed. It was very special, my twentieth birthday. I was working for *Philco* then, had a good salary, and had moved my parents (Yaya Neranzo had died) into a nice modern two-bedroom apartment, with living and dining rooms, a proper kitchen and bathroom, and a veranda looking over a small back garden with almond and apple trees. It was up the hill, near my childhood friend Sofoula's house and across from the mosque with the marble fountain. At Emin Camî 34/2.

Sofoula Papadimitraki, Poppy Marinaki, Erato, Katie Marinaki, my cousin Mihali .

My co-worker Yolanda Holloch, the *Philco* secretary, was invited to this party, along with Sofoula, her brother George, my cousins Mihali, Strato and Frossoula, and Evghenoula's nieces Poppy and Katie.

That afternoon Stavros sat beside me and offered me a cigarette. After a puff, I had extinguished it, retaining the lesson. And I adhered also to the other important advice he gave me that day:

'You see, Erato, my child, you are a beautiful, successful, smart girl. You will be sought after by many guys. We live in a cosmopolitan, multi-ethnic city. I know that the man you will give your heart to, the man you will choose to share your life with, will be worthy of you. So, it's all right with me whether he is Chinese, Italian, Turk, Muslim, Buddhist or whatever. But remember one thing. You marry not only the man, but his family as well. And society deals very harshly with mixed marriages. A man and a woman are already poles apart and you will struggle to smooth away your differences. But if you are from different backgrounds and different religions as well, the struggle will be very hard. And I can guarantee you that real friendship between a man and a woman does not exist. Given certain circumstances it will turn to romance, as happened to some friends you know. So my advice to you is, whenever you agree to go out with a guy, ask yourself if you would be happy marrying him. If not, avoid disappointment for both of you. Go out in groups only or to busy places, well-lit crowded places, never in a romantic *tête-à-tête* environment.'

It was a precious advice.

It was this particular day also, when Tito, my elementary school classmate, came uninvited, with a cactus flower as a gift, after George had told him there was a party at my house. He walked in with an illuminating smile, his huge black eyes ravaging, his wavy black hair messed up… He was handsome, a joker, a fantastic dancer and a great musician. He played the piano, the accordion, the guitar and he was the soul of every party. No wonder every girl he met was crazy about him, as I heard. It was after this party, my only real one, that we got romantically involved.

"Could you talk about *Ashkalé,* if you are not too tired?" I ask Father, to distract him from the cigarette fiasco.

"*Ashkalé?* It was for the *Varlık Vergisi*, the Property tax, under Ismet Inönü's presidency. There was a rumour – and this was only a rumour, I don't know if there is any truth in it – that Sükrü Saratsoglu, the Prime Minister then, was dining in a hotel at Yalova. At another table, close by, Greek dignitaries were ordering bottles of *champagne* galore. Saratsoglu asked who these people were. Kosmetos, Tsavouris and other Greeks, he was told. He realized that those *Giavours* had not been damaged by the war, or if they did, those infidels were back on their feet and had lots of money. So, in November of 1942, Saratsoglu passed a law, according to which those who had not participated in the Kurtulus Savashi (the Battle of Deliverance in the 1920s), in other words the ones who did not fight against the Greeks, were to pay a Property tax. The tax was aimed mainly at the non-Muslims of Istanbul and, in a small part also, against non-Muslims residing in Izmir, Bursa, Ayvalik and Ankara. It was planned against Greeks, Jews and Armenians and admittedly against a few rich Turks who had made fortunes after the war.

"The basis for assigning the amount of taxation was very arbitrary, just vague estimates. It was first to be paid within 15 days, then extended to one month. Committees were formed with lists of names separated as Muslims, non-Muslims (divided in sub-groups) and later some renegades who had become Muslims [?] were added. Whereas Muslims were taxed approximately 10 percent, non-Muslims were taxed 50 percent and renegades 25 percent. The amounts assigned were soon found to be not enough and the non-Muslims' taxes were increased by an extra zero. So that if someone had been estimated to pay 1,800 liras, the tax was recalculated to 18,000 liras. And the ones who could not raise the money and pay within a month, non-Muslims, had their property confiscated and sent to *Ashkalé* to work in forced labour camps building roads and railway lines. Many perished in those camps…"

Stavros stops, drinks his now lukewarm coffee, puts it on the side table with a grimace. Then he squeezes his eyes, taps his fingers on the armrest and gathers his *souvenirs*.

"Neshet Akol, my Albanian friend, and Hadji Çakir were on the tax committees. They were trying to lower the tax amounts. The mayor of Istanbul, Lütfi Kirdar, went to Ankara, the capital, to try to lower the taxes because they would harm Istanbul's economy. He only managed to decrease the amounts by ten percent. Tevfik [Yilmaz?], Yusuf and Nadji had it easy. Atlamazoglou was originally taxed 1,800 liras. With the added zero, it became 18,000 liras. He could pay. Others couldn't and were 'burned'. One of the richest men, Erato, was Kyriacos Teperikoglou. He was at one point president of the tax committee of Prinkipo. He must have had over 3 million liras. They taxed him 200,000 liras. He could pay, but refused to do so. (Cough bout) … One day, I see him. I tell him: 'Kyriaco, you can pay. I know, it is a big amount, but if you sell one of your buildings, you will be able to pay. You will make this money again, later.' It was for sure that Seferoglou and other Greeks would be able to earn – later – the money they owed. 'Leave it!' answers Kyriacos. 'But they will send you to *Ashkalé!*' I remind him. 'Let them. I will go,' he persists. He went to *Ashkalé*. Do you know what he did there? He organized a canteen and made money! "

Stavros laughs, remembering the innovative spirit of this man. Then he frowns: "But many died in *Ashkalé.* I know a few. Maybe you know this one too: Evghenoula had a ... Dimakopoulou, who had a villa at Ortaköy and had it rented. Her husband Dimakopoulos died in *Ashkalé.* And Alekos Mathirinos [?] and Fetzis who had a concussion... He was later at Baloukli Greek Hospital, staying with the elderly patients."

Cough... Stavros spits in a tissue that he folds and tucks in the empty coffee cup. "They even confiscated the dowries of young girls," he continues, in a vexed voice.

I know. I have heard that the Baloukli Greek Hospital and Residences for Retired Patients, Greek churches, Greek schools were all heavily taxed and many non-Muslim institutions had to close their doors after this tax.

Father adds: "They also wanted to tax the residents with Greek citizenship. But the (Greek) Ambassador Raphael played a big role in avoiding this... And this incident passed into history: When they tried to send a Jew to *Ashkalé* from the Haydarpasha train station, he cried: 'Heil Hitler!' In other words, 'Hitler is better than you'... *[What about the Holocaust?]*... But what happened in the end? *Ashkalé, Mashkalé,* taxes and all, Greeks stood up again... As for me, there was no problem. They wouldn't even find a single lira on me," he laughs. "Inönü was the greatest enemy of the Greeks. The twenty classes round up; then the Property tax; later the 1955 riots against the Greeks that his party instigated with the help of the English. But his weakest point was the Property tax, the *Varlik Vergisi,* where he separated Turks and Greeks and Jews [*and Armenians? It is known that they helped with Atatürk's deliverance army, yet they were taxed also*]. That was his downfall. And in the electoral speech of Adnan Menderes, there was also an idea of mine... Indirectly..." He smirks.

"How come?"

"Neshet Akol was on the electoral committee of the new Democratic Party. I told him, 'If Menderes wants to win the election he must aim at the Property tax incident which had no base, no excuse. Not at the 20 classes forced round up...' And Adnan Menderes won the election... His nickname was Antonis [*given to him by Greeks?*], Anthony..."

"Why do you say that the 1955 riots were instigated by Inönü's People's Party?"

"Because," Stavros explains with emphasis, "the People's Party members knew of the events before they happened. They had told me, 'Stavro Efendi, don't stay outside these days' ... But Menderes' Democratic Party members were in the dark.

Erato-Katina-Stavros ca 1955

"And when Istanbul's Mayor (Lütfi Kirdar) asked the Third Army Corps to interfere, its commander, who was from the People's Party, refused saying he could not interfere without an order from the National Assembly. You understand? ..."

I remembered Tito telling me that Redjep Bey, his father Gavril's partner, warned them to go home early that night and stay inside because dangerous things could happen or even better they should all go to his house.

Tito was at Izmir at the time and witnessed a march towards the NATO headquarters with the mob demanding to burn the Greek flag. General Clark then appeared at the entrance gate and tried to calm the crowds, telling them this was neutral ground and he was there to protect "all" the flags. When the crowd persisted, he ordered his military police to arm and aim at the gathering... After that the crowd dispersed.

Stavros goes on: "The only thing Menderes did (as Prime Minister) was to sign a permission for the University Students to march in protest for Atatürk's birthplace bombing in Thessaloniki. *[The belief was that the bomb was planted by Greeks, but as it turned out it was a Muslim Turk from Bulgaria who had planted it.]* He (Menderes) at that time had left [the country?] by train."

[*There was a rumour – that I could not verify – that Menderes was to sign a secret pact with Greece, Yugoslavia (and Bulgaria ?) to control the bordering seas so as not to be subjected to English and American control over them. The fact is Menderes was on a train trip that afternoon – according to some rumour to the West, some other to the East - and he had to interrupt his trip and return home, though not fast enough to stop the riots against the Greeks, and no pact was signed. So some concluded that the riots were instigated by foreign forces that were against that pact*].

The riots of the 6th and 7th of September 1955 did a lot of damage. All the Greek shops and firms along Istanbul's main arteries, thousands of houses and properties in the Greek suburbs as well, were smashed and vandalized; most Greek churches were burned or smashed, priests maltreated, girls raped, cemeteries desecrated. Some Greeks were killed, many wounded, and the mob advanced shouting 'Death to Greeks…'

"In Ortaköy," says Stavros, "there was this brave Greek guy, Polikarpos, a *dayi*, always carrying a weapon. When the mob plundered the Church of St. Phocas, Polikarpos asked a policeman in civilian clothes who was standing there, '*Bu né ish*? – what is happening? – ' '*Bu bashka ish,* – this is a different happening – answered the policeman. At that, Polikarpos aims his pistol at the policeman and wounds him, only in the foot… "

Stavros stops, leans forward, breathes heavily… Then, he lifts his index finger: "The English did it… I was having a drink at *Pascal*, before coming home. And I saw a dark Gypsy converse with two Englishmen. 'Strange,' I thought, 'very strange. Intelligence Service?'"

Father makes me think of the conversation I overheard in the subway the next morning between two men, probably Kurds, judging from their dialect: 'How many English gold coins did you get for last night?' asked one. 'Two' replied the other. 'You were cheated. I got four' answered the first one…

"You told me once, Father, that the Greek-speaking Turks did not take part in the riots and that they protected the Greeks…"

"Yes, the Cretans, and those from Yannina, from Thrace, or from Midilli Island, and some Albanians. Lots of Turks who spoke Greek liked Greeks. Ali Santi, for instance, when he learned about it, he gathered all the Greek women and children in his storehouse, in Edirnekapi, and stood guard with a two-sided sword claiming: 'In the name of Allah, if anyone dares anything against them I will slaughter him like sheep.' Then, there was another Cretan, Rüstü Zülfi who offered me shelter ... That evening Angheliki, who was a cashier at Saray cinema, and living with Avgheris (a cook at *Façyo* seaside restaurant) and his family on the second floor above us, arrived breathless. 'Kyria Katina, they are plundering Nea Agora, Artemis and Ankara Pazari' she cried to your Mama. Those were the largest grocery stores in Beyoglu. They belonged to Greeks... I was home already. Osman, a neighbour, reassured me: 'They may break some windows, make some noise, that's all. Don't be afraid.' But Yashar, an Albanian, from the house across from ours, who was married to a Greek, swore not to allow anyone in the neighbourhood to be plundered."

"And Hadji Osman Bey, Father, our new landlord. He sent us, all the tenants from the three flats, all Christians, to his fourth floor penthouse and ordered us to hide in his bedrooms while he kept his wife, daughter and granddaughter in the living room. With you. Then he kept guard in front of the main door at the entrance, with his rifle on his knees declaring: 'If anyone enters here, it will be over my dead body.' Do you remember?"

"*Yok Djanoum!* No sweetheart," exclaims Father using a Turkish expression. "We didn't go upstairs. I wanted to stay in our apartment and guard all of you."

He obviously had forgotten or had chosen to.

"Yes, you did want to stay, but Hadji Bey convinced you that you would be more useful upstairs, guarding his family and ours, instead of staying in our apartment. Since you were the only other man...You stayed in their living room, with his family, with a jar of powdered black pepper (to throw at the assailants' eyes) and a small utility knife as sole weapons. Don't you remember?"

Stavros shakes his head. He recalls Hadji Bey with his rifle in front of the main door – he had kept telling everybody about it – but not of us going upstairs ... *How could he forget this incident that scarred all of us so deeply? Did he choose to erase it from his memory? Why? Was it due to his Greek pride? Couldn't he bear to have been helped by a Turk?*

There were in fact many such incidents of Turks helping Greeks. The night guard of *Philco*, for instance, the international import company I worked for at the time, was owned by two Greek brothers, Niko and Stelio Katanos, and a Jew, Nathan Eskenazi. When the rampage started, this Turkish night guard raised the Turkish flag, stayed in front of the door and managed to keep the mob away declaring 'This is a Turkish enterprise'. Similar incidents, unknown to me and to my father, must remain in the minds of many Greeks after that night.

I cannot forget the sobs of my friend Ziynet (a Muslim Turk and a new immigrant from Bulgaria), when she saw me at the Austrian Sisters' summer camp at Antigoni (Burgaz) Island a few days after the incidents. She placed her hands around my neck and hid her head in my shoulder. 'Thank God, you are OK. I am so sorry, Erato, my sister! I apologize for what my people did to you. I am so ashamed! So ashamed to be a Turk, today!' she repeated between sobs. Deeply touched by her genuine sorrow, I hugged her and reassured her that it was not all Turks' doing and that there were some Turks helping Greeks also.

My mind stops now at X …, a villain and at all the damage he did a few years later.

"Father," I ask, "there was a rumour that X …, a known Greek, was collaborating with the Turkish Secret Service as an informer and that he betrayed many Greek citizens and caused their deportation. Do you know if there is any truth to that?"

Stavros sighs, nods his head, "Yes".

"Why did he do it? For money?"

"For what else? My child, this man was all the time at the Patriarchate. He had access to all the archival files of Greeks. So he knew all their secrets and was passing them on to the Turks."

"But why was the Turkish Government deporting the Greek citizens? What did they have to gain from their expulsion?"

"Why? For the Cyprus problem, my child. And deep down Turks [Turkish authorities] wanted all the Greeks decimated. Out! You see, they did organize the September riots. That didn't work. The Greeks regained all their might and all their power and on top of it they supported Menderes who tried to rekindle the Greco-Turk friendship and collaboration. So when Inönü came to power after Menderes was deposed… he did this. Inönü was the biggest enemy of the Greeks. "

"Why?"

"Because, whenever there were elections, whoever won in Istanbul won the elections. There were approximately 350,000 ethnic and religious minorities in Istanbul; Greeks, Armenians and Jews, spread across the city, the islands, the Bosphorus and the suburbs [mid-1950s]. In Beyoglu everybody supported Menderes. In the islands also. In Bosphorus the same. Inönü was waiting, hoping that as they - the minorities - had blamed him for the Property tax, people now would blame the Democrats for the September riots. But Menderes, after the September riots, won the elections again! So Inönü hated the Greeks for supporting Menderes."

"But, Father, the Greek citizens could not vote. Why deport them?"

"I told you, to decimate them. Greek citizens and Greeks of Turkish citizenship were inter-mingled, married to each other, relatives. And then what? Every Greek who was to be deported had to sign a blank declaration. The Turkish police filled it in the way they wanted, forcing the guy to state that 'I did this and that … I worked as a spy. I am a traitor,' etc. Naturally the authorities seized all Greek properties – they still owe them back. And the Greeks had no right to sell or buy any property in Turkey. By deporting the Greek citizens, Turks also incited many Greeks with a Turkish citizenship – relatives – to follow them. This was a way to put pressure on the Greek government."

Stavros has a cough crisis. Stops, spits, clears his throat, swallows some cold coffee. Then he continues eagerly, leaning forward, hands locked together.

"Because in the Cyprus problem, my child, there was a pact of '*serdeks*' where Karamanlis, then Prime Minister of Greece, was at fault. According to the United Nations protocols, when 75 percent of the people want a merger, it's a merger. Want independence? It's independence. There were 80 percent Greeks and 18 percent Turks in Cyprus. Karamanlis erred, and signed the Zürich pact. But he trusted Menderes. According to the pact, at certain points [*of Turkish Cyprus?*] there would be '*serdeks*' where the mayors would be Turks, but all collaborating with Greeks. This was the American plan. They wanted to get into the Balkans at any cost. And this pact was a way for them (the Americans) to get in. But the English – who wanted to keep Cyprus as an English protectorate – opposed this plan and reacted. Do you understand? ... And the airplane carrying Menderes to London, to sign the final treaty, crashed at Gatwick Airport! Cut in two! Most passengers perished, died. Yet Menderes survived by miracle … A genuine accident? Or again … So, since the September riots did not take Menderes down, the only way out was to eliminate him … He was becoming too powerful; he had taken Turkey into NATO, became a good ally of the Americans, offered them military bases…

"Menderes was to go with Zorlu to Athens Friday to sign the final details. And the military coup took place Thursday night, at midnight … The problem of Cyprus, my child, is enormous. And the Americans are still trying … And the game is this, Erato. They [*who?*] threatened Greece with the possibility that Turkey would take the Greek islands. And they threatened Turkey by possible inimical actions by Greece. If the treaty was ratified in London and Menderes remained in power, Cyprus would become a NATO stronghold.

But England had military bases there. They did not want anyone else there. And they still don't. If the Americans had been smarter and had paid closer attention to the Ankara-Athens axis versus the Tel-Aviv-Cairo one, everything would be all right. But there was money involved … As Ioannidis [?] had explained, the 'green light for the Turks to get into Cyprus was not given by the Americans but by the English.' … The only solution would be for Greeks and Turks to collaborate and keep a common front against foreign powers. During a war, whoever controls the straits, Bosphorus and Çanakkale, wins. Turkey protects Greece against a Communist invasion from the Black Sea. And Greece protects Turkey against a Communist invasion from the North and West. And another thing not to forget is that the Turks are a mixed race, and many Turks are friends of the Greeks. During the 1948-49 internal war of Greece against the EAM rebels (*Ethniko Antialvaniko Metopo* or the 1941 leftist National Liberation Front), many Turks fought alongside Greeks as volunteers."

"Really? I never heard about it, Father. You don't mean Greeks with Turkish citizenship, but Muslim Turks?"

"Yes, Muslim Turks … *[I could not verify this. Greek history archives mention that Turks helped Greeks by sending them food during 1941. The Turkish S/S Kurtulus made five voyages to Athens. It is also known that during the 1948 civil war, the Greek Resistance Movement, EAM, rounded up Greek children, aged three to fourteen, and sent them to Bulgaria and other northern border countries to raise them as Communists. Since many children of western Thrace would be Muslim Turks of Greek citizenship, it is plausible that Turks would fight alongside Greeks to liberate these children].* Now, why should Greeks and Turks sacrifice their children for the English or the Americans, or any other foreign power? Since 1821, wise political men of both sides tried to bring a rapprochement between Greece and Turkey, but the foreign powers were always against it."

I didn't quite understand all the political strategies but kept silent so as not to interrupt the flow of Father's thoughts.

"Remember Zorlu?" Stavros asks after a while. "How he was shouting 'I want the telegram' during his 1960 court proceedings?"

How could I forget? In 1960, I was working for Ipar Transport, and our CEO, the ship-owner Ali Ipar, was wrongly detained and tried as a traitor at Yassi Ada Island (*Plati*), by the Colonels' Interim Government, along with all the 1955 Democratic government members who were accused of being "*Vatan haïni*", traitors of the Nation. As a witness and executive secretary, I was following Ipar's trial and also all the proceedings for the other political trials. Fatin Rüstü Zorlu, the one time External Affairs minister of the government under Celal Bayar's presidency and Menderes (Prime Minister), was in London, during early September of 1955.

'All I want is the telegram I sent to Menderes from London, to warn him not to allow the students' march because foreign forces would try to instigate incidents,' he had exclaimed, to show his innocence. 'What telegram?' had questioned the judge. 'There is no telegram!' 'But there is! I have the receipts from the Post Office! They must be in the embassy,' insisted Zorlu. The judge explained that neither the telegram, nor any receipts were ever found in London. *The Post Office's fault?* The court implied Zorlu was lying to save his neck. It was understood that no telegram had ever reached Menderes before his (train) departure. No investigation ordered about it ... And strangely, I don't remember reading any report on the "telegram" issue in next day's news-papers...

In fact most of the proceedings were not reported in detail in the press... The 1955 Democratic cabinet members claimed that the incidents were provoked by foreign forces – without accusing any opposing group, such as the "Cyprus Is Turkish" organisation. The 1955 External Affairs Minister Fuat Köprülü maintained that the agitators were probably Communists, 'considering that over forty *Reds* had been involved in the riots and detained then'. Nevertheless all 1955 cabinet members were found accountable and guilty of not stopping the riot incidents. Therefore they were traitors, and sentenced to death by hanging in 1960. Only President Celal Bayar's sentence was changed to life imprisonment, due to his advanced age and failing health. In reality the Court appeared to be looking for scapegoats to appease the world public opinion about Turkey. In my CEO's case, they ignored the notary affidavits of Chase Manhattan Bank that his four ships were under mortgage to the bank which had financed their purchase, keeping the freighters as collateral. The court decided that no such thing was possible, that Ali Ipar must have taken money out of Turkey to pay for them, that he was using, in secret, the money of the Turkish people and of the Turkish Government for his own benefit. And that was a serious crime. Therefore, according to the court, Ipar was a traitor. The court seized the ships and kept Ali Ipar in jail, trying to force a "guilty" confession out of him. Ipar lost an eye during his interrogation ... He was only freed when the regime changed.

Stavros' indignant voice pulls me out of my own recollections:

"They did not believe Zorlu's telegram claim and considered him a collaborator in the events... Now, Zorlu's daughter lived in an upper story apartment, in Nishantash, Istanbul; and one floor below resided Ohanidis, the Greek pharmacist. The daughter was a beautiful girl and there was fear that the mob might abuse her. So Ohanidis raises the Turkish flag, puts Atatürk's portrait in view, takes the girl into his apartment to protect her and goes out and says to a soldier, 'Zorlu's daughter is in danger'. Now, is it possible that if Zorlu knew how things would turn out he would let his daughter be in danger? The Democratic government members were wrongly condemned... an excuse to be put away... sacrificed to the games of foreign powers."

Stavros sweeps the air with his hand and rests his head on the pillow.

I wanted to ask him how he knows about Ohanidis and the incident, though the pharmacist was known amongst Greeks. But Stavros is really tired now. So am I.

Stavros closes his eyes and plunges into the past. I let him live in this past world and dream about what it might have been if...

Stavros ca 1956-60

VII – The Doubt

Stavros looks haggard this cold, winter morning.

"What's wrong? Are you sick? Do you feel bad?" I ask him, worried

He gives me a strange look. A strange, lost look. "There is nothing," he says in a monotonous whisper. "Absolutely nothing. Just blackness."

"What are you talking about, Father?" I ask, a panic button ringing in my head.

"There is nothing, I am telling you. No afterlife or anything. Nothing after death. Nothingness. Chaos! Only Chaos!"

I shiver. I feel the floor slip under my feet, my heart pumps dangerously. I understand that, like most gravely ill persons, subconsciously Stavros feels the end is near. But his anxiety, his despair that there is nothing after, goads me relentlessly. I have been trying to help him physically, to keep his body strong, to help him live with dignity whatever time he had left, surrounded by love. But I have never tried to help his spirit! I have never tried to prepare him for the end, to help him face the end. What was I thinking? That he was so strong that he wouldn't need any preparation? Any help? *God, help us!*

"What makes you say that, Father? How can you say there's nothing? Don't you remember that Mama came to visit you when she died? That you saw her in front of you, in the flesh, waving 'good bye'? You told me so! Isn't that proof that life continues?" I try to steady my voice, to appear calm, quiet.

"That's different," he answers in a low voice, fidgeting with his wedding ring. "At the moment of physical death, when the heart stops, the brain is still alive. Alive and free to travel by thought. For a few more minutes, maybe an hour or even two. That's when she came. But after, when everything freezes, there is nothing. Nothing!"

"That's not true. You taught me the soul is immortal. Pythagoras, Plato. Christ... Did you forget the dream I had about Mama showing me her life in another world?" I ask, my heart pounding.

"That dream ... your wishful thinking, my child... You wanted to *see* your mother alive in another world... Listen, this is a mystery. If there is anything, anything at all on the other side, I promise you to find a way to let you know once I am gone," he says with a sad smile.

"I don't want to hear you talk like that! Don't talk to me about death—"

"We are all going to die one day, my child. This is the only way for the World to survive. Imagine if we were physically immortal? As for Christ..."

Stavros starts a lecture about Jesus, repeating what he had told me at other times, but elaborating now.

That Jesus was "the most exceptional teacher humanity encountered", that during the time of His absence – the so called retreat to the desert – He had travelled to Egypt and to India, learning all the mystic teachings that existed. That He was probably a *fakir*, yet only a normal human being, "like you and me", but not the Son of God. Jews expected a soldier-saviour to liberate them from the Romans. But Christ's goal was to bring peace through love and forgiveness. "Jesus was a divine gift to humanity," continues Stavros. "He taught a new precept which is a mixture of Greek philosophy and the best of the Old Testament. He said: 'I didn't come to abolish but to complete.'"

Stavros adds that, like Socrates, Jesus went to His crucifixion as a willing human being. "Because if He accepted the crucifixion as a God, as a son of God, knowing he couldn't die, His sacrifice would be worthless. But as a human... that makes him 'superhuman', as Renan said," states Stavros with emphasis.

"As for His resurrection," he continues, "I believe that Jesus did not die on the cross. He simply stopped his heart beating. And being physically fit and strong, He survived His wounds. We don't know what happened at the tomb and who moved the rock-door, but He reappeared to his apostles, alive... He moved though walls. It is said that *fakirs* could do that too. He let his followers touch His wounds; so he was not a ghost. He ate with them; so He was not a spectre. He was alive. And all Jesus did, all His miracles, had physical explanations...

"As for His transfiguration and lifting in Heavens... How? Where did He go? We don't know. They are mysteries for which there are no explanations... Now, his followers took all this and merged it into a new teaching..."

Dumbfounded I let him talk, reassured that his mind was wondering away from death, away from the darkness and chaos that disturbed him so much. I even find the courage to turn on the recorder, as usual...

"His (Christ's) followers were mainly Alexandrian Hellenists," Stavros goes on. "In this new teaching, they abolished the Greek Olympian Pantheon and replaced it with a new Pantheon, with the Prophet Elijah, Saint Demetrius, etc.

"To the forty or so Olympian demigods, the Christian Pantheon offers forty thousand saints. This is only for the simple human masses. And they (Christ's followers) link everything beautifully, taking the best and the most beautiful and discarding the rest, like bees gathering pollen only from the sweetest flowers. When the Apostle Paul addressed the Greeks he said: 'I came to talk to you about the Unknown God'...

"Now, how can a simple parish priest analyze all this and find what constitutes today's religion? Impossible!"

I listen. I'm not paying full attention to his discourse, my mind is whirling. I can't understand his doubt...

Stavros was always an agnostic, not an atheist. More than that. He considered himself a Christian, even if not one practicing properly. I knew he took me regularly to church just to accompany me, but I was sure he believed in God, "this Intelligent Power that created the Universe and kept it, and is keeping it, in harmony," as he had explained since my earliest years.

He had only stopped coming to church with me when I started going out with Tito. Thereafter, he would always accompany us to the Midnight Easter Liturgy – the Liturgy of the Resurrection and Enlightenment – and he would sing the hymns with us. And he believed forcefully in the immortality of the soul, or rather of the "*pneuma*", the spirit, as the Greek philosophers and many religious thinkers around the world had claimed.

Moreover, Stavros had maintained that the "spirit" could travel in the past or in the future, that it could delve into a parallel world.

He admired Jesus and all the great thinkers, the Apostle Paul, John's Gospel "of Love", and the Greek theologian Fathers of the Church that shaped our religion, adapting Greek and Mesopotamian rites and celebrations; thinkers like John Chrysostomos, Gregory the Great, St. Basil, St. Augustine, St. Thomas Aquinas, and the Patriarchs. He considered simple parish priests and deacons as not having a complete theological education and being, at times, speculators.

As for the long liturgical ceremonies, for Father they were theatrical gimmicks to proselytize and to keep the new faith for the simple folk, not for the intellectual man. Yet he still claimed he was a Christian at heart, and followed Jesus' teachings. Because, as he maintained, of all the philosophers and great thinkers and religious leaders, it was only Jesus who taught unconditional love and forgiveness.

"Not only love thy neighbour, but *love thy enemy*… if he slaps you, turn the other cheek…" would explain Stavros with admiration. "What magnificence! If applied, mankind would be really saved!" he used to say. Furthermore, he believed in reincarnation.

So why this nihilism now? Why this fear of chaos?

I don't know how I dragged myself through the day. That night I did not sleep at all, trying to figure out how I could help Stavros face the end. I could not rely on the spiritual help of a priest or a clergyman because Father, although surrounded by bishops in his youth, distrusted the robed men profoundly. And he had not a single other living relative left, not a close friend in this land, in short, no one but me.

I had to drag him out of this bottomless pit. But how? I realized that he had forgotten things that we lived together, spiritual awakenings of mine. And what about his own lessons on the Greek philosophers and great thinkers of the world?

I would have to remind him of all that and emphasize my own perceptions and experiences. Yet, how to make sure that he would pay attention to what I had to say? *Write it! A written message is read without interruptions. A written message leads to thinking.*

I started to write feverishly. And I devised a plan to force him to read my essay. I would pretend that I wrote it for a friend of his, Nicolas, whose kidneys were damaged to the point beyond dialysis and who now would finish his days calmly with his family. Nicolas was an atheist. This essay was to help Nicolas face the end, offering my own spiritual experiences, written as a memoir to my daughters, as a proof of the immortality of the soul. But Nicolas was an intellectual, like Stavros. If my manuscript showed spelling or grammatical errors, Nicolas would reject it as "worthless". So, I would ask Stavros to read it and correct my Greek syntax, before rewriting it "for Nicolas".

I let a week pass without any mention of the "chaos" incident to Stavros. He did not mention it again, either. So I guided our conversations and recordings to the Greco-Turkish War, his passion. The talks would always bring a sparkle to his eye, excite him and even improve his appetite.

During these political discussions, Stavros would explain how Metaxas, the then prime minister of Greece, had refused to lead the Greek Armed Forces and had advised King George of Greece to solve the problem peacefully with the Turks, because any attack against the twice stronger Turks was doomed.

Father would relate how Metaxas had to abdicate when the King had insisted on the plan to attack Turkey. How the Turks, when they lost to the Greeks at Ankara, asked Britain to cut their help to the Greeks in exchange for the petroleum of Mussul. And when Gounaris, the head of the Greek government, went to London to ask for economic assistance, how the British refused it, thus forcing the Greek government to change tactics, withdraw from Ankara and concentrate on the Aegean coasts.

Stavros explained that the Greek generals refused to withdraw, and that Hatzianestis was named head of the army at Smyrna (Izmir). Father elaborated about the tactics of Polymenakos and Harilaos Trikoupis. On how the Turks now attacked Izmir, and set it on fire with cannons, forcing the inhabitants (mainly Greeks) to flee to the sea while the British stood "gazing" and the Americans, the observers, "only took photographs". And when the fleeing Greeks tried, with boats, to reach help from the French Navy, stationed at the Aegean Sea, they were asked by the French, their 'allies', to "surrender!" To the Greek cries "But we are allies! We fought together," the French responded by breaking the arms of the Greeks who were trying to get aboard the French ships. Stavros then would analyze the ceasefire of Mudanya, followed by the 1923 Pact of Lausanne signed by Venizelos – a mistake according to many – and Inönü, and the exchange of Greeks.

So, during daytime, I kept recording, for the sake of Anghelos Kyriou and the archives of our Association. Not familiar with all this political entanglements, I made no comments and did not have the stamina to verify what Stavros was saying. I trusted his rare memory and his love of history and veracity. At night I was writing till the wee hours, rushing against time, anxious to finish my manuscript as soon as possible.

One day, I recalled to Father his friend Nicolas' case. "Do you know that they cannot do any more hemodialysis on him? Nor any treatment? He chose to finish his days at home, amongst his family…" I told Stavros.

"He is lucky to have a family to lean on," replied Father. "Imagine if he were left to die alone in a hospital or in a hospice? What a tragic end!" he added, biting the corner of his lower lip, his gaze fixed on the snowed-in garden.

I will never let you die alone, Father!

At last, my manuscript was ready, "*With Love as Guide*" as the title.

It is divided into three parts. The first is a preface to my daughters, where I explain that I wish to share with them my personal enlightening experiences so as to guide them through life. The second is a lengthy introduction where I try to answer Stavros' own questions about religion, the scriptures and Christianity, using the general leading ideas on the subject. Here I maintain that life on Earth is but a school towards perfection. I compare the historical and spiritual evolution of mankind to the educational progress from elementary school to university. Finally, with the advent of Christianity and Jesus' teaching of love, I maintain that for me, mankind enters through Jesus its post graduate studies. I concede that since I am not a theologian, I will simply relate the inexplicable phenomena I have lived that have renewed my hesitant, at times, faith and my certitude in the Divine Providence. Thus in the third and main part of the manuscript I recall the extraordinary happenings of my life – those that Stavros had lived with me but that he had either forgotten or misinterpreted, and those he had ignored. I conclude with the hope that these events would fortify the faith of my daughters, as they did for me.

I will present the manuscript to Father, tomorrow.

VIII - WITH LOVE AS GUIDE

The sun shines on the carpet of white snow and fills the room with a golden glow that makes me forget the chills of winter. Stavros seems to be in a good mood this morning.

"Look, I wrote an essay to help our friend Nicolas face the end of his journey," I say to Stavros, giving him the manuscript.

"Although our friend is an intellectual, he is a complete atheist, as you know. I hope this will help him. I've written it for my daughters and I based it on my personal beliefs and on my own spiritual experiences. I intend to just present it to him as a manuscript. Maybe even ask his opinion about my writing. I think it will work. Don't you? Would you please correct my grammar and syntax errors? Otherwise Nicolas will discard it. Also, would you let me have your comments on whatever you think I should omit or elaborate?"

Stavros weighs in his hands the rather heavy manuscript. "It's thick. It looks like a lot for a simple essay," he remarks, with a strange glance at me.

What are you thinking, Father? What have you guessed?

"It's quite an endeavour, Erato. If you expect to succeed, my hat is off to you. Well, leave it with me," he says, putting it on the side table. "Give me a pen. I will read it and correct it when I have some peace of mind and can concentrate."

"Did you think about an article for our Association's commemorative album?" I ask, to encourage him to do something cerebral. "You could talk about Katina, if you wish, or—"

"We could just reprint my article about the *Fate of Hellenism*," he cuts me.

I find the old article, as printed in Greek in a past bulletin, and hand it to him.

Η ΜΟΙΡΑ ΤΟΥ ΕΛΛΗΝΙΣΜΟΥ

> Ὦ παιδιά μου ὀρφανά μου
> σκορπισμένα ἐδῶ κι' ἐκεῖ
> πού μέ κόπους κατά τόπους
> τρέχετε γιά μιά τροφή
> "Ρήγας Φεραῖος"

<u>Ὑπό Σταύρου Εὐαγγελίδη</u>

<u>Μέρος Πρῶτον</u>

Μοῖρα χαραγμένη ἀπό μιά ἀνώτερη, θεία ἴσως δύναμη, συνηφασμένη μέ τήν τρισχιλιετή ἱστορία, τά πεπρωμένα καί τό αἰώνιο μεγάλο δρᾶμα τῆς Ἑλληνικῆς φυλῆς.......

Ἀρχίζει ἀπό τούς μυθικούς χρόνους, τούς Ἀργοναύτας, τήν Τροία καί τούς Μηδικούς μέ τόν Μαραθῶνα, τάς Θερμοπύλας καί τήν Σαλαμίνα. Ὅλη ἡ Ἑλλάς ἡνωμένη ἐκδιώκει τούς Πέρσας ἀπελευθεροῦσα τάς Ἑλληνίδας πόλεις τῆς Θράκης καί τῆς Ἰωνίας καί ἐάν δέν ἐπήρχετο ἡ σύγκρουσις Ἀθηνῶν καί Σπάρτης μέ τόν τριακονταετῆ πόλεμον, ὡρισμένως ἄλλαι θά ἦσαν σήμερον αἱ τύχαι τῆς Εὐρώπης.

Ἐξηντλημέναι ἀπό τόν ἔναντι ἀλλήλων ἐξοντωτικόν αὐτόν ἀγῶνα, αἱ δύο αὐταί Ἀκροπόλεις τοῦ Ἑλληνισμοῦ , δέν δύνανται νά ἀναχαιτίσουν τήν πρός στιγμήν ἡγεμονίαν τῶν Θηβῶν, διά νά ὑποκύψουν τελικῶς ὅλοι εἰς τόν Φίλιππον καί τόν Μέγαν Ἀλέξανδρον.

Μέ τό ὅραμα μιᾶς νέας αὐτοκρατορίας, ὁ Μ. Ἀλέξανδρος διαλύει τό Περσικόν κρᾶτος καί φθάνει μέχρι τῶν ἐκβολῶν τοῦ Γάγγη.

"Πᾶσιν Ἕλλησι πλήν Λακεδαιμονίοις" τά λάφυρα τῆς πρώτης του νίκης.

Ἀλλά μέ τόν πρόωρον θάνατόν του, διαλύονται ὅλα τά μεγαλεπήβολα σχέδια καί οἱ διάδοχοί του δέν δύνανται νά ἀντιταχθοῦν εἰς τάς Ρωμαϊκάς λεγεῶνας. Θαυμασταί καί λάτρεις οἱ Ρωμαῖοι τοῦ Ἑλληνικοῦ πνεύματος ἀφοῦ καί οἱ Αὐτοκράτορες κατέρχονται εἰς Ὀλυμπίαν διά νά στεφθοῦν Ὀλυμπιονῖκαι, ἔχουν ὡς πρότυπον πρός μίμησιν κάθε τι τό Ἑλληνικόν, ἀποδεχόμενοι πλήρως τήν Ἑλληνικήν παιδείαν καί τάς τέχνας, τήν ἰδεολογίαν των καί ἀκόμη αὐτάς τάς νέας των δοξασίας.

Ἡ ὑπό τῶν Ἑλλήνων ἀποδοχή τῆς Χριστιανικῆς θρησκείας, ἐάν ὀφείλεται εἰς τήν διαπίστωσιν τῆς ὀρθότητος τῶν διδαχῶν της, ὀφείλεται πρός στιγμήν καί εἰς λόγους πολιτικῆς σκοπιμότητος καί διορατικότητος.

Μέ τόν συνυφασμόν καί τήν ἀραχνοΰφαντον ἀριστοτεχνικήν σύνδεσιν τῆς Ἑλληνικῆς Φιλοσοφίας μέ τήν νέαν διδασκαλίαν τῆς ἀγάπης, ἐλευθερίας καί ἰσότητος, ἰσοπεδώνουν τήν διαφοράν μεταξύ κατακτητῶν καί ὑποδούλων. Καί ὅταν προχωροῦν εἰς τόν Χριστιανισμόν, οἱ πλεῖονες τῶν ἀξιωματούχων καί πατρικίων τῆς Ρώμης, εὔκολος πλέον ἡ νίκη τοῦ Μεγάλου Κωνσταντίνου καί ἡ Πρωτεύουσα μεταφέρεται ἐπί τό ἀσφαλέστερον εἰς τήν πόλιν τοῦ Βυζαντίου διά νά ἀποβῆ σύν τῷ χρόνῳ Πρωτεύουσα τῆς ΒΥΖΑΝΤΙΝΗΣ ΑΥΤΟΚΡΑΤΟΡΙΑΣ. Ἐπί δέ Βασιλείου τοῦ Βουλγαροκτόνου καθιεροῦται τό πρῶτον ὡς ἐπίσημος γλῶσσα τοῦ Κράτους ἡ Ἑλληνική.

Ἀλλά βάσκανος ἡ μοῖρα τῶν Ἑλλήνων.......

Ὁ Κώστας Φαλτάϊτς, πολεμικός ἀνταποκριτής τοῦ "Ἐλευθέρου Βήματος" τό 1920, περιγράφει σέ ἕνα του δημοσίευμα, πώς περιφερόμενος στά περίχωρα τοῦ Ἀϊδινίου εἶδε μιά ἐπιγραφή......"Μεγάλη νίκη τῶν Χριστιανῶν ἔναντι τῶν Ἐθνικῶν" καί διερωτᾶται μέ πικρία.....ποιό δρᾶμα ἀδελφοκτόνου πολέμου ἄραγε νἄτανε. Διωγμός καί ἐξόντωσις τῶν Ἐθνικῶν καί οἱ Ἀκρίται, οἱ ἄγρυπνοι φρουροί τῶν συνόρων φεύγουν τώρα σέ ξένες χῶρες καί ἀκούονται τώρα στάς Ἄλπεις, στά Πυρηναῖα, στόν Μέλανα Δρυμό καί στίς ὄχθες τοῦ Ρήνου τά νοσταλγικά ἀκριτικά των τραγούδια.

Μέ τήν ἔξοδο καί τήν φυγή αὐτή τῶν Ἀκριτῶν ἀρχίζει καί ἡ πρώτη καμπή τῆς αὐτοκρατορίας.

<u>Ἡ Μοῖρα τοῦ Ἑλληνισμοῦ</u>

Σελίς...2α

Πάθη, θρησκευτικός φανατισμός, εἰκονολάτραι, εἰκονομάχοι καί τελικῶς τό Σχίσμα. Ἀκολουθεῖ τό κῦμα τῶν Σταυροφόρων διά τήν ἀπελευθέρωσιν τῶν Ἁγίων Τόπων καί στό πέρασμά των ἀπό τίς διάφορες ἐπαρχίες λεηλατοῦν, διαρπάζουν, καταστρέφουν τά πάντα καί ἐπιφέρουν τήν γενική ἐξάρθρωση αὐτή τήν διάλυση τοῦ Βυζαντινοῦ κράτους.

Φραγκοκρατεῖται ὅλη ἡ Ἑλλάς μή δυναμένη νά συνδράμη τήν κινδυνεύουσα Πρωτεύουσαν. Καί τό Βυζάντιον ἀπομεμονωμένον τελείως μετά ἀπεγνωσμένον ἀγῶνα, πίπτει τελικῶς μαζί μέ τόν τελευταῖο του Ἕλληνα Αὐτοκράτορα, τό ἡρωϊκόν αὐτό τέκνον τοῦ Μιστρᾶ.

Μέ τήν ἅλωσιν ἀρχίζει γενική ἔξοδος ὅλων τῶν ἀριστούχων, ὅλης τῆς ἀριστοκρατίας, ἄλλων μέν πρός τήν Ρωσίαν ἄλλων δέ κυρίως πρός τήν Ἰταλίαν καί Ἰσπανίαν.

Πολλοί ἱστορικοί παρομοιάζουν τήν ἅλωσιν μέ τό σπάσιμο ἑνός πολύτιμου βάζου πού τά μῦρα του ξεχύθηκαν στή Δύση. Καί ὅπως οἱ Ἀκρίται διοργανώνουν στρατιωτικῶς τούς Γερμανούς, Ἰσπανούς καί Γάλλους, ἔτσι τῶρα καί οἱ ἀριστεῖς τοῦ Βυζαντίου συμβάλλουν εἰς τήν Ἰταλικήν " Ἀναγέννησιν". Ὁ ἱστορικός Παπαρηγόπουλος ὑπολογίζει ὅτι ἐπί Περικλέους καί Κίμωνος, ἡ Ἀθηναϊκή Συμπολιτεία μέ τάς Ἑλληνίδας πόλεις Θράκης καί Ἰωνίας εἶχεν πληθυσμόν ὀκτώμισυ ἑκατομμύρια πλήν τῶν Λακεδαιμονίων καί τῶν συμμάχων των. Καί τῶρα ; ; ; Ναί... αὐτή εἶναι ἡ Μοῖρα τοῦ Ἑλληνισμοῦ..... Τό δρᾶμα τό μεγάλο τῆς Ἑλληνικῆς Φυλῆς.

Ἡ Ἔξοδος...Ἡ Διασπορά....Ἡ Διαρροή.... σέ ξένες χῶρες σέ νέες πατρῖδες. Ἡ Ἑλλάς δέν ἀρκεῖ πού ἔδωσε τά φῶτα καί τόν πολιτισμό της,,, ἔδωσε καί δίνει καί τά παιδιά της, ἱεροφάντας ἄλλους, λαμπηδοφόρους μέ τή φλόγα τοῦ Ὀλυμπιακοῦ Πυρσοῦ καί ἀναμένη αὐτή λαμπάδα τοῦ αἰωνίου ἀθανάτου της πνεύματος.

Καί ἐκεῖ στά βουνά της, τήν ἱερή Ἑλληνική γῆ, διαιωνίζει τήν μακραίωνη Ἑλληνική Δόξα μέ τά λοιπά ἐπίλεκτα παιδιά πού τῆς ἀπομένουν.

Ἕνα ὑπερήφανο λακωνικό ΟΧΙ καί τό ἔπος τῆς Ἀλβανίας, τά ἑλληνικά ὀχυρά, ἡ Μάχη τῆς Κρήτης καί αἱ νέαι Θερμοπύλαι στά στενά τοῦ Ρούπελ.

" Ζητῶ ἑκατόν πενήντα ἐθελοντάς τοῦ θανάτου, ὅσοι δέν θά τούς κλάψουν γυναῖκες καί παιδιά" ὅλοι οἱ ἄνδρες τοῦ Συντάγματος ἕνα βῆμα ἔμπρός. Δακρύζει ὁ Στρατηγός Μπακόπουλος. "Δέν δύναμαι παρά νά κάνω ἐπιλογήν διά κλήρου" Κοινωνοῦν τῶν ἀχράντων μυστηρίων οἱ ἀθάνατοι μελλοθάνατοι καί καταλαμβάνουν τά στενά τοῦ Ρούπελ διά νά τά κρατήσουν ἐπί ἐξάωρον μέ μόνα τους ὅπλα τήν ἀδάμαστη ἑλληνική ψυχή.

Ἀρχίζει ἡ τρομερά ἐπίθεσις τῶν τεθωρακισμένων Γερμανικῶν μεραρχιῶν καί ἔπειτα ἀπό δεκάωρου ἀγῶνα κατορθώνουν νά περάσουν. Μένει μονάχα ἕνας ἀπό τούς ἥρωας μαχητάς καί ὁ Γερμανός Διοικητής τῶν μεραρχιῶν ἀποσπᾶ ἀπό τό στῆθος του τό ἀνώτατον παράσημον, τόν μεγαλόσταυρον τοῦ Κάϊζερ καί τό ἐναποθέτει εὐλαβικά στά ματωμένα στήθια τοῦ Ἕλληνος ἐπιλοχία καί τόν καλύπτει μέ τόν στρατιωτικόν του μανδύα.

Μιά χρυσή πλάκα ἀναρτᾶται..... ΕΔΩ ΚΕΙΝΤΑΙ ΟΙ ΗΡΩΕΣ ΤΟΥ ΡΟΥΠΕΛ καί τό χρυσοῦν της ὁμοίωμα ἀποστέλλεται εἰς τήν στρατιωτικήν Ἀκαδημίαν τοῦ Πότσδαμ. Φόρος τιμῆς πρός τούς ἥρωας ἀκόμη καί ἀπό τούς ἀντιπάλους. Ὁ Τσῶρτσιλ πλήρης θαυμασμοῦ λέγει ἐπιγραμματικά.....
"ΟΙ ΗΡΩΕΣ ΠΟΛΕΜΟΥΝ ΩΣ ΕΛΛΗΝΕΣ"

ΣΤΑΥΡΟΣ ΕΥΑΓΓΕΛΙΔΗΣ

Τό Δεύτερον μέρος στό ἑπόμενο τεῦχος μας.

ΕΛΛΗΝΟΚΑΝΑΔΙΚΟΣ ΣΥΝΔΕΣΜΟΣ ΚΩΝΣΤΑΝΤΙΝΟΥΠΟΛΙΤΩΝ

Stavros reads it approvingly. This was an article that brought moving criticism from Greeks from Istanbul. "Can you translate it?" he asks, his eyes gleaming.

"I will try," I say, "although it will definitely lose its spark in the translation. You write so well in Greek! And my English is not very good."

He smiles, content.

This is the nicest article he has written in the last couple of years. So I work on it as best I can.

I show him the English translation, next day. He approves, beaming. However, although the facts are well known to all Greeks, it might seem strange to foreigners. So I added some short explanations in parentheses.

THE FATE OF HELLENISM

"O my children, my orphaned ones
scattered here and there
who in pain are running for some
food in lands." – RIGAS FERAIOS.

By Stavros Evangelidis – Part One.

Fate traced by a higher, maybe divine, power, tamed in the three-thousand-year-old history the destinies and the endless big drama of the Hellenic race...

It starts from the mythological times, the Argonauts, Troy and the Medic wars with Marathon, Thermopylae and the battle of Salamis. All of Greece, united, ousts the Persians and frees the Hellenic cities of Thrace and Ionia, and if Athens and Sparta were not entangled in the thirty-year battle, Europe's fate today would certainly be different.

Exhausted from the fight against each other, those two Citadels of Hellenism cannot stop the momentary ruling of Thebes and they all finally succumb to Philippe the Macedonian.

Alexander the Great (son of Philippe), with the vision of a new kingdom, disperses the Persian dominion and expands to the edges of Ganges.

"To all Hellenes, except Lacedaemonians..." go the spoils of his first conquest. But with his timeless death, all his grandiose plans fail and his heirs cannot resist against the Roman legions. The Romans, admirers and worshippers of the Greek spirit – since even (their) Emperors go to Olympia to be crowned Olympians – aim to mimic everything Greek, fully engulfing not only the Greek education and arts and ideologies, but even their new beliefs.

The acceptance of the Christian religion by the Greeks, though dependent on the credit of the correctness of its teachings, is also relied, partly, to political aims and visions.

With the blending and the masterful web-like binding of the Greek Philosophy with the new teaching of love, freedom and equality, the differences between conquerors and enslaved subjects are levelled. And when the best of officers and Roman Patricians accept Christianity, the victory of Constantine the Great is now easy, and the capital of the Empire is transferred (from Rome), *to the city of Byzantium – as more secure – which will become, in time, the capital of the Byzantine Empire. And under Basil the "Vulgaroktonos" (*the Bulgarian Slayer*), Greek is established for the first time as the official language of the Empire.*

*But hit by evil eye is the fate of Hellenes... Kostas Faltaits (?), the 1920 war reporter of ELEFHERO VIMA, relates in one of his articles that in the vicinity of Aydin (Turkey) he came into this Greek inscription: "Great victory of Christians against Nationals (*or Heathen*)." And asks himself in bitterness what part of fratricide war was this? ... Persecution and extermination of Nationals (follows)*; *and the "Acrites", the sleepless guardians of the borders, are now leaving for foreign countries and their nostalgic border songs are heard now across the Alps, the Pyrenees, the Black Forest and the shores of the Rhine.*

With the exodus and flight of these border guardians starts the first decline of the (Byzantine) Empire. Pathos, religious fanaticism, icon worshipers, iconoclasts and finally the Schism. Next came the wave of the Crusaders for the deliverance of the Holy Lands who, in their advance through various provinces, plunder, destroy everything and bring the general dislocation and the dissolution of the Byzantine state.

The whole of Greece gets catholicized and cannot come to the aid of the ailing Capital. And thus Byzantium, completely isolated, after a desperate fight, falls (to the Ottoman Turks, 1453) with its last Emperor, the heroic son of Mistra (Constantine Paleologos).

With the Conquest (of Byzantium) begins the general flight of all the luminaries, all the elite, all the aristocracy partly towards Russia but mainly towards Italy and Spain.

Many historians compare the Conquest with the breaking of a precious vase whose perfumes rolled to the West. And as the way the Acrites, the boarder guardians, organized the military corps of Germans, Spaniards and French, now the luminaries of Byzantium contribute to the Italian Renaissance. The historian Paparigopoulos relates that under Pericles and Kimon, the Athenian State with the Hellenic cities of Thrace and Ionia had eight and a half million population, excluding the Lacaedaemonians and their allies. And today??? Yes... this is the fate of Hellenism... The great drama of the Greek Race.

Exodus... Diaspora... Flight to foreign countries, new homelands. Greece did not only give its light and its civilization, it gave and gives its children, the new hierophants, the torch bearers of the Olympic Flame, this eternally lit flame of the immortal spirit.

And there, on the mountains of the Holy Greek earth, this spirit perpetuates the centuries-long Greek Glory and the select children that remain with her. (Here we have) a proud laconic OXI (NO, *to Mussolini in the beginning of World War II*) *and the Albanian Epic, the Greek strongholds, the Battle of Crete, and the new Thermopylae at the straits of Rupel:*

"I am asking for one hundred volunteers of death, ones that will not be mourned by women and children." All the men of the regiment step forward. General Bakopoulos weeps. "I can only choose by draw..." The future immortals take Holy Communion, seize the straits of Rupel and hold them for six hours with, as their only weapons, the indomitable Greek soul.

The ironclad German divisions start a dreadful attack and after a ten-hour battle they manage to pass through. Remains only one of the heroic (*Greek*) *warriors. The German Commander of the division, tears from his bosom his Great Kaiser Cross, the highest decoration, puts it with reverence to the bloodied chest of the Greek sergeant-major, and covers him with his own military cape. A golden slate is raised on the spot: "*HERE LIE THE HEROES OF RUPEL,*" and its golden copy is sent to the Military Academy of Potsdam. A tribute to the heroes even from the enemies. Churchill, says, full of admiration... "Heroes fight like Greeks"*

STAVROS EVANGELIDIS

The second part in our next issue.

Η ΜΟΙΡΑ ΤΟΥ ΕΛΛΗΝΙΣΜΟΥ...

'Υπό Σταύρου Εὐαγγελίδη

Μέρος Δεύτερον

"Πουλάκι ξένο κι'ἐρημωμένο,
ποῦ πᾶς καί τρέχεις
ποῦ φωληάν ἔχεις;
Φωληά δέν ἔχω
πηγαίνω τρέχω ἐδῶ κι'ἐκεῖ
διά νά εὕρω τήν εὐτυχίαν
διά νά εὕρω τήν ἡσυχίαν
ποῦ κατοικεῖ"

'Αλέξανδρος 'Υψηλάντης

Γραμμένοι λές κι'εἶναι ξεπίτηδες οἱ πονεμένοι αὐτοί στίχοι γιά τό δρᾶμα καί τήν τραγωδία τοῦ 'Ελληνισμοῦ τῆς Πόλης. 'Η ἅλωσις καί τά μετά τήν ἅλωσιν ὡς σήμερα. Καί σέ μιά παρένθεση μερικές ἄγνωστες σέ πολλούς σχετικές ἱστορικές λεπτομέρειες ἀπό τήν πτῶσιν τῆς Βασιλευούσης.

'Εκεῖ στό λοφίσκο τοῦ Φαναρίου λίγο ψηλότερα ἀπό τήν Μεγάλη Τοῦ Γένους Σχολή, ὑπάρχει τό "Παπάς Τζαμισί" πού εἰς τήν κορυφή τοῦ μιναρέ του ἀντί τῆς ἡμισελήνου ἔχει καλυμμαύχιον διάκου. Εἶναι τό τέμενος πού ἔκτισαν οἱ Τοῦρκοι εἰς μνήμην τοῦ φανατικοῦ ἱερομονάχου πού ἤνοιξε τήν Πύλη τοῦ 'Αδριανοῦ διά νά εἰσέλθουν οἱ πρῶτοι εἰσβολεῖς. 'Ηθική κατάπτωσις πού ἔφθασε μέχρι καί αὐτῆς τῆς προδοσίας. 'Ο Παλαιολόγος τιθέμενος ἐπί κεφαλῆς τῶν ὀλίγων γενναίων τῆς Φρουρᾶς Του διά νά απωθήση εἰ δυνατόν ἔξω τῶν τειχῶν τούς εἰσελάσαντας ἐχθρούς,δέν ἀπευθύνεατι πρός αὐτούς. " "Ανδρες τοῦ Αὐτοκράτορος ἐμπρός" ἀλλά Ελλην αὐτός μέ καταφανῆ συγκίνησιν τούς ἀποκαλεῖ ""Ανδρες "Ελληνες" καί ἐπιζητεῖ τελικῶς ἕνα ἔνδοξον ἡρωϊκόν θάνατον εἰς τό πεδίον τῆς μάχης, θέτων οὕτω τόν λαόν του ὑπο τήν κηδεμονίαν τοῦ νικητοῦ ὅπως ὁρίζει ἡ θρησκεία τοῦ 'Ισλάμ μέ τάς ἐπί τούτω ῥήτρας τοῦ Κορανίου.

Αἰχμαλωτιζόμενος θά κατεδίκαζε καί αὐτόν εἰς αἰχμαλωσίαν μέ παρεπόμενα τήν δουλείαν καί τόν ἐξανδραποδισμόν. 'Η δέ αὐτοκράτειρα 'Ελένη μέ τό βαρύ πένθος τῆς ἀπωλείας τοῦ συζύγου της, καί φέρουσα εἰς τά σπλάχνα της τόν καρπόν τῆς ἀγάπης των τό παιδί τους, θέτουσα ὑπεράνω ὅλων ἀκόμη καί αὐτῆς τῆς τιμῆς της τήν τιμήν καί τήν εὐημερίαν τοῦ ἀπορφανωμένου λαοῦ τοῦ Βυζαντίου, δέν διστάζει νά γίνη σύζυγος τοῦ ἐρωτευμένου Πορθητοῦ. Καί εἶναι τόσον μεγάλη ἡ γοητεία καί ἡ ἐπιρροή πού ἐξασκεῖ, ὥστε ἀποσπᾶ τήν ἔγκρισίν του ὅπως ὅλα τά ἐκκοπτόμενα νομίσματα καί κέρματα φέρουν ἐφεξῆς τήν ἐπιγραφήν ΚΩΝΣΤΑΝΤΙΝΙΕ.

Δέν πρέπει λοιπόν νά μᾶς ἐκπλήξη ὅτι κατώρθωσε νά σώση καί τό παιδί της, καί ὅπως διατείνονται πολλοί ἀκόμη καί Τοῦρκοι μελετηταί τῆς 'Ιστορίας καί ἄς μήν εἶναι ἐντελῶς ἀποδεδειγμένον ὁ Μπαγιαζήτ ἦτο υἱός τοῦ Κωνταντίνου. "Ενας ἐπί πλέον λόγος αὐτῆς τῆς διαδόσεως καί πεποιθήσεως μεταξύ τῶν 'Ελλήνων εἶναι καί ἡ ἀμέριστος βοήθειά των πρός τόν Μπαγιαζήτ, ὅστις κατορθώνει νά νικήση τόν ἀδελφόν του Σουλτάν Τζέμ, ὁ ὁποῖος καταφεύγει τελικῶς εἰς 'Ιταλίαν. Τήν ἰδίαν εὐεργετικήν ἐπιρροήν ἐξασκεῖ ἀργότερον καί ἡ πριγκήπισσα Εὐδοκία ἀπόγονος τοῦ αὐτοκρατορικοῦ οἴκου τῆς Νικαίας.Σύζυγος Σελήμ τοῦ Β΄καί μήτηρ Μουράτ τοῦ Γ΄, ὅστις πρός τιμήν ἀνήγειρε τό μεγαλοπρεπές τέμενος "Βαλιντέ-Τζαμισί" μέ τούς "Ελληνας ἀρχιτέκτονας καί κτίστας του καί τό πλεονάζον οἰκοδομικόν ὑλικόν κτίζει τόν ἐν Χρυσουπόλει περικαλλῆ ναόν τοῦ Προφήτου 'Ηλιοῦ.

'Η 'Εκκλησία καί ὁ κλῆρος ὑπεραίρονται ἑαυτῶν μέ μίαν νέαν πνοήν δυναμισμοῦ εἰς ὅλους τούς τομεῖς συμπληροῦντες ὅλα τά κενά. 'Ο παπᾶς, ὁ μοναχός,ὁ καλόγηρος,ὁ ἀσκητής,ὁ ψάλτης,στήν πόλη,στό χωριό, στό μοναστῆρι,στόν κάμπο,στό βουνό εἶναι ὁ δάσκαλος μέ τό ψαλτῆρι καί τό συναξάρι πού μαθαίνει τά γράμματα στά 'Ελληνόπουλα.

Τό Πατριαρχεῖον μέ τήν παροχήν τῶν προνομίων,τά ὁποῖα καταλλήλως καί μέ θαυμαστήν περίνοιαν ἐπεκτείνει εἰς ὅλους τούς ὀρθοδόξους →

λαούς τῆς νέας Αὐτοκρατορίας,μεταφέρεται ἀπό τόν Ναόν τῶν Δώδεκα 'Αποστόλων πού εἰς τήν θέσιν του ἀνεγείρεται τό τέμενος τοῦ Φατήχ εἰς τήν ἱεράν μονήν τοῦ 'Αγίου Γεωργίου εἰς τό κλεινόν Φανάριον.

Φανός πράγματι ἀπαστράπτοντος φωτός εἶναι δι'ὅλους τούς ὑποδούλους. Φάρος τηλαυγής πού σκορπίζει τά σκότη τῆς ἀγωνίας καί ἀπελπισίας μέ τά ἐκπεμπόμενα ὑπό τῶν φαεινῶν του προβολέων ἀέννα κύματα τῆς ἐλπίδος καί τῆς ἐνθαρρύνσεως.

Οἱ λαοί τῆς Βαλκανικῆς οἱ ὁποῖοι ἐδιδάχθησαν τήν θρησκείαν καί τήν γραφήν ἀπό τούς 'Ισαποστόλους Μεθόδιον καί Κύριλλον,χάρις εἰς τό Πατριαρχεῖον,τούς ἀρχιερεῖς μητροπολίτας καί τούς Φαναριώτας ἡγεμόνας τῆς Μολδοβλαχίας καί τῶν Παραδουναβείων ἐπαρχειῶν,διατηροῦν ἀμείωτον τήν πίστιν καί τόν ἐθνισμόν των. Μία ὀφειλή πρός τήν Μητέρα 'Εκκλησίαν πού οὐδέποτε πρέπει νά λησμονοῦν,ἐδίδαξεν ἀλλά καί διετήρησε μέ χαλκέντερους Πατριάρχας καί ἱεράρχας,οἱ ὁποῖοι δέν ἐδίστασαν νά φθάσουν ἀκόμη καί μέχρι τῆς ἀγχόνης ὑπερασπιζόμενοι τό ποίμνιόν των.

Μέ τό ἐλεύθερον 'Ελληνικόν κράτος, ἀποβαίνει τό κέντρον ἡ ''Ανωτέτη Κορυφή τῆς 'Ορθοδοξίας μέ νέαν αἴγλην καί ἐκθαμβωτικόν μεγαλεῖον. Ἔρχονται ὅμως χρόνια δίσεχτα,χρόνια δύσκολα μέ νέες δοκιμασίες. Η ἀνταλλαγή περιλαμβάνει καί τόν περισσότερο 'Ελληνισμό τῆς Πόλης καί ἀκολουθοῦν τά γνωστά δραματικά γεγονότα καί μετά ἡ ἀπέλασις ὅλων τῶν 'Ελλήνων ὑπηκόων πού συμπαρασύρει καί δεκάδας χιλιάδων ἄλλων 'Ελλήνων. 'Η μάνα 'Ελλάδα πού ἔδωκε ἕνα κομμάτι γῆς καί ἕνα ξεροκόμματο στούς πρόσφυγας δέν μπορεῖ πιά νά σφίξη στήν ἀγκαλιά της αὐτά τά δίχως πιά φωλιά τρομαγμένα πουλιά. Ἔχουν στερέψει πιά τά στήθια της καί δέν μπορεῖ νά τά δώση τό μητρικό γάλα. Τά βλέπει ταξειδιάρικα μέ σφιγμένη καρδιά πού πᾶνε σ'ἄλλους τόπους. Καί ἕνα ἀχνό χαμόγελο στά μαραμένα της χείλη σάν νά βλέπη στή ζεστασιά μιᾶς ἄλλης μητρικῆς ἀγκαλιᾶς,τῆς ἐκείνης τῶν Πατρίδας. Ἕνα προσκύνημα κάποτε σ'αὐτή τήν πονεμένη μάνα 'Ελλάδα πού θά λάμψη τό πρόσωπό της ἀπό χαρά σάν θά δῆ τά ξενητεμένα παιδιά της εὐτυχισμένα. Ἕνα προσκύνημα στούς Ἁγίους Τόπους τῆς γενέτειρᾶς μας, στό Φανάρι,στό Πατριαρχεῖο μας πού ἄρχισε καί πάλιν νά ἀναλάμπη μέ τήν προβολήν τῆς παγκοσμίου του Οἰκουμενικότητος. Μιά ἐπίσκεψη, μιά χειραψία, ἕνα ἀγκάλιασμα μέ τούς δικούς, τούς φίλους,τούς Ἕλληνας τῆς Πόλης πού νέοι Ἄτλαντες βαστάζουν τό φορτίο μιᾶς τόσο βαρειᾶς κληρονομίας, πού..........

Καί θαρθεῖ μιά μέρα.................

Ὦ ψυχή παραδαρμένη ἀπό τό κρίμα...

ὅπως λέγει στόν προφητικό του ὁ ποιητής, αὐτοί οἱ λίγοι θά ἀποτελέσουν τόν χρυσοῦν συνδετικόν κρίκον ἑδραιώσεως τῆς δοκιμασθείσης φιλίας δύο λαῶν πρός ἕνα ἀδιάσπαστον σύνολον ἑνότητος......συντελεσταί ἀπαρχῆς μιᾶς περιόδου νέων διαμορφώσεων.

Εἶναι τά ἀνά τούς αἰώνας ἱστορικά διδάγματα μέ τόν διαρκῆ ροῦν τῶν ἐναλλασσομένων μεταλλαγῶν καί τῶν ἀλληλοδιαδόχων ἐξελίξεων εἰς τήν εὐλογημένην αὐτήν γωνίαν τῆς 'Ανατολῆς,νοτισμένη ἀπό τό ἀφρόδετο γαλανό κῦμα τῆς Προποντίδος, τοῦ Αἰγαίου καί τῆς Μεσογείου πού ὑπῆρξε κοιτίς τοῦ πολιτισμοῦ,πατρίς καί πηγή ὅλων τῶν ἀρχαίων καί νέων θρησκειῶν.

Καί ἡ 'Ιστορία δέν εἶναι δυνατόν νά διαφευσθῇ,
διότι......Η ΙΣΤΟΡΙΑ ΕΠΑΝΑΛΑΜΒΑΝΕΤΑΙ.

ΣΤΑΥΡΟΣ ΕΥΑΓΓΕΛΙΔΗΣ

THE FATE OF HELLENES
BY STAVROS EVANGELIDIS
Part Two

Little bird, estranged and isolated,
Where do you run and go,
Where do you have your nest?
I have no nest,
I go and run here and there
To find happiness
To find peace.
Where does it dwell?
- ALEXANTROS YPSILANTIS

One would think that these painful verses were written specifically for the drama and the tragedy of the Hellenism of Constantinople (Istanbul). The Conquest, and following the Conquest until today. And in a parenthesis some unknown to many related historical facts from the fall of the Reigning City.

Up on the low hill of Fanari, somewhat higher than the Great School of the Nation, there is a "Papaz Camisi," Mosque of the Priest, which bears at its crest the high-hat of a Deacon instead of the Crescent. This is the mosque that was built by Turks in memory of the fanatic monk who opened the Gate of Adrian to let in the first (Ottoman) invaders. Ethical despair that reached up to treason.

When Paleologos (The Byzantine Emperor, Constantine Paleologos) at the head of the few braves of his Guard, wanted to exhort them to withstand the battle as possible as outside the City Walls, he did not address them as "Men of the Emperor, go forth," but, a Hellene himself, he addressed them, with visible emotion, as "Greek men, go forth". He finally seeks an honourable heroic death in the battle field, putting thus his People under the protection of the Conqueror, as orders the religion of Islam with its related Koranic laws. Were he to be taken prisoner, he would condemn his Citizens to enslavement and to the extinguishing of its men.

As for the Empress Helen, mourning heavily the loss of her husband and bearing in her entrails the fruit of their love, their child, she puts above all –even (above) her own honour – the honour and prosperity of the People of Byzantium, and does not hesitate to become wife of the love-stricken Conqueror (Fatih Sultan Mehmet II). And so great is her charm and her influence that she gets his approval that all coins and gold pieces minted afterwards bear the inscription KONSTANTINIYE.

So, it should not astonish us that she also managed to save the life of her child, who, as many historians, even Turkish ones, maintain –though not proven– was Beyazit, the son of Constantine. One more reason about this rumour among Greeks is their undivided help to Beyazit, who manages to win – the throne – over his brother Cem (Djem) Sultan and forces him to flee to Italy.

The same beneficial influence is also applied later by princess Evdokia, a descendant of the Imperial House of Nikaia. She was the wife of Selim the 2nd and mother of Murat the 3rd, who built in her honour the grandiose mosque "Validé Camisi" – Mother's Mosque. *With the surplus material and the help of its Greek architects and masons, he (Sultan Murat) also built the beautiful Church of Prophet Elijah in Hrisoupolis (modern day Uskudar, Turkey).*

(Now) the Church, the clergy outdo themselves with a new breath of dynamism in all sectors, filling all voids. The priest, the monk, the ascetic, the cantor, in the city, in the village, in the monastery, in the field, in the mountain is the teacher with the Psalter and the prayer-book who teaches letters to the Greek children.

The Patriarchate, thanks to the privileges it gets (from the Turks) and that it extends with admirable intelligence to all the Orthodox Peoples of the New Empire (the Ottoman one), is transported from the Church of the Twelve Apostles, where is now built the Mosque of Fatih, to the Holy Monastery of St. George in Fanari (Fener).

Beacon, really, of bright light is (the Patriarchate) for all the enslaved subjects. A bright Lighthouse that illuminates with its light beams the darkness of agony and despair, offering waves of hope and encouragement.

The Peoples of the Balkans, who were taught the religion and the writing by the Apostles Methodius and Cyril, thanks to the Patriarchate, the Bishops, the Metropolitans, and the Fanariote Governors of Moldo-Vlach and the All-Danube provinces, manage to keep intact their faith and their nationalism. A debt they should never forget (they owe) towards the Mother Church who taught and maintained the indefatigable Patriarches who did not hesitate to even face death protecting their flock.

With the liberated Greek State, this centre (Fanari) becomes the highest Crest of Orthodoxy with new splendour and dazzling magnificence. But arrive leap years, difficult years, with new trials. The Exchange (of peoples) includes also the majority of Greeks of Istanbul. Then follow the known dramatic facts and later, the expulsion of all the Greek nationals that takes in its flow tens of thousands of other Greeks. Mother Greece, who offered a piece of earth and some dried bread to the immigrants, can no longer embrace in her chest those frightened nestless birds. Her breasts dried up and cannot offer them anymore their mother's milk. She looks at them, travelers, with heavy heart, as they leave for other lands. And a fleeting smile on her hurting lips, as if she sees them in the warmth of another motherly bosom, in their new Homeland. A pilgrimage (is due) sometime to this hurt Mother Greece whose face will illuminate with joy when she will see her estranged children happy. A pilgrimage to the Holy Lands of our Motherland, to Fanari, to our Patriarchate who started again to glare with the worldwide projection of Ecumenism. A visit, a handshake, a hug with our own (people), our friends, the Greeks of Istanbul who, like new Atlases, hold the weight of such a heavy inheritance, who.......

"And a day will come ....
O, soul beaten from the offence..."

as sings in his prophecy the poet, (that) those few will become the golden linking chain of consolidation of the battered friendship of two Peoples towards an unbreakable whole unity... coworkers into starting an era of new formations.

Those are the historic centuries'-old teachings with the continuous flow of alternating changes and successive evolutions in this blessed corner of the Anatolia surrounded by the foaming blue waves of the Propontis (Marmara Sea), the Aegean and the Mediterranean and which has been the cradle of civilization, motherland and source of all the old and new religions.

And it is impossible for History to be belied,
because... HISTORY REPEATS ITSELF.

STAVROS EVANGELIDIS

* * *

Stavros approves the translation with a nod.

"You don't want to write anything new? You may submit more than one article," I propose.

"Later, for the next one, I will write about Greco-Turkish Friendship. If I get better, though... If not... Because, it is one thing to write about it, another to prove it... I need to concentrate..."

My heart sinks. It is the first time Father admits his doubt returning to health.

"Did you read my manuscript? When could you correct it?" I ask, to change the subject.

He signals with his head the pile of papers on the side table. "I did the first part," he says. "Not much to correct, you made a good job of the research. Some minor things to be rephrased, mainly on page 6. And the syntax is all right."

I glance at my manuscript and his corrections:

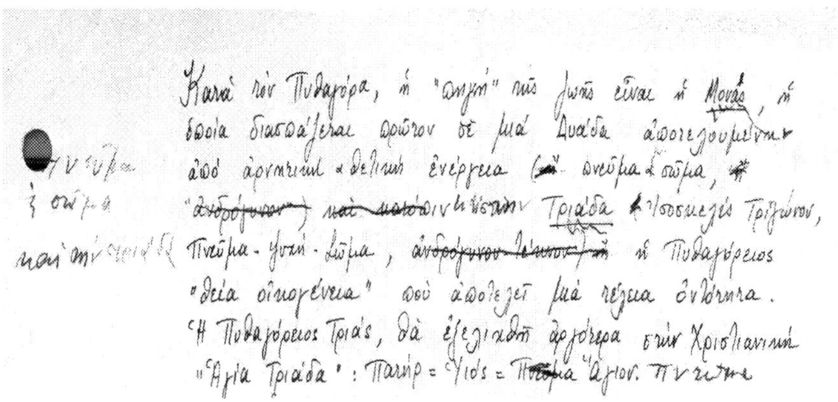
Κατά τόν Πυθαγόρα, ἡ "πηγή" τῆς ζωῆς εἶναι ἡ Μονάς, ἡ
ὁποία διασπάζεται πρῶτον σέ μιά Δυάδα ἀποτελουμένη
ἀπό ἀρνητική & θετική ἐνέργεια (πνεῦμα & σῶμα,
Τριάδα (ἰσοσκελές Τρίγωνον,
Πνεῦμα - ψυχή - Σῶμα, ἡ Πυθαγόρειος
"θεία οἰκογένεια" πού ἀποτελεῖ μιά τέλεια ὀντότητα.
Ἡ Πυθαγόρειος Τριάς, θά ἐξελιχθῆ ἀργότερα στήν Χριστιανική
"Ἁγία Τριάδα": Πατήρ = Υἱός = Ἅγιον Πνεῦμα

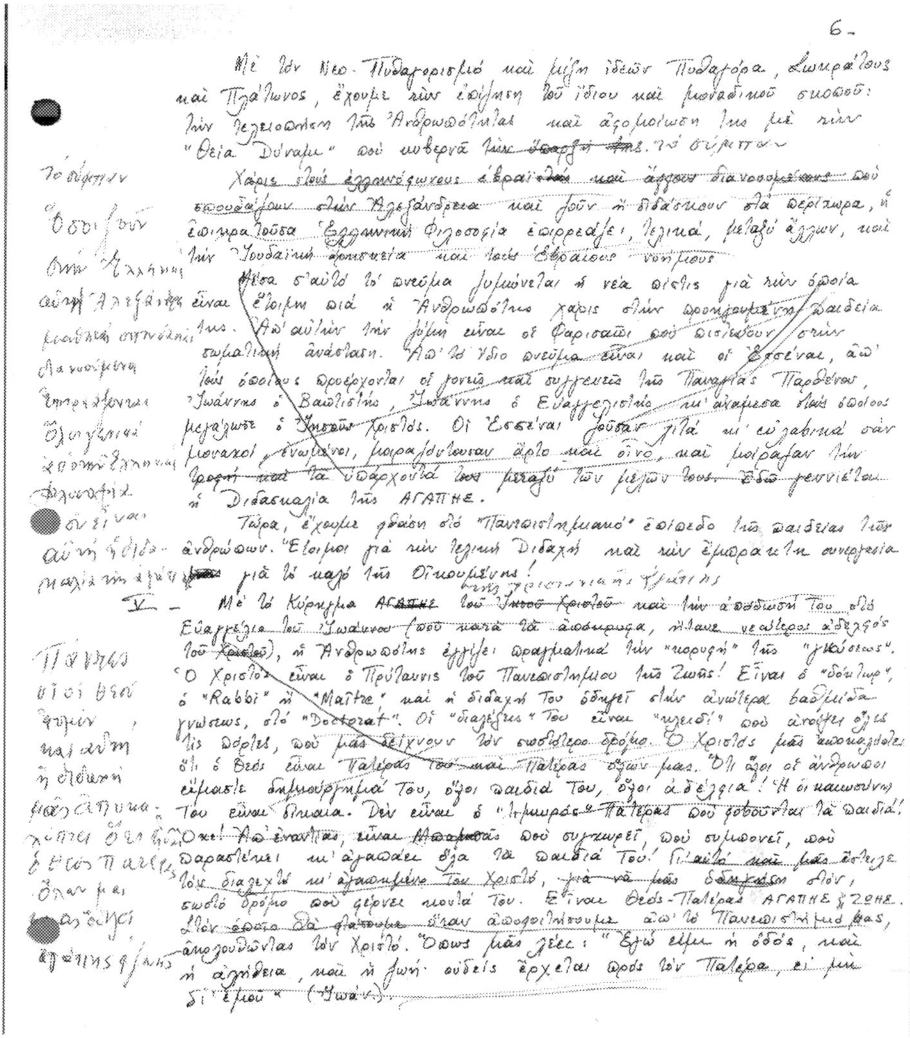

6-

Μὲ τὸν Νεο-Πυθαγορισμό καὶ μίξη ἰδεῶν Πυθαγόρα, Σωκράτους καὶ Πλάτωνος, ἔχουμε τὴν ἐξύψωση τοῦ ἰδίου καὶ μοναδικοῦ σκοποῦ: τὴν τελειοποίηση τῆς Ἀνθρωπότητας καὶ ἀφομοίωση της μὲ τὴν "Θεία Δύναμη" ποὺ κυβερνᾶ τὸ σύμπαν.

Χάρις στοὺς ἑλληνόφωνους Ἑβραίους καὶ ἄλλους διανοουμένους ποὺ σπούδαζαν στὴν Ἀλεξάνδρεια καὶ ζοῦν ἢ διδάσκουν στὰ περίχωρα, ἡ ἐπικρατοῦσα Ἑλληνική Φιλοσοφία ἐπηρεάζει, τεχνικά, μεταξὺ ἄλλων, καὶ τὴν Ἰουδαϊκὴ θρησκεία καὶ τοὺς Ἑβραίους νομικούς.

Μέσα σ' αὐτὸ τὸ πνεῦμα γυμνάζεται ἡ νέα αἵρεσις γιὰ τὴν ὁποία εἶναι ἕτοιμη ἡ Ἀνθρωπότης χάρις στὴν προηγούμενη παιδεία της. Ἀπ' αὐτὴν τὴν μύηση εἶναι οἱ Φαρισαῖοι ποὺ διδάσκουν τὴν σωματικὴ ἀνάσταση. Ἀπ' τὸ ἴδιο πνεῦμα εἶναι καὶ οἱ Ἐσσαῖοι, ἀπ' τοὺς ὁποίους προέρχονται οἱ γονεῖς καὶ συγγενεῖς τῆς Παναγίας Παρθένου, Ἰωάννης ὁ Βαπτιστής, Ἰωάννης ὁ Εὐαγγελιστής κι' ἀνάμεσα στοὺς ὁποίους μεγάλωσε ὁ Ἰησοῦς Χριστός. Οἱ Ἐσσαῖοι ζοῦσαν μιὰ κι' εὐλαβικὰ σὰν μοναχοί, ἐνωμένοι, μοιράζονταν ψωμὶ καὶ κρασί, καὶ μοίραζαν τὴν τροφή καὶ τὰ ὑπάρχοντά τους μεταξὺ τῶν μελῶν τους. Ἐδῶ γεννιέται ἡ Διδασκαλία τῆς ΑΓΑΠΗΣ.

Τώρα, ἔχουμε φθάσει στὸ "Πανεπιστημιακό" ἐπίπεδο τῆς παιδείας τῶν ἀνθρώπων. "Ἕτοιμοι γιὰ τὴν τελικὴ Διδαχὴ καὶ τὴν ἐμφάνιση ἐνέργεια γιὰ τὸ καλὸ τῆς Οἰκουμένης!

V – Μὲ τὸ Κήρυγμα ΑΓΑΠΗΣ τοῦ Ἰησοῦ Χριστοῦ καὶ τὴν ἀποδοχή Του στὸ Εὐαγγέλιο τοῦ Ἰωάννου (ποὺ κατὰ τὰ ἀπομνημονεύματα, ἦταν νεώτερος ἀδελφὸς τοῦ Χριστοῦ), ἡ Ἀνθρωπότης ἐγγίζει πραγματικὰ τὴν "κορυφὴ" τῆς "γνώσεως". Ὁ Χριστὸς εἶναι ὁ Πρύτανις τοῦ Πανεπιστημίου τῆς Ζωῆς! Εἶναι ὁ "δόκτωρ", ὁ "Rabbi" ἢ "Maître" καὶ ἡ διδαχή Του ὁδηγεῖ στὴν ἀνώτερα βαθμίδα γνώσεως, στὸ "Doctorat". Οἱ "διαλέξεις" Του εἶναι "κλειδιά" ποὺ ἀνοίγει ὅλες τὶς πόρτες, ποὺ μᾶς δείχνουν τὸν συντομώτερο δρόμο. Ὁ Χριστὸς μᾶς ἀποκαλύπτει ὅτι ὁ Θεὸς εἶναι Πατέρας του καὶ Πατέρας ὅλων μας. Ὅτι ὅλοι οἱ ἄνθρωποι εἴμαστε δημιουργήματά Του, ὅλοι παιδιά Του, ὅλοι ἀδέλφια! Ἡ δικαιοσύνη Του εἶναι δίκαια. Δὲν εἶναι ὁ "τιμωρὸς" Πατέρας ποὺ φοβοῦνται τὰ παιδιά! Ὄχι! Ἀπ' ἐναντίας, εἶναι Πατέρας ποὺ συγχωρεῖ, ποὺ συμπονεῖ, ποὺ παραστέκει κι' ἀγαπάει ὅλα τὰ παιδιά Του! Τὸν διαλεχτὸ κι' ἀγαπημένο Του Χριστό, γιὰ νὰ μᾶς δείξει τὸν σωστὸ δρόμο ποὺ φέρνει κοντά Του. Εἶναι Θεὸς-Πατέρας ΑΓΑΠΗΣ & ΖΩΗΣ. Στὸν ὁποῖο θὰ φθάσουμε ὅταν ἀποφοιτήσουμε ἀπ' τὸ Πανεπιστήμιό μας, ἀκολουθώντας τὸν Χριστό. Ὅπως μᾶς λέει: "Ἐγώ εἰμι ἡ ὁδός, καὶ ἡ ἀλήθεια, καὶ ἡ ζωή· οὐδεὶς ἔρχεται πρὸς τὸν Πατέρα, εἰ μὴ δι' ἐμοῦ" (Ἰωάν.).

As I thank him, Stavros sweeps the air with his right hand and says: "If I were you, I would omit this whole part," pointing to my introduction.

"Why?"

"Because Nicolas is a scholar. He knows all this. It is… 'doctrinarian'? You are not a theologian, so…"

"But I want to keep this part for my daughters. Specifically what relates to the influence of Greek philosophy," I protest.

"That's another story. Shorten it to a few paragraphs. It will be more interesting if you start from your own experiences. My opinion."

Well, at least he had read it.

I rewrite the Introduction into a foreword, and resubmit it to Stavros the next day. [For the purpose of this part, I edited and translated the manuscript into English].

"Here," I say. "I condensed the whole 17 pages of my introduction into my foreword. I couldn't cut it more than that. Do you approve?"

He takes my manuscript and starts reading. He nods his head, as he turns the pages...

WITH LOVE AS GUIDE

By Erato Evangelidis Sahapoglu

1986©

PREFACE

To My Daughters!

The astonishing scientific, technical and material advances of our century – in bitter parallel to the famine, sickness, injustice, disasters and wars that cause agony and fear that, in spite of all our progress and knowledge, Mankind may be heading towards its final destruction – have crushed the faith and hope of many.

Many of our youngsters believe either that they can do, like gods, everything, or that they are condemned by fate to a life without moral evolution or hope.

The occasional message of religious leaders addressed to youth, stating that youth can, if it sincerely wants to, change the progression of the world, with its own means and with the support of faith and of hope in God, have some repercussions. However, without tangible proof that God does indeed exist and guides our lives, 'faith' remains to many only a word, empty of any deeper meaning.

During the past 50 years, I have had the chance to 'live' personally this love and guidance and to witness extraordinary events that could only be produced by a divine power. And I wish to share here with you, my children, my personal experience, hoping to convince you as well, the way I was convinced myself, that this Superior Power, is not only overseeing the path of our 'schooling' existence in this world that we call Life, but has also assigned to us incomparable guide-teachers, to help us in our progress.

January, 1986

FOREWORD

To me, the evolution of Mankind appears as steps in an educational progress. It starts with the oral traditions and is followed by historical steles and papyrus. Later, we have the written word with writings such as the Book of the Dead of the Egyptians, the Vedas of the Asiatic peoples, the Old Testament of the Hebrews and the Laws of Moses, the Greek legends and myths, and the Upanishads of the Hindus. These writings are followed by the Torah of Judaism and the Bhagavad-Gita of Hinduism. They all have a common point: How super celestial or infernal forces control the lives of men.

Follow the teachings of Buddha in India, Zoroaster in Persia, Confucius (K'ung Fu Tzu) in China and of Greek philosophers like Pythagoras, Socrates, Plato and Aristotle, in Greece. They all generalize "ethics" for the benefit of Mankind, and they separate citizens' laws from individual spiritual evolution.

With Alexander the Great, Hellenism spread to Alexandria and the Middle East, and there is a synthesis of all previous teachings merged with the Greek thought.

For instance, Pythagoras, the mathematician, in his school in Crotona (Calabres or Calabria) Italy, around 500 B.C. taught that the Universe is governed through the balance and harmony of the adverse energies that compose it and according to the will of a Creative Mind. He maintained that the source of life is the "Monad" or One, broken into a "Dyad" of positive and negative energy (Spirit and Body) and thence into a "Triad", symbolized by the isosceles triangle with two equal sides. It forms a perfect entity or 'divine family'. This Pythagorean Triad will later inspire the Christian Holy Trinity of Father, Son and Holy Spirit. Pythagoras, like others before him, maintained that the Spirit is immortal, that it can impose upon the physicality of the body and that it can take another form (reincarnation or transmigration of the soul). In Crotona, Pythagoras formed elite families aiming at the betterment of Mankind according to a divine plan.

Socrates with his "know thyself" principle and dialectic teaching, believed in a "daemon", an immortal protective spirit. His student Plato, who was also a Pythagorean follower, believed that the Soul-Spirit evolved continuously through different stages or reincarnations until it reached Perfection. Plato's student Aristotle proposed a synthesis and unification of logic or rational thought with the intuition of the divine will.

Between 30 and 101 A.D., Christianity will spread from Judea and the Near East and will evolve into this synthesis of old universal teachings and the modern merging of Greek philosophy, especially in Alexandria, Egypt. Over the years this new synthesis will merge into Neo-Pythagoreanism and a Neo-Platonism which, translated later by Arab scholars, will be rediscovered and influence the Renaissance movement. It was Alexandria's Hellenism that definitely helped the spreading of Christianity in its beginnings.

Most of Jesus' followers were either Essenes or Hellenists and some of the first Gospels, the Acts of the Apostles, St. Paul's Epistles, and St. John's Apocalypse, were written in Greek.

But Jesus' teachings surpassed all past ethics. He teaches us not only faith, respect, integrity, simplicity, humility and magnanimity, but also altruism, tolerance and, above all, "love". He was indeed one of the greatest Master-Teachers and Prophets of Mankind. He did possess extraordinary energy and knowledge. Whether He was indeed the "Son of God" as stated in the Gospels, or if He meant that He and all of us are children of the Unique and Sole God, and therefore we are all brothers, makes no difference. He remains the Christ, the Chosen one, because with His life He achieved the most Divine Perfection. He assures us of the immortality of our soul. And He is only asking us to follow His love for humans and to have faith in God, our creator, as our sole means of achieving what He has achieved. I believe that this Love of our neighbour, and the forgiveness of our enemies, as Jesus teaches, is the sole means that will unite Mankind into a harmonious and peaceful coexistence which will bring us close to God, to the "Divine Perfection" (Matthew). Jesus will be called the 'Prince of Peace', although, ironically, his followers, not grasping the real meaning of His teaching, will perform, in His name, the most terrible atrocities.

Mankind's atrocities make doubt creep into the hearts about the existence of God. Some claim that the prophets were mythical people and that Jesus did not exist. Others claim that Elijah, Moses, Jesus and the Angels are teachers from another Planet and that they were sent to Earth to help men and later returned to their birthplace by "ascending" in spaceships. Some even claim that Man is a clone of this superior inter-galactic species.

I am not a theologian trying to prove the historical existence of Jesus (though more and more historians are coming to this conclusion) nor the veracity of the four gospels where, although there are some differences in details, the essence is the same.

But I see that, in our modern rational half-knowledge, we try to explain all the inexplicable or 'miraculous' events that we encounter (from telepathy to materialization of the dead, to miraculous healings) according to the knowledge we believe we possess. And we either consider these 'miracles' as human accomplishments or we simply discard them. We consider them to be the effects of individual or mass excitation, mass subjection or hypnosis, and we deny the mere existence and works of 'holy entities' or 'saints' – accepted over thousands of years by the authorities of different religions.

This scepticism towards the 'wonder' stems mainly from the fact that there were (and still are) some individuals who, for the sake of fame or greed, have staged so-called 'miraculous' phenomena. They are using religion simply to satisfy their own ambitions. In spite of aims of scientists and researchers to prove them wrong, their wrongdoings spread disbelief. Therefore, people who are sincere and who have experienced miracles, keep silent, afraid to be characterized either as "crooks" or as "irrational" and "crazy".

I was also one of those 'witnesses' who experienced inexplicable phenomena but kept my lips sealed out of fear of judgement by my fellow humans when they heard what I had to say. When my prayers were answered or premonitory dreams materialized and inexplicable events occurred, I either chose to ignore them or attributed them to my personal will and to the surge of my subconscious. And each time, I tended to forget, to even consciously reject other miraculous events that had guided my life.

Until, finally, my university studies brought me to the lectures of a Christian professor, Reverend John Rossner. He was a philosopher-man-of-the-robe who was analyzing in parallel all the world's religions and all the inexplicable phenomena occurring in our world. In his classroom, we 40 students admitted and confessed to others, at last, the strange events that we all had experienced at some time, but that we had silenced, even ignored, either out of genuine ignorance or out of fear of judgement by others.

And for the first time in my life I realized the extent of my vanity; all those years I had been trying to explain some of these events as my "own accomplishments" or my own telepathic capabilities, or even as a power of my subconscious. I did not accept them as proofs of divine guidance.

The majority of my classmates had had reactions similar to mine.

It is only now, after my ongoing studies had offered me some basic knowledge and reassured me that I am not "irrational" that I dare to freely discuss these extraordinary phenomena which have resurrected my Faith in God, in Jesus, and my certitude in the Divine Providence.

"So? How do you find it?" I ask, Father.
"Hmmm. Better than before," he admits, and turns the page.

WITH LOVE AS GUIDE (Continued)

Marked events of my life

I am recalling these events for you, my beloved daughters, with the hope that they will give you strength during difficult times in your life and that, moreover, they will fortify your Faith if it ever weakens, giving you the certainty that God's Love will always be with you and guide you.

Most of the experiences that impressed and molded me were announced as "prophetic" dreams. In the beginning, they either amazed me or frightened me. Only later did I realize that, like the biblical prophetic dreams, like those interpreted by Joseph or those of seers, my own dreams were also meant as a forewarning to prepare me in every way for what was to come. Like the lighted "Fasten your seat-belt" sign on an airplane or the announcement by the captain to brace for turbulence during our flight. As a result of these warnings, when the turbulence hits we remain calm, without panic, having faith in our pilot and the aircraft. At other times our dreams are like the captain's pleasant announcements of flying over a landmark so that we would not miss its importance or its beauty. In this life-journey, our life-pilot is God's Divine Assistant – for me Jesus. And our physical bodies are the aircraft that our soul occupies, travelling in space towards our destination, our Creator.

Here are the experiences that marked my life.

1. *I was barely four or five years old, maybe younger, when I had a nightmarish dream. An old man, very tall and skeletal thin, with waist-long white hair and beard, was stretching his chained boned arms to me and asking me, silently, to free him from his chains! I was terrified at that tender age. Today I would explain the dream as an archetype image: either a Jungian image of "Eternity" or "Father Time", or as a traditional image of God or the "Eternal Higher Self" struggling to be freed from oblivion. Had not Jesus said that He "existed before Abraham"? Even "before the beginning of time"? That He was the "Alpha and Omega", the "Beginning and the End"? (John).*

Or, in other words, the "cause and effect"? And that we were all linked, like Him and through Him, to the same Creative Force, to "God our Father"?

Yet, through the years that passed, I wondered why I had had such a symbolic dream. My rational being inclined me to believe that for our own "sanity", our memory of the very remote past should be buried in oblivion, otherwise we would not be able to function properly day by day.

Today, I feel that all the experiences that accompanied my childhood and my mature years have finally prepared me to face anything – past, present or future – and that I am now ready to assess those special events in the light of my whole life, in what I believe is a pre-ordained divine path for my own spiritual growth. If the first projection, or image, was scary and baffling by its inexplicable meaning then, it did change to become understandable and "adapted' to my own age in the years to come.

2 - I must have been five or six years old when I was overwhelmed by a marvellous vision: I woke up during the night, to go to the washroom. When I looked out of the window, I saw, in the starry night, a strange panorama of brightly lit skyscrapers (non-existent in the Istanbul of the late 1930s) and a huge suspension bridge lit with round blinking lights. The bright lights changed the dark night into a glorious, glowing, deep sundown. Suddenly, on the horizon, emerged, from the waist up, a young person with a young child beside him/her (?). They were both wearing glowing golden helmets and were smiling and waving to me. I was fascinated. It surpassed in beauty any special film effects at that time!

Yet, when I returned to my room and looked again out of the window, there was only the dark sky with the twinkling stars. It was not a dream then! Or was it? Was it a vision? I spent my childhood recalling this marvellous 'vision' and trying to explain it over the years according to the knowledge of the "unknown" that I would gather on my way.

Till lately, I could not interpret this vision. Yet I still remained under its spell. At times I believed it was a reminiscence of another life, or even the symbolism of "Father and Son", the Creator and the Creature that are part of all of us.

Later, I thought this vision could be a premonition of Istanbul's future 'suspended' bridge over the Bosphorus, erected just a few years ago, and always lit. However, I was not living in Istanbul any more, so what linked the dream to me?

Then again, very recently, when riding along a side road on the South Shore of Montreal towards the Champlain Bridge, under the glorious deep orange-red-blue northern sky of an advanced sundown, I realized I was re-living my childhood vision! The Champlain Bridge looks indeed like a suspension bridge, lit by the cars crossing it both ways at nightfall! And Montreal skyscrapers are reflecting the rays of the setting sun and the red radiant clouds.

So then, what I saw 50 years ago was a glimpse of my future city where I am living now! With, at my side, *my first child who was born in Istanbul! Doesn't that prove that it was our destiny to come and live here? That our life is planned in advance? That our destination and the paths to follow it are traced beforehand, no matter how long or how fast or by what means it takes us to reach it?*

Finally, if we consider the original vital cell as "asexual" or "androgynous" as Pythagoras and others claimed, then maybe the Youth and the Child might represent "Me", my own duality: the Child I was then and the Young Person who would migrate to Canada in her mid-twenties. But then the vision was to attain a cosmic meaning whereby the life pattern of each individual is set from the beginning of time and the individual or "entity" is split into the physical body that lives in this pattern and the spirit that molds it, guided by the Divine Teacher to Whom it stays linked.

The questions beginning to arise and the assumptions (since I cannot use the word conclusions) are dazzling and marvellous.

Yet, I have to admit that my whole life, to this day, is following a preset path, with a "dream" preparing me beforehand for its several stations.

The same thing must be happening to most of us, whether we are conscious of it or not. Let me recall, chronologically, the major events that were shaping my life.

"I don't see the relation of those two examples to the existence of God," remarks Stavros, raising his eyebrows.

"They show a preset path in the journey of our life," I explain. And if there is a preset path, it implies a plan, guided by a Supreme Intelligence."

He makes an unconvinced pout.

"You will see, further down... It will all fall into place," I insist.

He goes on reading, without any comment.

3. *When I was still a very young child, without any idea about the Bible and Gospels, I had the following dream: I was in our House in Emin Djami, Istanbul, standing at the foot of the indoor stairs of the entrance-hall, with the light out.*

Suddenly, I see three Turkish women, in black robes and cloaks covering their heads but leaving their faces open, coming down the stairs towards me.

Each one holds a lit candle illuminating her face. They pass me by, saluting me, and they signal me to follow them. Turned to stone, I can't move!

Only as late as 1985, did I understand that the dream must have represented the Three Women visiting Christ's Tomb of the Gospels: the Virgin Mary, mother of Jesus, Mary Magdalene and Mary of Klopa (or Salome, the Gospels differing about the third woman). They were the first to find the Holy Sepulchre empty and bear witness to Jesus Christ's Resurrection.

This dream was my first "baptism", my first 'enlightenment' in Jesus Christ's teachings. In the years to come, I realized that the Virgin Mary was to be my Guide and my Protector. And, when I would come to grasp the meaning of the Gospels, I would also realize that Christ, God's "Verb" (or "Cause" and "Justification" according to the etymology of the Greek word "Logos"*) would be the greatest revelation and consolation and would give a meaning to my life. (By a strange coincidence I also have three names: Erato for the muse of love songs, Evanghelia meaning good news and/or good angel, and Maria...)*

Furthermore, during this past year (1984) I was offered a seventeenth-century icon, representing the Three Women at the empty tomb of Jesus Christ, lit by the halo of the Angel of the Resurrection...

4. At eight, I have an extraordinary dream, appropriate to be grasped now by a child of my age. It still takes place in our apartment dwelling of Emin Djami.

The door bell rings. I open the iron street door of the apartment. In front of me I see the Virgin Mary, young, beautiful, with a dark cloak covering her head. Behind her I make out a cloud of thick white smoke. The Virgin smiles faintly, moves to the side, and with her hand she motions to what is taking place behind her. The dense white smoke becomes translucent and starts to disperse. In the middle, I now see a "bonfire" and around it small children, dressed in the garments of the Roman epoch, dancing in a circle. Suddenly they break the circle and from its centre there advances towards me a small boy of divine beauty, with short curly brown hair, surrounded by a halo of light. The boy stretches his arms towards me and tells me silently, telepathically:

"Take me! Me! Not the other children!"

I look back at the Virgin Mary in astonishment. As an answer, She hands me a small yellowed roll of paper. I unroll it. It has some letters printed on it, but they are illegible, faded, half-erased. I turn to the Virgin Mary to ask Her to help me decipher what I believe to be a prayer. She is not there... The whole scene has vanished.

I wake up agitated. Incapable of interpreting my dream, I describe it to my mother.

My mother, although she seldom goes to church, is very religious and has a deep faith in the Virgin Mary as our protector and our intercessor to God, as sung in our liturgical hymns. She takes me to the Church, of the Presentation of the Holy Virgin of Pera (Beyoğlu) –called in short "Panaghia" – and asks me to light a candle to the icon of the Holy Virgin holding the Christ Child.

Later, she tells my dream to Kyria Elenitsa, the very devout mother of her best friend Evghenoula. This elderly lady, whose hair has whitened over the years of praying with her Missal and whom I called "Aunt'", gives the following interpretation to my mother:

"In your iconostase (the cabinet where we Greek Orthodox keep icons that we light with a votive oil-lamp or candle), behind the votive light, you probably have an icon other than that of Christ. Bring the icon of Christ to the front, so that it can be illuminated directly from the flame."

The same afternoon, Mama asks me to clean the iconostase and check the icons. Although I know that we had no icon of Jesus, I bring the iconostase down, take out all the icons and start cleaning them one by one. Behind the glass oil-lamp, we had the Virgin's Dormition; to its right an icon of St. George; to its left the icon of Ste. Barbara and a small icon of St. Pantaleon. I don't find any icon of Jesus.

Then, while dusting the iconostase itself, I sense something under my small fingers and I find, stuck deeply between the wood panels of the left corner, a yellowed piece of paper. I take it out with care, pushing it with a long pointed knife. It is a thin yellowed roll. I unroll it. What do I see? A colour picture of our Virgin Mary with Jesus in her arms! He is a little child, with brown curly hair, exactly as in my dream! And the right hand of the Holy Mother is holding the right hand of the little Jesus! The icon represents the Virgin Mary as the "Odeghetria", the Guiding one, with our Christ in her arms.

We have the icon covered with silver foil by a silversmith. When we get the icon back, I place our votive oil-lamp in front of it to light it. Since that day, all my sincere and desperate implorings to our Jesus and His Holy Mother are being answered... This is the only icon that I took with me when we immigrated to Canada...

This whole event could not have been a simple coincidence since it was revealed to me in advance, in a dream. It was neither telepathy nor a pre-statement from anyone, since nobody in our family knew of the existence of this hidden rolled icon. That rules out the possibility that I was being used by someone else's power of subjection.

It also excludes my own self-induction by my subconscious for any reason. It was simply an "unsolicited preconscious dream" with an unsolicited divine message materializing in substantial evidence. I accepted this manifestation as "divine will".

It changed me deeply, shaped my beliefs and those of my mother, strengthened my faith in Jesus and the Holy Virgin, and offered me support, trust and guidance in life. I did not know yet, at that time, that Jesus had said, according to the Gospel of John:

> The one who has my commandments and keeps them,
> That one is the one who loves me;
> And the one loving me, is also loved by my Father;
> And I will love him too
> And will reveal myself to him.

To how many of us did He indeed reveal Himself, but had we failed, perhaps, to recognize Him? I was privileged to have the guidance of Aunt Elenitsa, that devout elderly lady, to sustain and guide me in my first "encounter" with Christ. I was too young yet to ask myself "Why? What was the purpose of this revelation?" Was it just to sustain me during future personal ordeals the way He surely is sustaining most of us, even when we do not realize it, as He promised He would do? Or was I part of a "link" between Him and the ones needing His help? My parents? My friends? Strangers? I did not know.

Stavros, visibly moved, puts the manuscript on his knees. "I took that icon to the silversmith myself to have it all covered in silver; except of the faces of the Virgin and of Christ," he says in an altered voice.

The icon is now in the iconostase, in Kathy's room. Lit by a votive oil-lamp.

"Do you want me to bring it to you, Father, to examine it?"

"No. I just had forgotten the circumstances… Strange… Strange indeed."

He crosses his hands on the papers and rests his head on the back of his chair. Closes his eyes. *Daydreaming? Introspecting?*

I deposit a light kiss on his forehead and leave him with his thoughts.

IX - Slow Deterioration

*I*t is a grey, cold, winter day. Stavros has had a busy morning. Earlier, he had the weekly visit from his G.P.

"No change", she remarked to Stavros.

"The sickness progresses as predicted", she told me.

Then Robert came to give Father his regular bath and massage. We appreciate Robert's help. This energetic young man is always cheerful and smiling. Father feels much better after his visit.

At noon, as always seated in his reclining chair, Father ate the meatball soup and the vanilla rice pudding I prepared for him. He is becoming more tired and no longer joins us at the dining table.

The TV off, Stavros is resting his head on his neck-pillow. His eyes are closed, his breathing heavy but regular. He smells good. But he has lost weight. His cheeks are hollow now, the facial bones are etched. His skin is almost translucent. The veins in his forehead and hands stand out, hard, blue. I stare at him, my heart heavy. I try to tip-toe out of the room. His hand grabs my arm as I am leaving his side.

"Don't go," he says. "I'm not asleep. Just relaxing."

"You don't want to sleep?" I ask. He shakes his had "No."

"Feel like talking?"

He smiles, nodding.

"Do you want a coffee or a Spider, before?"

"Yeah, a Spider would be nice," he answers.

I come back with his favourite vodka and mint cocktail to which I added lots of ice, the way he likes it nowadays. Strong alcohol disturbs his oesophagus. He takes the glass and slowly savours a few sips smacking his lips on the sweet green liquid.

"The Association's commemorative album is printed," I say. Your article "*The Fate of Hellenism*" appeared in its original Greek version. My "*Do You Believe in Santa Claus*" was also printed in its original English. Lack of space for bilingual articles, I guess."

"That's all right," says Stavros.

"Did you write anything new?" I ask, eager to see him occupied in an activity he loves.

"No. But I read a large part of your manuscript. Interesting. Here", he says, handing it to me.

We go over it together.

WITH LOVE AS GUIDE (Continued)

5. *I will never forget that day of March 24. As I came home from school, I saw my mother behind the door, eyes red from crying and distress on her face. Mama rarely cried.*

   "What's wrong?" I asked, alarmed.

   "Renoula – Marianthi's daughter – is sick with very high fever. Her throat is covered with a white membrane, she can hardly breathe. It's diphtheria, says her doctor uncle. It's very difficult now to find a serum against it. It's serious. She may die. Do you want to go and pray at the miraculous Annunciation Icon at the Evanghelistria Church? Today is the Vigil for the Feast of Annunciation. "

"I will go," I answered. I handed her my school bag and off I went. The Church of Annunciation was at Yenishehir, on the outskirts of Kurtulus, a half hour fast walk. Almost running, I passed along the narrow streets lined with fishmongers and fruit merchants. Deaf to their cries, I passed the long barren stretch, before seeing the NeoGothic spiral of Evanghelistria's bell tower. I walked past the religious ware vendors who crowded churchyards at every big feast, and ignored their cries of "Keria, Fitilakia*" (Candles, wicks).* "Thimiama*!" (Incense)* "Karvounakia*" (small pieces of charcoal)...*

I walked with difficulty through the entrance and the narthex flooded with churchgoers where volunteers were asking for donations to charities: "For our hospitals," were crying some uniformed nurses... "For our public kitchen," cried others. "For the maintenance of our church," cried the church volunteers offering, on a silver platter, oval icons of the Annunciation scene embossed on silver leaf. Others were distributing flowers and sprinkling us with rose water, soliciting our "obole*".*

I finally made it to the "solea*", the main interior of the church. The icon was at the back, at the left, close to the altar. I elbowed my way to the front of it. The icon was covered in silver-leaf. It was full of votive offerings attached to three rows of strings – from the faithful who had been miraculously healed. Two embroidered white batiste curtains protected the old image from light. Sweet-smelling white flowers crowned its frame. I fell on my knees and started to pray. I prayed for a long time, isolating myself from everything around me. Tears flooded my cheeks. I asked the Virgin to help save the life of my little friend. Renoula was the first baby I ever held, the first baby that I fed with a spoon, that I took out in a stroller. She was more than a little sister to me...*

It was night when I left the church. When I returned home, Mama was beaming. She announced, with tears of joy in her eyes, that Renoula was sleeping peacefully, with no fever, her throat cleared... Healed miraculously...

This was the most marvellous gift I received on that Vigil of the Feast of Annunciation, the 24th of March, the anniversary of my birthday.

Didn't He say?

> Whatever you will ask, in prayer,
> Believe that you will receive
> And so will be done to you! (Gospel by Mark)

Jesus' most important commandments were to love God, have faith in God and in Him, and to love our neighbour. It is true that I loved Renoula very dearly and I had great faith in Christ and the Virgin Mary as our mediators to God.

However, at that age, I was not thinking of what Jesus had said.

I had never thought that my own prayer could have had anything to do with the "healing". Yet my latest experience with the icon of the Madonna and Child had just reinforced my faith that God would do something to save the life of little Rena anyway, and I was thrilled that He did so.

Later, much later, I asked myself whether I could have been used, at times, as an instrument to help fulfill His divine wish. I would find the answer to this query even later.

6. As a young teenager, I had another thought-provoking dream.

I was in our first floor apartment, in Emin Djami. The inside doorbell rang. I opened the wooden door and saw Jesus in front of me! In the height of his youth! His long wavy brown hair with auburn highlights brushed his shoulders. He wore modern clothes, black trousers and a dark blue coat.

"My Christ!" I whispered, and fell on my knees. He stopped me. "I came to tell you that you are going to get married and go far away. And to reassure you that I will always be with you and your parents."

7. The dream came true fifteen years later.

I did get married to Tito, my soul mate since grade one, and we did migrate to Canada. The fact that I was foretold about it fifteen years earlier excludes any "subjection" or "telepathy". Once more, it was the divine will. As to why it had to be revealed to me so early, it was simply an answer to my question whether I should not have been called to become a nun. This was something I was asking myself secretly, probably influenced by my religious dreams and the admiration I bore for the bee-like life of the nuns of the Catholic School I was attending then.

However, I had never discussed it openly with anyone, not even with my mother. Jesus' words were the divine answer to my secret query at that stage of my life.

This was the second time that Jesus had appeared to me in a dream. And this time in an appropriate image for the teenager I was. But would I have recognized Him as being Jesus had I not experienced whatever preceded this event? Would anyone have recognized this "rock-and-roll" stereotypical youth as being, in fact, Christ? And therefore weren't all my experiences forming the links of a chain that was pulling my life by an invisible hand?

Yet, the main thing that I sensed then, and realized later, was, indeed, that Jesus Christ never left the side of my parents and of all of us.

As He promised, He is "staying with us, till the end of time..."

"I never had a clue that you wanted to become a nun!" says Stavros.

"Your Mama was right then, in her fear to enroll you in a nuns' school. The daughter of one of her friends had become a Carmelite nun, and your Mama was afraid that the nuns would proselytize you also. I had to fight with her to let you go to Sainte Pulchérie. I was sure you had a strong character and strong beliefs and would not let yourself be manipulated."

"It had nothing to do with proselytizing, Father. It was mainly my dreams and past experiences with the divine that influenced me. And seeing that the nuns had dedicated themselves to Jesus and to prayer, while leading a useful life in the community, I just wondered if there was a calling for me too, a calling that I did not recognize. That dream was an answer to my question.

"The only thing the nuns – actually Soeur Marthe, the nun closer to me – did, was to include me in the church choir for special performances and teach me how to draw and paint. Soeur Marthe taught me how to use black and red ink, charcoal, chalk highlights and pastels. She would let me sit in the last row of benches in class, provide me with all the art material I needed, excuse me from lectures, and let me draw. I was making greeting cards to be sold at our school *kermesses* to raise funds for the poor. I even reproduced, in charcoal and white chalk, a blonde Madonna by Boticelli that a visiting expert from Italy took for an original treasure!

"The other thing Soeur Marthe did was offer me free piano lessons that Mama asked me to refuse because it would make me come home almost at nightfall. Unless she was afraid that they would make a nun of me, as you say. I often asked myself why she was so over-protective of me."

"You were our only child. She adored you. And you were in poor health. You were very thin and sick most of the time. So, if she could not be around you to protect you, she feared something bad could happen to you," explains Stavros in a dreamy voice.

Come on! You were over-protective too, Father.

You wouldn't let me go to the movies with Tito for the first time, without you accompanying us! I was over twenty-one! To protect my "good name" apparently. 'Except if you are officially engaged!' you had said.

"Soeur Marthe also enrolled me in the Daughters of Mary organization," I continue, not mentioning his own behaviour.

"This was a Christian group like the Girl Scouts for a few chosen students. We were dedicated to helping the poor, sewing layettes for the babies of the orphanage. We helped at "open house" events, preparing a bazaar for the poor children with games and toys and organizing a St. Nicholas feast with sweets and crafts for them.

"The child who found the 'bean' in the special cake would be crowned King or Queen for the day. We would also make and sell cards and crafts to raise money for the school's charities. Nothing bad. Except for the Oath of Allegiance we, the Daughters of Mary, had to make at the end of the year. The printed oath was distributed to all of us at the last minute. It stated that each of us was to pledge allegiance to the Virgin Mary, to the Pope and to the Catholic Bishop. We were to sign a 'will' stating that we wished to be buried, when we died, according to the Catholic rites!"

"God! What did you do? Did you sign it?"

"No," I laugh. "You know me better than that. But I was angry. I felt cheated. First, I saw it as a trap by the Sisters to convert us to Catholicism. Then I tried to excuse them, telling myself that this was a typical pre-written oath given to everybody attending. It couldn't mean that the non-Catholics would have to abide by it or sign it. But I wanted to see what other non-Catholic girls would do. So I went to the ceremony, expecting to be treated as a guest without being called for the oath. However, I saw that some non-Catholic girls took the oath, maybe thinking it would be of no importance. When my name was called, I was surprised. I rose, walked to the centre of the room, faced the audience, and read from the printed oath I held in my hand but changing the words. I stated that I pledged allegiance to the Virgin Mary, to the Greek Orthodox Patriarch and the Orthodox Bishop, and that I pledged to be buried, when I died, according to the Greek Orthodox rites..."

"Hey, Hey!" laughs Stavros. "Why didn't you ever tell me about it?"

"Because you would have withdrawn me from the school. Wouldn't you?"

"Probably. Or I would denounce the Sisters to the authorities as proselytizing and mind-controlling. Did your Mama know about this?"

"I didn't tell her either, for the same reason."

"What happened when you read your own text?"

"The audience gasped. Mother Levine almost fainted. The Bishop moved uneasily in his chair. Then Soeur Marthe rushed to my side, grabbed my hand and took me out of the room, without a word. After that incident I was banished from attending any further gatherings of the Daughters of Mary – supposedly finished for the season – or singing in the church choir. Always very politely, without any blame and without any questions or explanations."

"Hmmm... And I had to fight with Katina Stamatiadou, your final year Greek teacher at Tarsis Varidou, for sending you to a foreign high school instead of a Greek one. Particularly in Athens! Remember? Stamatiadou told me you had a rare writing talent and that I would be committing murder if I didn't help you nurture it."

"I remember. She was herself from Arsakion – Athens – and wanted me to go there. She claimed I could even study there for free.

"You see, in the beginning, my teachers at Tarsis Varidou, thought that you were helping me with my compositions. But after reading what I wrote during class exams, they were convinced that I was talented."

"Yes, and they fought our decision to send you to a foreign school. I guess Katina Stamatiadou acted as your school's spokesperson. She called me a 'murderer'! I explained to her that writers, especially Greek writers, could not survive in these post-war times. That we were poor and that the best thing for you would be to become versatile, learn many languages and be in commerce, earning enough money to be independent. This, I explained, could not be achieved with further studies in Greek only. I told her that if you were really as talented as they claimed, the French language would open doors for you to French and to world literature. Thus, foreign languages would, on the contrary, be valuable and rich assets for you. And I reassured her, that once you mastered French and English as well, you could, later, write in any language you chose."

"And you were right, Father. French and English really opened doors for me. And after you made sure I had access to good Greek literature, my mother tongue is still the best one I use."

He laughs, content.

We continue on my manuscript.

WITH LOVE AS GUIDE (Continued)

8. *At age 15 or so, I had a strange dream.*

It was springtime. I was on top of a steep mountain covered with pine trees. Suddenly I slipped on the pine needles and started to fall, rolling down towards a precipice. At the edge of the precipice I saw a young man. He was blond, and wore a shirt with horizontal red and yellow stripes, and white shorts. He was kneeling down on the ground, his arms open, and he managed to stop my fall when I hit his chest with a thump! His name flashed telepathically in my mind: George.

I explained the dream to my mother. She thought it might be related to Saint George, as my protector against a future sickness. She advised me to go and light a candle to him at the Church of St. George, on top of the pine covered hill on the Island of Prinkipo, in Istanbul. I did so, and then I forgot about the dream.

Six months later, Mama decided to take a trip with me to Athens, to visit her sister Irini. It was August now.

That Saturday my cousins Stamo and Dimitri asked me to join them in an excursion to Mount Pendeli. On the morning of the excursion, their best friend joined us. When I saw him, I had a shock. He was the youth of my "falling" dream! He was wearing that same yellow-and-red striped shirt and white shorts. I knew what my cousin would say next: "This is George!"

As I stood there, frozen, a shiver ran down my spine at hearing his name. My cousin Dimitri looked at me and asked me, worried:

"Are you all right, Erato? What's wrong?"

I thought in a flash that if I told them about my dream of six months ago, they would think I was crazy. So I lied.

"Oh, nothing. I felt dizzy for a moment, that's all. I'm OK now."

For an instant, I hesitated about joining them in their excursion. Then, remembering that I did not perish in my dream, I followed them.

When we reached the steep piny slopes of Mount Pendeli, I recognized the scenery – the stony ground covered with pine needles. I became very vigilant and watched my every step. At one point, as I was climbing I turned my head and saw a precipice at my back. My eldest cousin Dimitri had remained behind. The next moment, my flat leather shoes lost their grip on the slippery ground and I started to fall, tumbling down towards the precipice! My cousins panicked. Dimitri ran to the bottom of the precipice and shouted: "I will catch you, Erato! Here! Try to fall here!"

Re-living my dream in a flash, I located George. He was kneeling down, at the edge of the precipice, his arms open, ready to stop my fall. Subconsciously I directed my fall towards him ... Seconds later I landed on his chest with his strong arms closing around me! The incident ended with deep sighs and nervous laughs. I kept silent about my dream.

However, had I not had that warning dream and had known its outcome, would I have been able to keep my cool and direct my fall towards this stranger and not towards one of my cousins? Or simply let myself fall down the precipice?

The sceptics can argue, of course, that in my subconscious I wanted to re-live my dream and that I staged my fall. Yet, I choose to believe that this incident, for an unknown reason, was to happen anyway, that it was part of my evolution and that George was placed there to help me.

The most important lesson of this event? It forced me to trust my dreams as means to help me understand and face, without fear, the difficult moments I would encounter in the path of my life.

"Again, I don't see how this incident relates to the existence of God," remarks Stavros, rather sternly.

"It's another link in the chain of my life pulled by an invisible, protective hand. It's the promise of Jesus, that He will always be with me," I answer. "The dream and its materialization teach me to trust my future, to trust in God and have faith."

Stavros shakes his head, unconvinced, but doesn't tell me to cross it out. We continue.

9. *At 16, an inexplicable event happens. It is an event that will prepare me for my next "test" and will banish the fear of death from me.*

   It is Holy Friday night, at the Church of Sts. Constantine and Helen, in Istanbul. During this night, the service is very long. It lasts approximately three hours. All twelve gospels are read and the symbolic body of Christ, painted and embroided on red velvet, rests on a portable altar under a four-post canopy adorned with flowers. It represents the Holy Sepulchre: the "Epitaphios". It is taken in a candle-lit procession to the streets or to the church's courtyard. After the stations of the Passion, the Epitaphios is taken back to the church where the Mass continues.

   When the procession returns, I am standing with my father next to the flower covered Epitaphios. I am just beside the high candle stand. The atmosphere is heavy with scents of flowers, rose water, candles and incense.

   Suddenly, I don't feel well. The week-long fasting and the long standing during the liturgy may have affected me (we had no church benches then, just 'stassidia' or standing high-chairs belonging to some paying parishioners). At once, I sense my legs growing weak and I black out.

   *The next thing I know, I see my body fall on the floor with a crash, while I am floating "without a body", light as a feather, above, on the ceiling of the church! I look down as my father and a stranger lift up my "body". My father shouts: "*Anixté*! Open up! Let us pass!" I see them transport my body to the narthex. Without realizing how, I pass through the wall of the solea as if it were made of air, and I find myself on the ceiling of the narthex. Then, I follow them, in the same way, passing through solid walls, as the group goes outside. I keep asking myself why all the fuss, since I am so well and feeling like a little bird up here ...*

   We pass the outside court. I continue to follow them – always "above my body" and passing through walls – to the separate administration building. From the ceiling, I look down at them, as they spill water on my face. I hear my father call me with anxiety:

"Erato! Wake up! My child! Erato!" He slaps my face, hard. Another slap ...

There is a flash of light. A beautiful white light. A shape of light... Someone orders me telepathically to go back. Then I black out again, feel a jerk, a sensation of emerging from water, and I wake up inside my body!

This is an out-of-body experience that is also mentioned in several parts of the Old Testament, in the Gospels, and in the letters of the Apostle Paul, as well as in the Apocalypse of John. It will help me realize that whatever events we read in the Bible and other religious books are in fact real, lived, experiences. But most importantly, it will make me identify death with this liberating feeling of floating and of peacefulness.

I am ready now for my next trial.

"I vividly remember you fainting. It scared me, because it took you too long to wake up. But you never told me about this special experience," protests Stavros. "You were really hiding things from us when you were young, weren't you?"

"I didn't hide it, Father. I just didn't know then. I thought that when anyone faints, they live through the same thing. It was much later that I made the connection with an out-of-body experience. But by then, there was no need to talk about it anymore."

Stavros takes another sip from his Spider. He keeps it in his mouth before swallowing it. Licks his lips. Closes his eyes and seems to meditate.

I don't move. I don't utter a word. A full minute or two pass. Finally Stavros re-opens his eyes. "Let's see your next trial," he says.

10. It was July of the same year.

Two weeks after our own year-end exams, the extra government school exams had just finished. I felt tired and very weak. I experienced blackouts, fainting spells, anorexia, irregular heart beat, perspiring shivers, chest pain, difficulty breathing and a feeling of drowning at night.

My regular doctor, Lazaridis, could not find the cause of these symptoms.

So my parents took me to a recommended chest specialist. After examining me, and without relying on any tests, the doctor, exclaimed to my mother, as if I was not present: "It's lightning tuberculosis. Your daughter has only about ten days to live!" And he added, "We will try a new medicine, Streptomycin, intravenously, and hope for the best. In ten days your daughter will either be cured or die! There is nothing else we can do," he concluded without a single glance to me.

My parents went to pieces! My mother was trying not to succumb to a nervous breakdown and my father rushed to search for the difficult to get (then) Streptomycin. Yet, I remained surprisingly calm and said to Mama: "With the little that I learned at school in biology, I am sure that I don't have severe tuberculosis. So, don't be alarmed."

That night I dreamed that I was in the church of Panaghia, the Presentation of the Holy Virgin, at Péra. I was standing by the right aisle, in front of the life-size icon of the Virgin Mary. Suddenly, she became flesh! She came out of the frame, stood in front of me, still clad in her blue mantle, put her hand on my head and said to me:

"Don't be afraid. Have faith in me! Don't take the medicine given to you by that doctor. I will heal you!"

I woke up and decided not to take that medicine. I told my father that I was refusing to have the injections, despite the odds, and that I wanted a second opinion about my illness. My mother, not knowing any specialists, took me to her gynaecologist to ask for his advice. He referred me to his son Alex, who had just returned from his internship in Paris.

Alex Sakellaridis put me through a mirror-X-ray machine and took some blood and saliva samples. He diagnosed a general weakness, possibly due to the burnout of my final exams, and adenopathy, or inflammation of the lymph glands. My white blood cells or leucocytes were abnormally high compared to my red cells.

"In short, your white cells are eating up your red cells. We will have to stop that. Trust me, follow what I prescribe, and I will cure you," he told me. And he explained that under these circumstances, intravenous Streptomycin injections could have been fatal ... In other words, our Holy Mother did indeed save me with Her warning. She saved me thanks to my faith and trust in Her, using Alex as her instrument.

Alex was also a heart specialist and he diagnosed a heart ailment: a genetic malformation of the aorta plus a chronic cardiac inflammation and a heart murmur caused by a childhood rheumatic fever that had induced some of the symptoms I was experiencing. He managed to control them with medicine. He warned me, however, that after the age of forty, the symptoms could return with strong pain. "Keep it in mind and seek appropriate treatment then" he said. He was right, as we shall see.

Yet, other than being refused life insurance, my ailments did not bother me for a long time.

Alex ordered a special rich diet of vegetable soups, steaks, grilled liver, purées, poached fruit compotes, yogurt and eggs, plus thalassotherapy and controlled sun-bathing.

And he prescribed mega-doses of vitamin C and intravenous calcium serums, plus a wine-syrup made of horse blood.

He also ordered complete rest for four months on the pine-covered Island of Prinkipo. My parents took his advice and rented a villa near the sea on the island – very costly, then. In other words, a regimen to boost my immune system and help produce red blood cells. It took Alex over a year to cure me completely.

As I recall my past life I see that what saved me then from panic and from giving in to despair was that whole chain of past dreams and events. They had prepared me not to fear death, to trust in my dreams as beneficial forewarnings, to have great faith in God, in Jesus and in His Holy Mother, and to know that whatever I had to experience would be, in the long run, for my own good.

"This was a most trying period, not only for you, but for your Mama and me," utters Stavros. "We were really afraid we were going to lose you … That scoundrel lung specialist! ... I was ready to denounce him as incompetent, but he was recommended by my friend Neshet Akol… So, I explained what happened to Neshet and I left the matter in his hands. I believe he made sure the doctor lost his licence. But you were surprisingly calm and courageous through the whole ordeal. You had explained to me your dream with the Virgin Mary to convince me to forget the medicine and seek another doctor. Impressive. Pity you lost your bursary at Robert College," remarks Stavros.

"Losing the bursary was, indeed, the hardest part for me," I agree. "I still see Dr. Alex telling me, 'It's your life or your studies! You can always continue your studies later, once you are completely cured.' But when I was finally cured, after the long months spent at home studying shorthand, commercial correspondence and drawing, I did not want to return to school. I wanted to get out and work and earn some money. That's what I did. And I had the opportunity to complete my studies, later, here, in Canada. No regrets," I say with a smile.

Stavros nods. "That Parisian teacher of yours, Alfred De Mülder, and his wife, were nice people. Their private school courses – by correspondence - were unheard of in Turkey. They helped you get a very good secretarial job with Carmello Allegra, in spite of your youth and your inexperience."

"Yes, I was lucky with that first job. Signor Allegra was an excellent boss. Very trusting. Very kind. He taught me invaluable life lessons, like not to attach any importance to money, when I had my purse with my first salary stolen, and to have faith. As for the Mülders, they were exceptional people. They visited us in Istanbul and after that, they called me their adopted niece. When we moved to Canada they loaned us the money to make the down payment on our house in Brossard. Without any interest! 'You do the same thing some day for someone else' they said as a sole explanation."

"I always said people are born nice," confirms Father with a gleam in his eye.

I am so happy to see him relaxed and in good spirits!

"Are you tired? Do you want us to stop?"

"We can go on a bit more," he says.

11. The years passed with prophesied-or-not events. I got engaged to Tito, my future husband when I was in my early twenties.

The wife of the newlywed partner of my second cousin Cass was diagnosed with an abdominal tumour. After the operation, the surgeons explained to her husband that the tumour was malignant and that it had spread to all her organs. So, they closed the abdomen without touching anything. They would give her one or at most two months to live. After consultation with the husband, the surgeons told the young woman that they had removed the tumour, which was benign, and that if she had no other complications she could leave the hospital in a week.

The young husband was desperate. Although sobbing when out of his wife's sight, he was clowning and laughing in front of her. He even sold his share in his partnership with my cousin, and bought two cruise tickets to take his wife on a last wonderful trip when she would be discharged from the hospital. "To celebrate your escape from this brushing with death," he told her.

My mother-in-law, Amélie, was deeply moved like all of us by their drama. The second day after the operation, she visited the young woman. She gave her a piece of cotton embedded with the tears of the Holy Virgin, offered to her by a priest who had just returned from Italy and who had taken it from a miraculous weeping Madonna statuette. "You need it more than me. May it heal you completely," said Amélie to the young patient, who took the piece of cotton piously in her hands, kissed it, put it inside her nightgown, on her chest, and exclaimed: "I feel that I will be healed completely, indeed, and will fear nothing from now on."

Well, the young woman did take the cruise with her husband.

They returned... Years have passed since... And as far as I know the couple is living happily ever after...

"Faith", taught Christ, "is the biggest force in the world".

Faith, with the will of God and the intercession of the Virgin Mary – and Amélie used as a link – saved the life of the young woman.

This event was a proof to me that Jesus spoke the absolute truth about the force of faith. Faith could achieve miracles. Whatever else I experienced before faded at the force of this miracle.

My own faith strengthened even more after this healing. In the years to come, it would help me, and those close to me, in a more specific way.

12. A few months later:

Frossoula, the daughter of my aunt Marika, was diagnosed with a serious heart ailment. She had always had blackouts and congenital heart problems. But now her condition worsened. My widowed and very poor Aunt was consumed with despair. We all hoped for a miracle. Based on all the past happenings, every night I prayed with faith to the Virgin Mary for help.

Suddenly a wealthy lady appeared, Mrs. Anagnostopoulou, who decided to help my sick cousin. She took Frossoula to Athens and arranged to have her operated at the Hospital of Evanghelismos by the best heart-surgeon in Greece. May God bless this lady! The doctor performed the open-heart operation free of charge. He removed the unhealthy mitral-valve and replaced it with a plastic one! Revolutionary surgery, for that time.

My cousin stayed a whole month in the hospital, with free treatment. Honours should go to the hospital and its surgeon. In the meantime, this angelic lady took care of Frossoula as if she were her own mother. At the end of the month, she brought her home to Istanbul by plane. Mrs. Anagnostopoulou was doing then, on a smaller scale, what Naomi Bernstein did in Canada for ill foreign children.

Frossoula lived another fifteen years and enjoyed life fully. She got married. Was happy. She died two years after her marriage, at the height of her existence, leaving us the memory of a joyous, shining, young woman.

This event fortified my belief in the goodness of men and women on Earth, and came as one more proof that sincere prayers are answered even if in unexpected ways.

"Frossoula's operation was almost a medical miracle for those days," says Stavros. "But it couldn't be done without the goodwill of people like Mrs. A., the heart surgeon and the hospital. My hat's off to them," he adds, imitating a bow with a hand holding a hat.

I laugh. He grins.

I dearly loved that sweet, beautiful cousin of mine. Her warm smiling brown eyes, contrasting with her honey hair, were always sparkling. I was teaching her French and English. She was bright and very studious. A fast learner.

I loved all my cousins. Mihali, Strato, George… They were my only and best companions during my youth. They are all in Greece now, happily married, with families. Life is good.

Stavros touches my nose with some loose sheets of my manuscript… We both laugh. Back to the present, we resume our reading.

13. *Many clairvoyant dreams followed sporadically, materializing in my every day life.*

Some included accidents, like plane or train crashes, or tragedies. Those scared me. I could do nothing to stop them from happening. So, in spite of the comfort and the benefit I had drawn in the past from my dreams, I was starting to become more and more anxious about them.

My biggest fright came when I dreamed about the Universe and saw our luminous Earth burst into three flaming parts that fell into the darkness... I lived in terror for days fearing the end of the World!

The dream materialized at the time of the dissolution of Philco, the company where I was working. The three partners, Nikos and Stelios Katanos and Nathan Eskenazi, separated suddenly, overnight, over a heated argument. I realized then that the "logos" *or trademark of Philco was a golden globe representing the Earth in the Universe. The symbolism of my precognitive dream was thus explained.*

I did not know yet, however, that only dreams of valuable importance to me or to my family were projected to me during my sleep. I did not know that their sole purpose was to warn me beforehand of what was to come. To warn me about what I would have to live through without being able to change it. And that all was a plan for growth, my own or that of the people linked to me. I did not realize then that I should, therefore, trust my dreams as precious God-sent tools. And alas, I gave in to fear. Fear of my not being able to control them, to interpret them correctly, or to stop what was to happen.

Thus, not being able to cope with this "gift", I prayed with all my heart and tried to brainwash myself, with all my will-power, to get rid of it. And I succeeded in forgetting my dreams completely for about five or six years.

"You never mentioned that dream to me! Nikos and Stelios were good friends of mine," says Stavros. "Soon after the partnership dissolved, the brothers closed the company and left for Greece, one after the other. And you went to work for TAE, the National Greek Airline."

"Good memory, Father!" I exclaim.

"However, I don't think this event should be mentioned here for Nicholas' sake," he adds.

"It shows my ups and downs, Father. And the doubts about myself and my rebellion towards a divine gift that scared me. It has its place here. It will show how my faith in my dreams will return in a few years. It is a chain of events culminating in faith and in Divine Guidance," I defend myself.

"You find an answer to everything..." says Stavros with a sigh.

14. *Almost a year after my marriage, and about the second week of July, I have, again, a marvellous dream. This time, I remember it.*

In front of me lies a road covered with sparkling diamonds leading to the peak of a mountain. On the summit, I see an extremely sweet being, with short curly brown hair, wearing a white robe. The being waves to me smiling. I hear one word "Gabriel!"

Since I was born on the Eve of the Annunciation, I interpret the dream as a revelation from my guardian angel Gabriel who is probably showing me the future path of my life. Moreover, my husband's father's name is Gabriel as well. So I decide to name our first child, if it happens to be a boy, "Gabriel".

I am so overwhelmed by the beauty of this dream that I don't even ask myself how and why it broke my 'tower of oblivion' and how I ended up remembering every single detail in it.

The following spring, on April 18th, our first child is born, a beautiful girl with curly brown hair. Following our custom for the first born, we want to name her Amalia – for Amélie – the name of Tito's mother. But my mother-in-law refuses vehemently. She claims that she hates her own name! And that for nothing in the world will she inflict it upon her grand daughter!

We finally choose for our baby the name Gabriella, in fact the name of my father-in-law Gabriel...

However, I still do not relate the name to the dream that I had had a few months ago. After we come to Canada, and manage to become successful, I explain the "diamond path" of that dream as a prophecy to me by my guardian angel Gabriel about this future achievement.

It was not until 1985, 22 years later, that I finally understood what that marvellous dream was all about. It simply announced in advance the birth of our daughter Gabriella! And only then did I realize that the 13th of July, the date of my dream, was about nine months before she was born and our Church was celebrating the Feast of the Assembly of Archangel Gabriel. So the event was probably announced to me on the day of her conception. And no matter what our wishes, the child would be named Gabriella anyway!

Aren't the directions of our lives pre-ordained and guided by a highest Divine Power? Despite the fact that the dream reinforced my belief in our chosen "destiny" and in "divine guidance", it also reinstated my trust in the revelations sent to me in the form of dreams, by God's will. Moreover, I know that the dream has a special meaning or purpose for our daughter Gabriella. She will interpret it correctly herself, some day, with some help from Above.

"Very impressive," comments Stavros. "It seems to be beyond a simple coincidence. I never knew about it," he adds with an accusing glance to me.

I open my hands in incapacity. "Let's stop for today," I say, and I lean to kiss his forehead. He nods and pats my shoulder...

X- Stirring Memories

It is a glorious sunny, cold, end-of-January day. There was freezing rain last night, and this Saturday morning the garden is a glowing fantasy with the bare branches of the trees glistening under the sun like diamonds

I am content as I prepare a rare Turkish concoction for my father and myself: *Sahlep*. I found a ready-mix sample in Brossard, at Vlado's, our Bulgarian grocer at nearby *Marché du Village*. It brings back warm memories of street vendors carrying a samovar on their backs, strolling the Istanbul streets in the early winter mornings, clinking their thick glasses and shouting "*Sahleptchi, sıdjcak sahlep*" to announce themselves and their hot concoction. We would open our windows in a hurry, call to them and rush to have our own glasses filled with the piping-hot soothing drink made with cornstarch, milk, honey and poppy-seed powder, and sprinkled with ground almonds, pistachios and cinnamon. It was creamy-thick and delicious. It will be good for Father's throat and cough, I think, as I rush down with two large glasses of homemade Sahlep.

"Look what I brought you!" I exclaim with enthusiasm as I enter the TV room. "Sahlep! Real Sahlep! One for you, one for me!"

But Father is gloomy, doesn't even glimpse at my hands. "What's wrong?" I ask, worried.

"Here," he says, sternly, tending me a hand written page. "I didn't sleep all night. I am tired of talking. Read it."

It is a letter of complaint about the doctors' inadequacies, the medicines that aren't working, how instead of getting better he has difficulty breathing, about being uncomfortable sleeping in the reclining chair, about changing doctors, and so on.

I try to stop the tears in my eyes.

"I will call your doctor, see what he can do. In the meantime, I will fix these thick pillows on the high-back sofa. Maybe you will sleep better here. If we remove the pillows, it becomes as large as a single bed; plus it has the high back for support. Will you try it? Or, since it is a sofa-bed, I can open it out for you into a bed, if you prefer," I offer.

He walks to the sofa, tries the pillows, agrees to lie there, half-sitting, unhappy, with a pout on his lips.

"Will you try the Sahlep? It is really good and it will soothe your throat..." I offer.

He nods, and accepts the glass. Takes a sip, nods his head in agreement, but still bites his lips in defiance.

"What's wrong, Erato?" asks my husband when I return to the kitchen. I show him the letter. He hugs me, his hand caresses my hair. "Call Noella, see if she can offer any advice to help him feel better," he admonishes. Then he goes to see Father and tries to reassure him, writing in his pad.

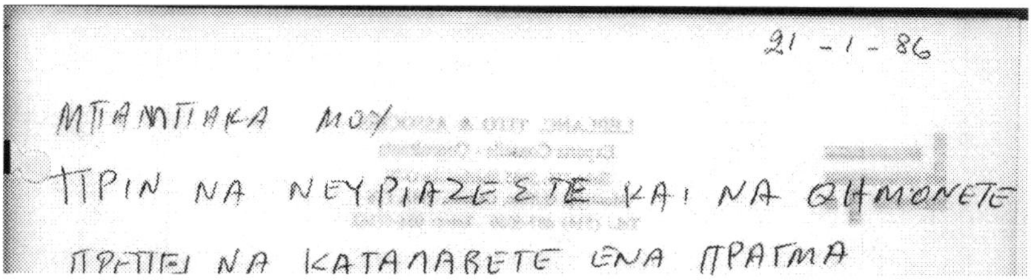

21 - 1 - 86

ΜΠΑΜΠΑΚΑ ΜΟΥ

ΠΡΙΝ ΝΑ ΝΕΥΡΙΑΖΕΣΤΕ ΚΑΙ ΝΑ ΘΥΜΟΝΕΤΕ

ΠΡΕΠΕΙ ΝΑ ΚΑΤΑΛΑΒΕΤΕ ΕΝΑ ΠΡΑΓΜΑ

"Babaka mou – My little (dear) Father," he writes. He tells him how much we love him and explains the side effects of all drugs. They affect not only him, but Tito also. And how, both Tito and Father being heavy smokers, the smoke has caused damage to their lungs. He explains how the doctors try to help him and that Father should at least try the medicines they prescribe before rejecting them.

"We are all trying to help you. Please try to understand that and help us do whatever we can to make you feel well. We love you," he signs, and assures him that we will talk to the doctors to see what can be done.

Thank you, Tito mou!

Noella comes that same afternoon, even though it is Saturday. God bless her. She brings some lung-dilating over-the-counter *dragées* and a spray for Father. Stavros refuses the spray, but keeps the pills and drops one into his mouth.

Noella assures him the doctor will come to see him on Monday. She approves of the bed-sofa and in the meantime she recommends a urinal, so that Father won't have to walk to the bathroom. Stavros calms down a bit.

Later, Father doesn't feel like eating our meal but asks for his preferred *Papara* instead, the bread pieces in hot milk, with lots of sugar, that I fortify with *Ensure*.

As he eats, I point out to him the beauty of the garden. He shakes his head "What's the use…"

"Well, the winter and the freeze offer some beauty too, Father…"

He shrugs his shoulders.

I let him have a nap.

He seems calm and refreshed when he wakes up.

"I had a strange dream, Erato. I saw a beautiful young woman, with long wavy black hair, leaning over me. Her long pale dress left her arms bare. She stretched her arms towards me and asked me 'Stavré, kiss me! Come to me! I am longing for you, my love! I love you!'… What a strange dream! Who could she be?"

"Katina?" I ask, with a shiver… *Is his time up?*

"No, your Mama did not have long hair…"

"She had long wavy hair as a teenager. We have some photographs of her. And she probably is worried about you and trying to help you…" I say, trying to sound reassuring.

Father shakes his head, dumbfounded. He stares at the garden, glowing orange with grey-violet hues under the low sun. He keeps silent for a few moments. Then he asks for a fresh glass of hot Sahlep.

At least he has a positive reaction! That calms me…

"Where is your manuscript?" he asks after having a sip from the Sahlep.

I bring the manuscript over to him, and together we go over the transcription of my past experiences.

WITH LOVE AS GUIDE (Continued)

15. The next three events precede our migration to Canada.
Here I should explain why we decided to migrate. After the military coup in Turkey (1960-61), the Turkish political leaders were taken prisoners by the military.

They were held on the island of Yassi (Flat-Island) in Istanbul. During these trials, human rights were violated and anything but 'justice' was granted to the Turkish politicians and prisoners. The political leaders were executed at the end by hanging, except for the elderly President of the Republic, Celâl Bayar.

Ali Ipar, the director of Ipar Transport, the shipping company I was working for at the time, was also on trial in Yassı Ada, for so called "treason" – outrageously unjustifiable! I was there... I was following the proceedings as an executive secretary and witness for the company. But I was not called to testify, neither the company excecutives... Ali Ipar lost his right eye there to 'questioning' sessions aimed at getting a 'false' admission of guilt from him. He was, however, spared his life and sentenced to prison for life; he was 'pardoned' after some time, a year or years I don't remember, by the succeeding new regime. The injustices shattered the lives of the accused and their families sometimes even leading to suicides.

In the meantime, the Cyprus problem arose. That made life difficult for the Greeks of Turkey. Life in general, then, took a downhill turn and many Turkish intellectuals began to leave the country. Under these circumstances what was to be the fate of the non-muslim minorities in Turkey? We thought things over and decided, for the sake and the future of our Gabriella, to leave Turkey for Canada. My parents were to accompany us.

The Sunday before leaving, Mama asked us to pay a visit, all together, to the very old Byzantine church of Vlahernae. This startled me because Mama, though a fervent believer, avoided entering a church, overwhelmed as she was by her own feelings of guilt for what she considered wrongdoings in her life (as I would discover later).

So, every time she did enter a church she suffered. She suffered excruciating moral pain, yet, as I look back, I realize she silenced her torment and did go to church for me, for my 'well-being'.

According to an old belief, when you enter a church for the first time, if you make three wishes and keep completely silent, your wishes will be granted. So, when I entered this church that I had never visited before, although I had lived nearby for over a quarter of a century, I made the vow of silence.

After the service, Mama asked the priest to read a health and success prayer for us, in intercession to the Virgin Mary, in front of Her centuries' old Byzantine icon. This icon was, according to legend, the very same one that the Byzantine emperors used to elevate in procession around the city's ramparts, asking Her to protect Constantinople, the capital dedicated to Her, from its assailing enemies.

As I looked at the very old icon, I saw it had a split in the middle of the face, towards the right. Could that be a wound from a blow she could have received from the mob during the 1955 September upheaval in Istanbul, when they attacked the Greek churches? Or had the split occurred before?

At the end of the prayer, as my family was leaving, I bent to kiss the icon.

Suddenly I saw a tear, clear as a crystal bead, roll down the cheek of the Virgin Mary. I stood there, frozen, speechless, wondering if this was a trick of my imagination. I did not dare touch it. It would be a sacrilege... I made the sign of the cross and walked out.

At the outside narthex there was a small replica of the same icon, on a portable high icon stand. As I bent to kiss it, I saw again a tear roll down the cheek of the Virgin! And then another one roll in the same groove! ... I was not dreaming! This was not my imagination, then! It was real! ... I made the sign of the cross and walked backwards out of the door, dumbfounded!

Outside, in the courtyard, my husband asked me what had taken me so long. Breaking my vow of silence, I explained what I had seen. He shrugged his shoulders as if saying "It's your imagination!" But Mama signed herself whispering "Hail to you, my Holy Virgin!" making no other comment. I asked her if we should return to the church and bring the event to the attention of the priest. She shook her head

"No need, my child! She will shed a tear for him too, if necessary..."

I am still questioning whether I did the right thing in not reporting the 'event' to the priest. Unless if he also 'knew' and did not reveal it, according to a non-understandable to me 'divine wish' as Katina was so sure about.

But why the "tears"? After so many years, I still wonder, trying to find an explanation.

The fact is that Istanbul remains almost empty now of its original Greek founders. Following the political upheavals of 1955, and the political uneasiness of the 1960s, after we left, the Greeks migrated in large numbers out of the city of Constantine. Was then the Virgin crying over the fate waiting Her worshippers? Or over the fate of humanity in general? Were the "tears" meant to stir me or whoever witnessed them, to make us conscious of the state of Man and try to do something about it? I don't know... I felt like a helpless ant in the path of the giant moving feet of selfish, powerful, cynical political machines that were, and still are, ruling the world, instead of the godlike humans we should have been by now...

"I don't remember paying attention to this event," exclaims Father. "Maybe I dismissed it as a figment of your imagination, like Tito," he adds, pensive.

We continue...

16. A few days before we leave Istanbul, I have an impressive dream:

I am in the hall of an old, two-storey, apartment-house.

At the right, a staircase with an iron balustrade leads to the second floor and surrounds it like a balcony. Upstairs, in the middle, behind the iron balustrade, I see three doors. The central door is wide open and shows a room lit by a single suspended light bulb.

I take the stairs... I enter the room... Around me, bundles of clothes. In the middle, a rope, fastened between two walls; hanging on the rope, clothes, pillowcases, sheets... At one corner, a fat old lady is curled up against a bundle of clothes...

I see soldiers and women around me grasping and taking everything they can lay their hands on from the bundles of clothes and whatever is hanging on the rope.

Suddenly, on the white sheet hanging in the center of the rope, I distinguish an icon imprinted in brown tones. It is the head of <u>Jesus Christ!</u> With the crown of thorns on his forehead! At once, His eyes lock with mine, His lips move, He becomes alive, and He speaks to me without a sound, telepathically:

"Take me! I want You to take Me! <u>You</u>, and nobody else!"

I wake up in turmoil. Based on my past experience with the icon of Virgin Mary with the baby Jesus, I try to find an icon representing Jesus with the crown of thorns, in order to take it with me to Canada. But I can't find such an icon anywhere in Istanbul. Besides, the iconography of the theme is European, Catholic rather, and not Byzantine...

Before leaving Istanbul, I explain my dream to Maman Amélie, my Catholic mother-in-law, asking her to try and find me such an icon from her Catholic nun friends or priests, and send it to me to Canada.

Once in Canada, I also look around for such an icon, but without success. Then, in about two weeks later, I receive an agitated letter from Tito's mother.

As a volunteer with the Petites Soeurs des Pauvres organization, Maman Amélie had to visit an old lady, who was unknown to her, in order to help her move to the sisterhood's hospice. As soon as she entered the door of the two-story building housing the lady, Amélie realized she was in the building of my dream...

Re-living my experience in real life, Maman Amélie climbs the stairs with the iron balustrade and enters the open middle door. The room is lit by a suspended single light bulb... On the floor, bundles of clothes and things that the old lady was giving away since she could not take them with her to the hospice. In the middle of the room, a rope! With some clothes suspended on it...

Maman Amélie approached the old lady who was sitting in a corner. She was small, fat and blind! But she talked as if she knew and could see my mother-in-law:

"I was waiting for you! I have something to give you ... In reality, it's not for you, it's for a young woman who left the country. But I know it will reach her through you." And she put in Maman Amélie's hands a little icon. The same one I had in my dream! The face of Jesus Christ, a crown of thorns on his forehead!

It was a very simple, small image, printed in brown on off-white background, the kind the Catholics distribute to children and parishioners. It was mounted simply over a green veneered glass and was obviously an object of devotion.

And it did reach me indeed, when my mother-in-law brought it to me when she came to visit us in Canada.

I tried to frame it. It does not hold any frame... But it is miraculous and it does answer the desperate prayers I address with faith to Jesus...

This was again another unsolicited divine and forewarning dream. I did not know the house, nor the old blind lady. We might have been related in another life, but have never met in this one. As for the words she spoke, they proved that she was also warned telepathically about me, as I had been about her.

Why me? For what purpose? I still don't know...

It was the third time that Jesus "revealed" himself to me in my dreams, and every time with features relevant in analogy to my age of the moment.

When He appeared to me for the first time, so many years ago, to the child that I was then, He offered me His icon as a Child in the protective arms of His Mother.

During my youth, He appeared to me as a teenage-idol symbol, as a Youthful Counsellor, promising me that He would always be by our side and telling me that I would go far away.

And now, in my mature years, He came also 'physically' by my side, with His icon in the sorrowful image of the Passion face with crown of thorns, as a symbol of the injustice and pain inflicted on Him by men, that He had overcome. He came as 'my' helper for the difficult moments that I would face in the future, as final proof of His Love and His assistance that we often ignore or even 'reject', convinced that we are not worthy of it. Yet, His love is limitless, like the love of a parent for his child.

As the Evangelist John reports His saying:

The one that has my commandments and keeps them,
Is the one who loves me;
And the one who loves me, will be loved by my Father;
And I will also love him,
And I will reveal myself to him.

I accepted this 'miracle' again as a 'divine interference and guidance' into my life and trusted it as such. It was also probably meant to fortify my faith, and through me, the faith of my mother and of my loved ones in the guidance of Jesus and in the blessing of God...

In it both my mother and I found strength, twelve years later...

"Yes," says Stavros, "this is the small icon you have in the iconostase and that you seem to venerate more than the others… I must admit", he adds, "I was never fond of it, because I thought it was given to you by Amélie as a reminder of her Catholic faith. I was even annoyed that you seemed to prefer it to our Byzantine icons. Did you ever tell me the whole story behind it?"

"Sure, Father!"

"I don't remember it. Or perhaps I never grasped the whole thing. Unbelievable! Extraordinary! The world is full of unexplainable mysteries…"

We both sit silent for a while, meditating. Then Stavros gives me a sign to continue.

"This next episode will be painful," I warn him. "Do you prefer to go on tomorrow?"

He gives me a puzzled gaze. Then, "Go on," he says.

17. I was not disturbed by reminiscences of any dream for a straight period of twelve years. Then, eleven years ago, I lost my mother to a massive coronary heart attack.

My Mama was very special. She had a strong character. She had a difficult childhood, taken out of the primary school and put to work, because her family was so poor. She had suffered a lot, indeed. And she devoted her life to giving me everything she had been deprived of. So, even when my father was taken away (under a soldier's uniform) in a special Turkish camp considered doomed, during the 1941 war and after, my mother worked day and night, often till dawn, but managed to offer me adequate food and clothing and the best education in the best private school in the city.

Despite her lack of time and despite our meagre means, she also managed to care about and assist less fortunate people around her. She was deeply religious but she considered herself to be the biggest sinner on Earth because she had had an abortion to stop a pregnancy when my father was taken away. And she judged herself unworthy to even enter a church. She claimed that no priest, no human on this Earth could do anything to lift her burden, and that she would have to face her Creator alone and accept the consequences of her act once in the Other World.

Yet, no matter what she had to face or to suffer, my mother kept an unshakable faith in God, claiming that we should "believe and not investigate". And she taught me to pray only during unbearable crises. Strangely, all her deepest wishes materialized... especially all those concerned with the well-being of her loved ones. I believe now that her Creator forgave her despite herself, and that my religious experiences were probably partly an evidence of His forgiveness and meant to lighten her heavy burden in this earthly life.

To come to the point, when my mother was hit with a devastating heart attack, I prayed for twenty-four hours outside the door of the intensive care unit of the hospital. Mama seemed to recover completely, despite the doctor's "hopeless" diagnosis.

On the tenth day of her stay in the hospital, the cardiologist announced that she was well enough to return home in three or four days. Yet, my mother did not rejoice. She was sad.

When I asked her why, she told me of a strange dream she had that morning. She was lying on her back at the bottom of a very narrow ravine, two high dark walls mounting on either side. Suddenly an avalanche of frozen pieces of earth, stone and snow started to fall on her. It filled the ravine... She could not move nor scream... I shivered. It appeared as a scene of entombment to me, seen with the eyes of the deceased being put into the winter earth! However, having forgotten by now all about my previous premonitory dreams, I denied any inner meaning to it. So I calmed my mother saying that a dream is usually the "reverse" of reality, and that this one should be taken as an omen for a long healthy life ahead. Yet, I left her uneasy, questioning the competence of the cardiologist in releasing her so soon.

Next morning, an icy Canadian winter day, I visited my mother. I was planning to return again in the early afternoon, as I had done the whole past week. But this morning, I decided to miss work completely and stay with her all day.

I fed her some soup. At noon, she asked me to help her go to the bathroom in her room.

Considering that, with her doctor's permission, she had been doing this since yesterday, and that she was carefully moving around with assistance, I helped her go slowly to the bathroom, holding her. Then I half-closed the door waiting by it.

At that time, Dr. Mehmet Kafadar, our family doctor, walked in, beaming with the good news that Mama would soon return home. Suddenly we heard a noise in the bathroom. I opened the door and we saw Mama lying on the floor... Despite the "Stat" revival attempts by the physician and the cardiologist who ran in almost immediately, and the slit in her throat to revive her (by opening the trachea), my mother died of a sudden cardiac arrest caused, I was told, by a clot in her head...

I was a wreck. No matter what the doctors said – "that this type of clot could strike unexpectedly and that it was always fatal, or that it would happen anyway even during her sleep" – I felt responsible for her death.

I was convinced that she must have hit her head and that caused her death. I felt so guilty! If I had asked the help of a nurse to take her to the bathroom, instead of taking her myself, my mother would still be alive! Or at least, it would not have happened "through my hand"... I felt like her murderer! ...

Frantically, I asked for a priest. They could not find one... In my despair and my guilt at having failed even to arrange for the presence of a priest, I remembered my "out-of-body" experience when I fainted years ago, in the church. I realized then that my mother's soul, her spirit, was still there in the room, seeing and hearing me, but incapable of speech. So, I talked aloud to her. I told her to ask her own beloved mother to come to her, to ask the help of her protector the Virgin Mary, to trust in the forgiveness and love of God, to ask Jesus to come to her aid, and finally to follow Him with trust and faith in the little light that would become a dazzling sun in this unknown journey towards her Creator... And I prayed, aloud, to Jesus and to the Virgin Mary to come to my mother's help and I entrusted her to their care...

When I kissed her, Mama's face was still pink and warm and reflected a very deep peace...

"I killed my mother!" I said, minutes later, to my husband, on the phone.

"I am coming," he said simply, guessing my turmoil. He was by my side in no time.

"She gave me life and I gave her death! I am responsible for her fall, that fall that caused her death! ..." I cried on his shoulder.

He hugged me, caressing my hair. He made me take the tranquilizers the doctor had prescribed. I did not know how I could live with this atrocious, unbearable guilt! My husband and our doctor did not know how to relieve my pain, how to get this guilt obsession out of my mind.

Finally, my husband tried to reason with me:

"With all your faith in God, and the proofs of His love He has given you, how can you believe that He would let you cause the death of your own mother? ...

"Don't you accept that it was to happen anyway, and that on the contrary He chose a moment that you were there so that you could help your mother in your own way? You are the one who never doubts God's help and guidance. How can you doubt *now and blame yourself? Are you playing God? He could have saved her* despite *you, if He wanted, couldn't He? If He didn't, it's because her time was up!"*

His words found their way into my heart.

And then, I remembered Mama's dream the day before! ... This was a God-sent dream to prepare us both for her departure! The remission from the first stroke in the intensive care unit was only a delay, an answer to my prayers, to give me time to brace myself for the end. But after the dream, we both knew, deep inside, that she was to die in the next hours. That's why I chose to stay with her that whole day! And had I found a priest, she could have been more tormented than the peace I brought her by my loud talk and prayer... This realization saved my sanity.

For the first time I understood that if we remember a dream that impresses, if it passes through the memory-blocking filter of our mind, then it is because the dream has a special purpose. A purpose to prepare us for the next events in our future. It is 'striking us' because of a divine will to help us. In fact, beside all my faith and my past marvellous experiences, it was my mother's prophetic dream that liberated me from my false guilt and helped me regain my peace of mind. As Jesus said:

> Father, the Ones you gave me, I will take care of,
> So that wherever I am, they will too be with me,
> ... In the world you have pain,
> But be of good cheer, because I overcame the world.
> (Gospel by John).

* * *

When I came home, my father asked me anxiously what had happened, as at "noon sharp", he saw Katina in front of him, headless, waving 'good bye' to him...

"She was right here! In flesh and blood! But headless! ...

I was sitting! Not asleep! What happened?"

I shivered.– It was the 4th of December, the feast of Sainte Barbara, the decapitated sainte for whom I had lit the votive candle years ago when she had whispered "I am thirsty"...

I asked Father to sit down and I told him...

I did not know then that what he experienced was what is called a "crisis-telepathic-apparition", but I attributed it to telepathy, anyway. Naturally I was beside myself, stricken with grief and guilt.

Stavros sighs. "It was eerie to see your Mama in front of me, alive, headless... It was a hard blow for me... Her departure was unexpected since we thought she had recovered. But you only told me that she had asked you to take her to the bathroom where she fell. You didn't tell me anything about your turmoil... Poor child!"

"I didn't want to upset you more. You were stricken. And I was a wreck..."

"And that dream she had... Weird..."

To change his thoughts and not to let him dwell into his own wound, I continue to check my manuscript with him.

18. The deep meaning of the previous Gospel's passage became clearer that afternoon when I told my seven-year old Kathy that her grandma Katina had died. She sobbed for a long time – they adored each other... Then she stopped, dried her wet cheeks with the palms of her little hands and exclaimed:

"We should not cry! She is not dead! She is alive! She lives now!"

I was shocked. She must be in denial, I decided. "Darling, you don't understand. She is really dead. She won't come back from the hospital. She is with God."

"NO! You don't understand! Don't you see? In order to live, to really live, we all have to die first!"

I was flabbergasted. I didn't know how to explain Kathy's words. Where did Kathy get them and how could she understand their meaning? These words were like a 'divine impulse', a healing balm to my aching heart, although I didn't grasp then their full impact. I realized much later that these words were a proof of Kathy's life and mind being still controlled by her own Higher-Self, her Higher-Spirit. That she was still keeping her spiritual intuitions, the ones we are all born with but that we discard later under the bite of rationality. That her soul was open enough to communicate with my mother's spirit who could have whispered these words to her; thanks to a divine intervention to lessen our pain.

"Now, you never told me anything about this!" protests Father vehemently.

"I guess I was too overwhelmed. Besides, at that time, I didn't know what to think of it myself, not understanding its full meaning…" I say.

"What happened after is even more overwhelming. Do you want to go on?"

Father looks pale, drained. But he nods…

19. What followed was a tangible proof that my mother was in fact "still alive" somewhere, in a dimension that I could not sense, and that God is forgiving, loving and taking care of us!

It was the first or second night after my mother had died. I was lying in bed, fully awake, a small night-light on, Kathy sleeping beside me.

Suddenly I am torn by a very sharp pain, like a dagger plunging straight in my heart. It squeezes me like an iron clamp. The pain gets stronger and stronger and spreads through my chest, paralyzing my left arm completely. I lose my breath. I choke.

A heart attack?

Here, I must explain, that during the whole period that my mother was in hospital, I had had constant pain in my heart, accompanied by tachycardia, blackouts and fainting spells. At the beginning I paid no attention to them. I attributed them to my chronic heart ailment caused by an acute attack of rheumatic fever in my childhood.

Ten years ago, the airline I was working for had refused me life insurance, after a thorough check-up and X-rays of my heart. What I was experiencing now, reminded me of the prognosis Dr. Alex Sakellaridis had given me in my late teens – that, past the age of forty, my condition could worsen. Just the week before, at my husband's insistence, I had had an electrocardiogram. It showed an irregular heart beat and I was advised to be hospitalized for observation. I didn't follow this advice. I was positive that my symptoms were induced by my wish to experience my mother's pain.

So now, lying beside my daughter, I try to control my pain with willpower, reasoning that this pain is not real; it is only a psychological identification with my mother's suffering.

But soon, the pain and the iron grip become unbearable… I am sweating in an effort to breathe! This is real! ... Unable to cope alone I finally gasp, "My God, help me control it! For Kathy's and Gaby's sake! ... Mama, help me!"

Suddenly, I see my mother's hand hovering above my chest! Real flesh! A real hand. In my mind I hear her voice say: "Don't be afraid! It will be light like Kathy's hand..."

Before I realize what is happening, I feel my mother's hand pass through my clothes. I sense it pass through my chest! I first "feel" my heart in her large palm, touched gently. Then I "feel" her hand grasping my heart firmly. I experience immediately a robust rhythmic invigorating massage on my heart, applied by the strong squeezing palm! ... My mind stops....

The iron grip loosens little by little... The pain calms, recedes... My arm moves, my hand opens up... My breathing becomes normal, liberated... The pain slowly disappears completely... A warm and soothing feeling of peace comes over me... "Mama!" I whisper. At once, the touching stops and her hand disappears...

Kathy wakes up at the sound of my voice:

"Did you call, Mammy?" she asks me.

"No, darling. It's nothing. Go back to sleep," I reassure her.

Agitated, I stay awake until dawn, trying helplessly to interpret what I had just experienced. It was not a dream! I re-live in my mind what had happened that afternoon when I told Kathy that her Grandma Katina had died... Now, Kathy's words hammer in my mind: "She is not dead; she is alive!" Is it possible that not only my mother's spirit is alive, but that she can physically manifest herself in order to help me, her only child? And could my poorly educated mother give me a life-saving open heart massage? Tired, I push away the thought of any 'divine intervention' and I throw myself into the trap of reason. "It must have been a hallucination or a creation of my subconscious," I tell myself.

In other words, despite all my past 'miraculous' experiences, where events proved to be produced unsolicited and outside of my personal control, my faith bowed to the rational logic and rejected any inexplicable divine interference! I was entangled, confined – believing that I was the sole and powerful creator of the phenomenon!

A few days later, at my husband's and my family doctor's insistence, I have a complete cardiac check-up at the Montreal Heart Institute. After many tests, X-rays, ultrasounds and echo-cardiograms, the head surgeon of the Institute announces that my heart is in perfect condition.

"You have the heart of a twenty-year old athlete", he tells me. "No sign of any chronic ailment, birth defect or anomaly!"

For a moment I am speechless. Then I explain to him how, because of heart trouble depicted in past X-rays, I had not even been eligible for life insurance for the past ten years.

He looks at me in disbelief.

"I don't know what the X-rays showed before. I did not see those X-rays... But now, you have absolutely nothing! Whatever you had is not here anymore! No trace of it!" he says with authority. He adds: "I will give you a report, and no insurance company will deny you a life insurance policy." (I do have a life insurance policy now.)

This confirmation makes me realize that my mother's hand was not a hallucination. It was not a creation of my subconscious. It was something outside of my personal control. It was my mother's doing! With the help of God. Katina is not dead. She is alive!

From that special night on, to date, my heart has not bothered me anymore, in any way. No arrhythmic heartbeats, no pain, no dizziness or blackouts, no drowning sensation, nothing!

Questions start to rise in my mind. Could the whole healing event have been triggered by my mother's deepest wish?

And how could she, Katina, who had such a low esteem of herself, who had believed herself to be a great sinner, and who had no formal education, how could she, alone, find the knowledge and the supernatural energy to materialize her hand and perform a life-saving "open heart" massage on me if she was not allowed and guided to do so by a Higher Divine Power? And if that Divine Power listened to her prayers and helped her fulfill them herself, in a miracle, wasn't that a proof of forgiveness, of Divine Love and of Eternal Life?

The mixed feelings of marvel, hope and "rational" scepticism remained with me.

Yet, Jesus had said (in Gospel by John):

> "... the one believing in me, the works I am doing,
> will be doing them also,
> and even greater of them will he do.
> Because I am going to my Father;
> and whatever you ask in my name, I will do it;
> so that the Father be glorified in the Son."

Father looks at me, troubled. He shakes his head, silent... Sweeps the air with his hand, then he rests it on his knee.

"Unbelievable!" he whispers. "I knew she adored you, but that... that... And again, you never explained it to me..."

"Didn't I? I don't remember. However, you knew I was being followed at the Montreal Heart Institute. And I told you I passed all the tests with flying colours and nothing was wrong with me and that I could have life insurance now —" I protest.

"No, you never did tell me about your mother's hand. I couldn't have forgotten something like that..." he whispers with reproach and sadness.

I lean over and kiss him on the cheek.

"I am sorry, if I didn't. I knew it would be important to you. But I was depressed, under great stress, shocked. I probably couldn't think properly. Forgive me..."

He closes his eyes. I really do not remember whether I did tell him or not at the time. I am afraid he feels cheated, betrayed... My heart sinks. I hug him, trying to soothe him. He pats my shoulder... He seems to forgive me... But does he really? ...

The week passed quickly. Father claimed to sleep better on the couch, but his hands started to shake a little and lose their grip. He didn't seem to notice it. Or was he pretending not to, for our sake?

When, this same week, we went to the hospital for follow-up X-rays, I grabbed a wheelchair and offered to move him around with it so that he wouldn't tire himself needlessly.

"I don't need it, I can walk," he protested.

"Most patients use it, Father. It's a long walk through endless corridors. Why not try it? Even Tito and I use it at times," I insisted.

He agreed, and I breathed a sigh of relief. In reality, I just wanted to get him accustomed to a wheelchair before he actually needed it, in case his health deteriorated rapidly.

As usual, I insisted on being in the room with him for the X-rays, and afterwards we went to see the doctor. The doctor put the films on the light screen and studied them. Stavros looked at them also, trying to decipher them.

"The end is near," the doctor warned me, as I placed myself between him and Father so that he could not read his lips.

"The disease has already covered all the lung cavities and it may go to the brain now. You must be prepared," he added.

"What can I do to help?" I asked, feeling an iron grip in my chest.

"We can only try to comfort him," answered the doctor. "Feed him well, try to help him walk around so that he doesn't lose his muscle power completely. Let him do or eat whatever he wants and keep his morale high. For pain, we can prescribe small doses of morphine, in pills, that you could give him at your judgment," he continued.

I thanked him, trying to keep my composure and braced myself to face Father.

"No change," I told him, in answer to his questioning eyes. "The doctor wants you to eat well and walk around a bit to fortify your muscles," I concluded.

Father insisted on walking his way out of the hospital.

I took him to our usual Greek psarotaverna, *Molivos* – which was on Park Avenue then – for a much loved grilled fish lunch, to keep his mind away from hospitals and doctors and sickness. Stavros "forced" himself to eat…

When we get home, Stavros hands me another piece of paper. As I take it, worried, I see that it is an article for our Association's Bulletin. It's about the Greco-Turkish friendship. *Good! At least his interest is still alive.*

"It's very good," I tell him, "although some of our friends may think that you are a Turcophile…"

"Let them think what they want. This is history. You cannot change history to please individuals…" he answers with a faint smile.

"I will translate it into English," I promise.

⋆ ⋆ ⋆

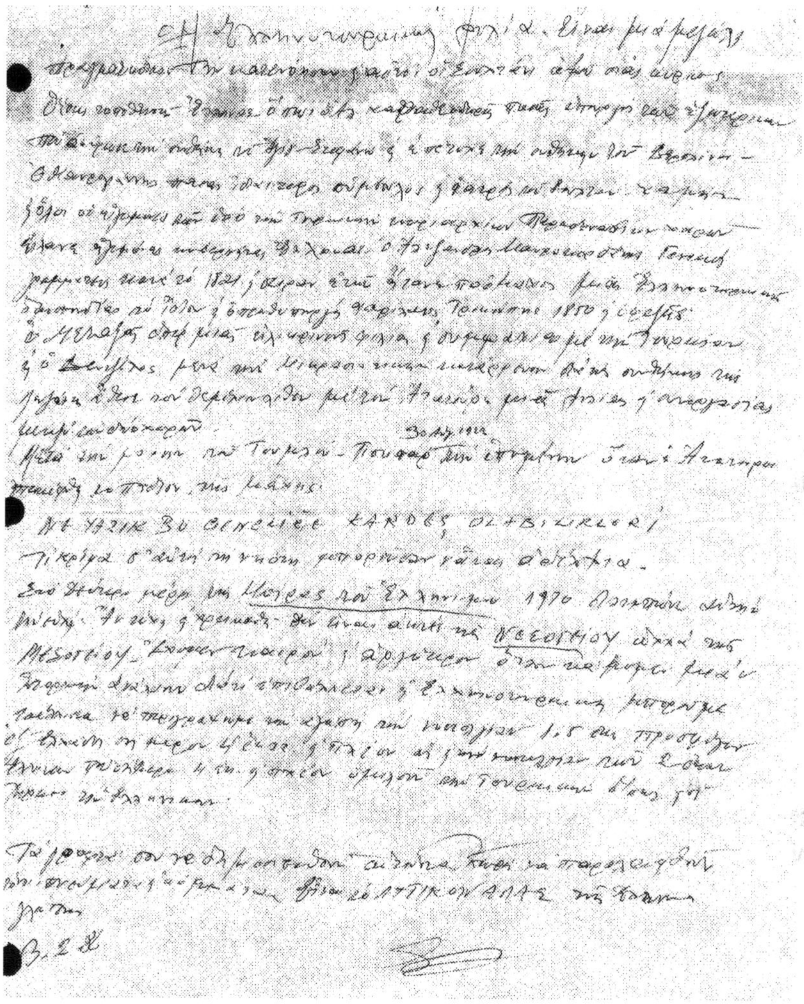

"The Grego-Turkish friendship is a great reality. Even the Sultans understood this since they placed Greeks in strategic political positions, like Al. Karatheodoris (?) Pasha as Foreign Minister, who nullified the St. Stephen Pact and ratified the Berlin Pact. Or, Mavrogiannis Pasha, personal adviser and doctor of Sultan Hamit. And all the provinces or lands under the Ottoman jurisdiction had Greek government rulers.

Alexandre Mavrokordatos, the (Sultanate's) General Secretary ca. 1821, was, for years, the defender of a Greco-Turkish confederacy (?)

The same (goes) for the Greek Prime Minister Harilaos Trikoupis around 1850. And after that Metaxas (the Greek Prime Minister) was *for a Greco-Turkish friendship and treaty with Turkey. Later, Venizelos, after the Asia-Minor collapse, with the Lausanne treaty, put with Atatürk the basis for a friendship and collaboration between the two countries.*

*The next day of the battle of Dumplupınar on 30 August 1922, when Atatürk walked through the battlefield (and saw the fallen Greek and Turkish soldiers) exclaimed "*NE YAZIK BU GENÇLER KARDEŞ OLABİLİRDİ*" (meaning), "What a pity, these youngsters could have been brothers". In the second part of "The Fate of Hellenism" (first print in 1970), I formulate this wish.*

[In an earlier essay dated 10 November 1983, Stavros mentioned the same historical anecdote that he believed appeared in the Turkish Newspaper *CUMHURIYET* and/or the Greek *APOYEVMATINI* in September of 1922. In that 1983 article, Father had maintained that genealogical research on Turks would show that only a percentage were heirs of the Ottoman founders Ertugrul and Osman, and that the rest came from mixed marriages, especially with Greek women. Consequently many Greeks and Turks were indeed, according to Stavros, step brothers. He further mentioned that we, the Greeks of Istanbul, could be the embodiment of this fact and that if his health allowed him he would like to undertake an analytical historical research that could help bring the understanding of these two nations who were nothing less than siblings. He added that this belief made him eager to study everything about these two countries.]

If necessary (correct this typo): it is not "Nesogeiou" but "Mesogeiou" (Mediterranean). We have time, and later we will make a historical analysis for why the Greco-Turkish friendship is imperative. We can very well describe the love and nostalgia of 1.5 million refugees from Greece (Turks) – today 4 millions and more – as well as the nostalgia of 2 million Greeks who today, 4 million and more, are speaking Turkish like the Turks are speaking Greek.

(Note): The writings should be printed as are. Without omitting accents, ellipsis and commas. These are the ATTIC SALT of the Greek language.

13.2.86 – Signature

XI - The Beginning of the End

This Monday noon, Stavros pushes away the soft-boiled eggs and minced tomato and cucumber salad I had prepared for him, saying that he was not hungry at all.

I explain that eggs are the most complete meal and he should try eating if he doen't want to lose his muscle strength. I realize that eating eggs from the shell is tricky, so, I empty them into a tea-cup and re-offer them to him to eat with a spoon.

Stavros takes the spoon, and tries. Then stares into his trembling hand and stops, gives up…

I take a deep breath, trying to hush my heart's pounding. "Let me help you," I say. "You helped me when I was a baby… I did not protest. So, now, let me help you too," and I direct the filled spoon towards his lips.

Was this the wrong thing to say? Don't think how he feels, Erato, or you will burst into tears and that won't help either of you…

Father gives me a long strange look, then stares again at his hands. When his eyes meet mine again, his gaze is that of a wounded animal… Without a word, he opens his mouth, and lets me spoon-feed him…

Finally, I arrange the pillows behind his back and his head, put the TV on mute with sub titles, and let him rest.

He must have napped. He seems in a better mood in the glowing afternoon sun when I bring him a coffee with milk. Wanting to take his mind off his problems, I ask him if he wants to go over my manuscript. He nods, and puts his hearing aid on. Obviously today he prefers listening to reading.

With Love as Guide (Continued)

20. "Whatever you ask in my name, I will do it…" *Indeed.*

Some time after my heart check-up, I was confronted with a difficult choice. I was over forty and it would be unwise, according to my doctors, to have more children. It would be risky for me and I could also run the risk of giving birth to an abnormal child. My husband and I were debating whether I should get a preventive ligature of my fallopian tubes or should he get a vasectomy. I wished neither. Yet I knew I would never consider an abortion.

Then suddenly, events escalated out of my control. My gynaecologist called to tell me that he suspected an abnormal growth in the neck of my uterus. A biopsy showed pre-cancerous cells. I got scared. An immediate hysterectomy was necessary. Back in the hospital room, after the operation, as I was awakening from the anaesthesia, I saw my mother hovering above me. She smiled and told me telepathically:

"It is over. And all is well. You don't need me anymore. I am going to rest on the shores of Bonita Beach..."

Then, she disappeared.... (Bonita Beach is a seashore resort in Florida where we used to vacation with her. She adored the place. She would spend hours in her rocking chair gazing at the sea and the seagulls' games.... or walking with me on the warm sand collecting shells.) Was I hallucinating? Dreaming? Or was it possible that she had in a way 'interceded' on my behalf to get the best solution for my dilemma, so that I would never have to face an abortion like the one she had had and that tormented her all her life? Was it possible that she "asked in His name", once more, and He "did it"? Was it possible that the sickness was sent purposely to me for a better quality of life?

"Another detail you never talked to me about," remarks Stavros.

"What for? I was questioning myself whether it was a hallucination or a dream—"

"What for? God! Everything about your Mama was important to me! You knew that."

"Sorry, Father. I didn't think of it at the time. I haven't even told my husband about it..."

Father shakes his head in disbelief and sweeps the air with his hand, a gesture he performs every time my behaviour disappoints him. Then he bents his head and without looking at me, "Go on," he says in resignation. Or is he eager to find out what else I did "hide" from him now that he discovers so many things I had not judged important enough to tell him? But these were happenings about which I was questioning myself as well and I had burrowed deep in me, maybe by the fear of being judged "abnormal" even by my loved ones.

I feel guilty now especially having kept from him whatever concerned my mother. So, it is with a hesitant voice that I continue:

21. Soon after the operation, I had a strange and impressive dream.

I was peeling vegetables over the sink, in front of our kitchen window. Suddenly, I look over in the garden and I see in front of me Mama, from the waste up, huge, covering my whole view and the whole sky! She is not smiling. She is serious, solemn. Her lips open and she tells me, emphasizing every syllable:

"Make sure your daughters remain Christian to the end! ..."

My heart was pounding. It was the first time that I heard my mother's voice for real. Until now, her messages always reached me silently, telepathically. Why the difference now? Why all the solemnity now? She obviously wished to impress me more than ever. But why? Are we not Christians? Was it because she had not received the last sacraments in her death-bed? Or was it because she found relief and peace through Jesus? My rooted beliefs made me accept the latter. Yet, why my daughters? Were they in danger because I was too liberal in regards to religious traditions and we did not go to church every Sunday? But didn't Jesus say that His Father was inside us? And that our body is His Temple? And did not the Apostles repeat the same thing? And wasn't Jesus angered with the lawful Jews who were going regularly to the Temple but instead of God's will were following the traditions and wills of men?

Were my daughters at risk of not remaining Christians, even though we were following Jesus' teachings?

Father shakes his head again in disbelief, sorrow in his eyes as they lock on mine. Another important dream involving my mother that I never shared with him... Is he also thinking about the meaning of Mama's message? ... I bit my lower lip in remorse but also with a glimpse of hope that maybe this exercise is reaching his soul and bringing some hope to him about the "afterlife" and "Faith". I continue:

The dream's meaning was revealed to me a few months later.
Our eldest daughter, Gabriella, declared herself an atheist!
The dream's message did strike me then! This is what had happened:

22. A classmate of Gabriella, the best student in class and her best friend, was fatally injured in a car accident.

He was thrown out of the car and landed on the road.

Denis was a lovable young boy, only seventeen, with a golden heart and no vices. He did not drink or smoke; he was always laughing and eager to help others. A source of pride to his parents, his classmates and his teachers.

Gabriella asked me to pray to Jesus for her friend's life. I did, with all my heart. And since Denis was in the same hospital and the same intensive care unit where Mama had been, I asked her to intercede for him too.

That night I dreamt of Katina. She came down, from above, on the elevator, to the intensive care unit floor where I was walking up and down. She stood in front of the elevator's open door, and motioned to a scene behind her: The elevator's walls disappeared and I saw a highway. A car was smashed in the middle. A young boy was lying on the asphalt. A pool of blood surrounded him, and he seemed to be drowning in his own blood. "Nothing can be done for him," Mama answered my mute question.

When I woke up in the morning, my Gabriella had already left for school.

That noon, Denis died from a lung haemorrhage that literally drowned him... The doctors' verdict was "He drowned in his own blood!"

This was a very heavy blow for my daughter. She was asked to deliver the eulogy during the service, in the name of her classmates. She did it, with pride and grief. When she came home after the service, heartbroken, she exclaimed: "Don't you ever talk to me again about God! It's not possible that God exists and allows criminals to live and commit crimes and, on the other hand, takes the lives of young people, like Denis, who are doing only good on earth!

"Seventeen years old! He didn't even have time to enjoy his youth! To taste life's joys!

"No! There cannot be a God who allows so much injustice in life!"

I tried to reason with her, telling her that according to the message of the dream with my mother, Denis was to die anyway and that nothing could have changed the tragic outcome.

I told her how life is like a school... With good but also with bad students. That we all have a purpose to fulfill before graduating from life's school, and then only after absorbing the knowledge and experience from our teachers. I told her that Denis was so good, so mature and experienced for his age that God must have made him skip classes and graduate earlier, calling him to His side... That Denis fulfilled his own purpose while very young. I asked Gabriella why blame God for human weaknesses and human mistakes?

God gave us all a reasoning mind and also teachers and guidance to follow. The way we choose to live and the path to follow is solely our human responsibility; our free will. God does answer our prayers from time to time and gives us a hand, like a loving parent to a demanding child. But generally, He lets us face the consequences of our actions, because this has to be so, for perfecting our education, our growth.

I explained to her that even if we analyze the event only rationally, once we admit that men have the faculty of judgment, then we must also admit that men are the only ones responsible for how they govern their own life – notwithstanding divine help or not. So that men alone decide on their acts and have to bear their consequences.

Therefore, men alone are to be blamed for their judgments and actions, and not God! Why don't we blame our society for creating criminals? Why don't we blame men for choosing cynicism and egocentrism over the love and altruism recommended by God?

If blame were the issue, then Denis' own father could feel guilty for allowing his young son to take out the family car on a rainy day. Although Denis was an excellent and careful driver, could he have yet acquired the experience and fast reflexes of a mature driver during bad weather? ... But in reality no one was to blame. It was to happen, it was simply pre-ordained to be so.

Naturally I was speaking for nothing. My daughter was not listening to a word I said. Finally, I took her in front of the icons of the Virgin Mary and Jesus, and had a long talk with her. I told her of all my past experiences, with these two icons coming to me from nowhere, as substantial evidence of Divine Will and Power, and of their guidance; in our case, the guidance of Jesus.

My daughter believes in God today. She still doesn't regularly follow Sunday liturgies, but she often prays fervenly in empty churches, or during important feasts like Easter and Christmas, and in solitude.

Wasn't this whole tragedy touching Gabriella 'unavoidable'?
And didn't my mother try to prepare us for it, thanks to a 'divine' guidance that she continued to receive although she has left our Earth?

Could I deny then the 'immortality' of her soul, of all souls?

And could I deny the Love and Forgiveness of a Mighty God?

"Well, that was quite an ordeal for Gaby!" exclaimed Stavros. "And what a tragic loss for the parents of this boy…" he continued. "How can a parent live after a child's death? And what a child! Denis was really a very nice young man... I remember him always smiling, always polite, with a nice word to me whenever he was visiting. I understand why Gaby felt that way... And those dreams with your Mama..."

"Do you want me to continue?" I ask, after a while.
"Yes, please..." he says, in a dreamy voice.

23. *For years after, I did not dream again of my mother.*

Except, a few times, in Bonita Beach, where she had told me she would be resting. In fact, on the beach, one day, there appeared a beautiful white heron which came towards me and did not go away when I approached. I wondered, against logic, whether that special bird could be my Mama's spirit, or a message from her. And every time we visit Bonita Beach, the white heron is always there, staying close to us...

There, Katina was also "sensed", one night, by 12-year-old Gabriella – adored by Mama as her first grand child – as a warm breath near her face. When Gabriella came to my bed, scared, I explained to her it was surely Yaya Katina who wanted to see her and be near her, because she loved her so much. I told Gaby to think or say "Yaya, you are scaring me, please do not come so close!" and Grandma would stay at a distance. That's what Gabriella did, and Katina never came so close to her again.

During the rare dreams that I had in Bonita Beach, Mama foretold some dangers we would encounter and how to avoid them and not fear them because they would not harm us. Like hurricanes hitting Bonita Beach, fire blocking the highway we were to take, fire on our aircraft's engine... Her forewarnings helped me not to panic and to remain calm at every incident when it happened as she had predicted.

Yet, besides all past experiences, doubt still crept into my heart concerning the phenomena related to my mother. I still asked myself, now and then, in a sceptical rationalism, whether the phenomena were not indeed created by my own subconscious... Created in order to appease my own pain and guilt about her death. I was willingly forgetting my experiences with the two unsolicited icons where my subconscious could have played absolutely no role, and that consequently my 'precious' subconscious could not be as powerful as I believed it was!

24. *My mother tried once more, during those years, to reassure me that the happenings were <u>not</u> controlled by my will, when she materialized for me again during a family crisis with my husband.*

It was one of those stupid arguments that afterwards we never remember how they started...Yet, it made him storm out of the house. I collapsed on our bed and began to cry bitterly, with hushed, heavy sobs. The night light was on. Suddenly I feel a warm breath near me and a fuzzy form appears at the side of the bed. It's like a pearl-white dense luminous cloud in the shape of a woman in a large cape. She approaches, bends over me, lifts me gently from the bed, and starts to rock me on her bosom as if I am a baby... I feel great peace... All my pain is gone. I feel soothed, protected, loved... I know, without being able to explain it, that she is Katina, my *Mama... "Mammy!" I whisper. She leans forward and puts me back to bed... Gently ... And the magical form disintegrates... I sleep through the night like a baby, not even sensing my husband coming home.*

The next morning I take a taxi and go to the cemetery to visit my mother's grave. To my surprise there is a beautiful pot of flowers on the red granite stone. I wonder who could have brought them. That evening when I tell Tito about it – we are on adoring terms again – ,"I brought the flowers myself, this morning," he explains.

"How come?"

"I had an urge to communicate with your mother... Maybe I saw her in a dream or something."

Tito never remembers his dreams... Yet here was another manifestation of my mother, now affecting also my husband. Again, it had nothing to do with my wishful thinking or my subconscious.

Stavros looks at me pouting. He seems now to be used to my secrecy about Mama's appearances… I stop, waiting for a scornful remark. He stays silent, nods for me to continue, his fingers drumming the armrest.

I resume:

25. *Finally, years later, during a comparative religion course at Concordia University, given by Dr. John Rossner, an Anglican minister, I realized at last that the "supernatural" happenings of my life had nothing to do with my willpower or my subconscious.*

We were about forty in his class, and most of us, if not all, had experienced comparable inexplicable and non-natural phenomena. Dr. Rossner explained to us that we all have naturally, by birth, the ability to see or live in the past or in the future, and to communicate with souls who live in different dimensions than our own. This ability remains with us till we reach the age of seven or eight. About this time, we are overpowered by the tendencies of our society, by the supremacy of analytical logic we are taught and by the materialistic experiences of life. And we suppress those special abilities that we were born with.

Now I understood why Jesus said that the Kingdom of Heaven belongs to children. Because we have to become little children again, pure, ignorant of society's rational teachings and prejudices, so that we may rely on those innate abilities and be open to discover life's mysteries once again.

Now I remembered again the outcry of our seven year old Kathy upon my mother's death: "She is not dead! She is alive! Now she really lives!" Those words were not the words of a seven year old child but the words dictated to her by her still alive intuitive instinct and Higher Self, in knowledge or in simple communication with souls (Mama's...) that were no more in our visible world.

Soon after, a dear deceased friend, Michael, repeated in a dream, to his adult daughter, Kathy's words; 'Not dead!'

"Look, I am not dead! I am alive! Death does not exist!
Life goes on!"

When his daughter Maria repeated her dream to her mother, Anna, they both – like all 'rational' humans – attributed the dream to Maria's subconscious wish to deny her father's death...

But for me those experiences were proof that life is indeed "eternal". Why do we stubbornly doubt it? Why do we reject all the proofs, from antiquity to the present time?

Even those who believe in Jesus Christ are puzzled by the many interpretations given to His own words and teachings, and are hoping (or are they really?) for a very distant "resurrection" at the end of time.

What did Jesus mean when He said "whoever believes in Him... will have eternal life"? I interpret it now as "whoever believes in the teachings of Jesus and follows His difficult example of unlimited and unconditional love – love even toward one's enemies – will not be lost in the cycles of perfectionist evolutions by reincarnations, but will have eternal life". "Whoever believes in Him." ... In other words, whoever has Faith. That means even the sinner? St. Paul analyzed and explained that "Faith" to our Teacher will save us and that in this "Faith to Jesus", men, as His brothers, imitating His example of self-abnegation and unconditional Love, were becoming "godlike". Once they reached this stage, even if they had sinned before, men were now on the path to eternal life.

Jesus said, according to the Gospel by John:

> The One who believes in me has eternal life .
> (...)
> The one who listens to my word
> and believes in the One who sent me,
> has eternal life, and is not coming to judgment
> but goes from death to life.

That is why it is affirmed in the Acts, by Paul, that not only the "Righteous" but the "Unrighteous" as well will be resurrected. Because God is "good" to all, to bad as well.

This path toward immortality must have been granted to my mother, and to Michael, and to so many others whose lives had been marked by love for their fellow humans and faith in God (or cosmic energy or whatever name we want to give to this force), even if they considered themselves bad.

Naturally, I could not even try to analyze all the theological implications, to discover all the answers where for nearly two thousand years, theologians and philosophers have not come to any agreement on the question. All I wanted to be reassured about was whether my mother, a sinner, could still be 'alive' in another dimension. Whether she was freed from the torments of her guilt for the 'murder' of her own child by abortion. Whether she was able not only to communicate with me, but also to perform the "miraculous" phenomena that I experienced.

Without giving any details as to my anxiety about my mother's soul, I dared recount to Dr. Rossner the materialization of my mother's hand, my total recovery from my chronic heart ailment after her intervention, and how I had attributed the entire episode to the power of my subconscious.

He smiled and gave me a short lecture:

"The majority of people are under the spell of modern teachings and modern psychology, and they attribute paranormal phenomena to the power or subjectivity of the subconscious. *But, don't you think that you are presumptuous in believing that you are capable, you alone, to create the materialization of your mother's hand and to heal a natural sickness which, as you say, had been recorded in X-rays – years ago – and diagnosed as such? Don't you admit that what happened was ordained from a power much higher than your own? Much higher than your mother's?"*

Then I remembered, again, the icons and how they were revealed to me. By a Divine Will. Without any solicitation or subjection on my part...

Dr. Rossner studied my face in silence then said:

"I see that your soul is still troubled for your mother. My wife is a medium and is helping, free of charge, those who need relevant help. If you wish, come to our gathering Sunday afternoon, at the Mount Royal Hotel. It starts at 3 p.m. She may be able to help you."

26. That Sunday, I went to the gathering at the Mount Royal Hotel.

I sat at the end of the very last row. There were about a hundred and fifty people in the audience. Marilyn Rossner was petite, youthful looking, with piercing eyes and neatly braided long blondish hair. She had a pleasant, clear, musical voice and was speaking at a very fast pace. She appeared to be very natural, not at all in a trance. Yet, she had a message of relief for many people in the audience.

I let a very rational doubt creep into my mind: 'Since she is a medium, what more natural for her than reading our own mind and repeating to us exactly whatever we wish to hear,' I thought. 'So, I would like her to bring me a message from my mother. Therefore, she will only tell me: "I have a message from your mother", and she will repeat to me verbatim my own thoughts!' I had to admit though, that it would have been difficult for Marilyn to single me out in the crowd of about a hundred and fifty people, even if her husband, Dr. Rossner, had described me to her – who, finally, was not present, and thus could not have seen me entering the room. Nevertheless, to my surprise, in a little while, Marilyn addresses me:

"You there, on the last row, the second seat from the right!"

"Me?" I ask.

"Yes, you! What's your name?"

"Erato," I answer and think to myself, now she will tell me, 'Erato I have a message for you from your mother!'

She tells me indeed:

"Erato, I have a message for you!" She stops and reflects in silence, as if she is listening to someone. Then she adds:

"But it is <u>not</u> the one you are expecting!

"You are expecting a message from your mother. However the message you have is from an old aunt of yours, who died recently!"

Aunt Harikleia! I shiver! Harikleia; Eleni Rigas' mother – Tito's great aunt and my mother's beloved confidante! Not for a single second had I thought of her!

Marilyn continues:

"Your Aunt is telling me that your mother is in the same 'world-sphere'

as her. And that your mother asked her to transmit to you that 'she is well, and that you should stop worrying about her'. Many loving spirits are praying for her and helping her, so she is all right."

I was speechless! Had the message come directly from my mother I would indeed be convinced that I generated it myself and that Marilyn had simply read my thoughts or my wishes! ... But coming from this Aunt about whom I was not thinking at all, changed the whole concept! ... My mother, and the Divine Power, knowing the process of my reasoning and my disbelief, found a way to prove to me that everything was produced and controlled "outside of my own power", through a Higher Power rising above all...

> (...) The one believing in Me, the works that I do,
> he will make them too, even greater than these, will he do.
> (...) and whatever you ask in My name, I will do.
> (Gospel of John)

and,

> Everything that you will ask in prayer
> with faith, you will receive. (Gospel of Matthew)

and,

> Whatever you ask in prayer,
> believe that you will receive
> and so will be done to you. (Gospel of Mark).

"Stupendous! The happening in this gathering is really important! It forces you to think... "

"Think what, Father?"

"That... there may be something beyond... I know about telepathy and mediums. And like you, I always believed that mediums read our own minds and repeat to us what we want to hear. But this... this message from Harikleia, cancels that theory... A pity... How could you keep all this to yourself? How could you ever presume that it wouldn't matter to me?"

I bow my head and chew the corner of my lip without responding. Stavros withdraws in some deep thinking.

"It's getting late," I say after a while. "I'd better start cooking. We'll continue tomorrow."

He nods, tired.

* * *

This morning Father seems to be waiting for me eagerly, bathed in the rays of a strong sun. He accepts my kiss on his forehead, pats my hand, and doesn't protest as I partly help him with his morning toilet and then help him eat his *Papara*. His eyes stay fixed on me as if studying my face.

"Give me my hearing aid," he asks when he finishes his breakfast.

"What do you want to do?" I ask him while adjusting the small device to his ear.

He motions to the manuscript on the coffee table.

Does he have difficulty with his eyes? Or does he really prefer that I read it to him so that he can discuss some points with me? I hope it is the latter. I make myself comfortable beside him on the sofa-bed and pick up my manuscript.

WITH LOVE AS GUIDE (Continued)

27.- A few years passed again.

About nine months before Father's sickness was diagnosed, my mother appeared once more in my sleep.

It was the eve of Ste. Catherine's feast, the 24th of November 1984, nine years after the 'same' day, that Katina (Catherine, my mother) entered the coronary unit of the hospital upon a massive coronary heart attack to which she succumbed after eleven days, on the feast of Ste. Barbara. I had this strange dream:

I am at the end of an unexpected trip to the unknown.

I am at the all-white marble hall of a Temple. There are no windows, just a strange soft irridescent light which pours in from nowhere and embraces everything. The hall reminds me of a Turkish Hamam, but without running waters or hot steam. As if it were a dry cleansing bath of light! ... Or a "baptism" of light ... I look around me. There are people of all ages, wearing sparkling white toga-like robes...

I distinguish, at the back, a large thick metal door, half-open. Someone signals me by hand... invites me to come close. I advance, pass through the gate, and go down a few marble steps to a passage-way adorned with flowers and bathed in a soft filtered light. At the end of the corridor, another door...

On my approach, the heavy door opens by itself and suddenly I am engulfed in blinding light! ... When my eyes become accustomed to the bright sun, I see, in front of me, a fairy landscape...

Green mountainsides, woodlands, flowered hills which convey a sweet smell, natural waterfalls that tumble in an hypnotic rhythm, brooks that sparkle.

Far away, a long deep river (or sea?) that shimmers under the sun, in front of misty, fading shores... No houses, no huts, no buildings anywhere... Only people. People of all ages... Men, women, old men, old ladies, young men, young girls, children... Alone, or in small groups, they walk, talk, or do something... They all smile, appear happy... Some of them laugh loudly... Children dance in circles... Young boys and girls run after each other with shouts of joy... Others bring baskets full of fragrant flowers and luscious fruit to dress the tables for a simple country feast. Clay pitchers are filled with fresh water...

Suddenly, my mother is by my side! ... She is young, beautiful, happy. Very happy! Her lips part in a bright smile, and her black eyes sparkle from an unspeakable joy and an inner peace. Her whole "being" is vibrating with an indescribable beauty... She embraces me with that tender gaze that was so much part of her. She speaks to me in a low, soft, calming voice:

"You see? We are all happy and carefree, here! Are you relieved now?"

I whisper, in wonder, "but then, life continues?"

"Yes, Life continues!" she confirms.

"But it is so beautiful! Why do they forbid us to come, Mama?"

"Nobody forbids you to come. The door is always open. But you have to be READY to be able to step in. And once one is in, one cannot go back. In reality, there is nothing to stop us from going back. But we know well that we SHOULD NOT! ..."

"And why not?"

"Because that would disturb the order of things! Everything has its time. And only those who are READY can come here. That is why we should not communicate with 'your' world."

"And me?"

"You must go back, Erato. You are not ready yet. You will come here later..."

As we talked, we had retraced our steps back. I was now at the threshold of the flowered corridor... Katina, stayed on the other side, below the blinding light... I forced myself to walk towards the white marble hall, the temple maybe of spiritual catharsis.

I woke up with a feeling of great peacefulness....

Was it only a dream? Or a message from the after life?

Yes, I was sure now that Katina, my dear mother, with God's grace, had once more found a way to reassure me that she is "all right", that she has the forgiveness and Love of God, and that I should not worry any longer about her peace and the salvation of her soul. Passages from Jesus' sayings in the Gospel of John now became clear to me:

> Where I am going, you cannot follow me now;
> you will follow me too, later.
> (...) Because so loved God the world,
> that He gave away His only Son
> so that whoever believes in Him
> is not lost, but has life eternal.
> (...) Believe in God, and believe in Me.
> In my Father's house there are many dwellings.
> (...)
> I am going to prepare a place for you.
> (...) (But) you know where I am going,
> and you know the way.

Now, with that dream, it was as if I was offered the privilege of having a glimpse of that "eternal life" in one of the dwellings promised by Jesus and by teachers of other religions.

And I am convinced, once more, that our life is pre-ordained and guided according to a divine design that will bring us to perfection. All we have to do is trust our Extraordinary Guide who showed us the way and follow His path.

Jesus said:

> Blessed be the ones who believe without proof.

And my mother, with her deep embedded faith, used to say:

"Believe and don't investigate!"

Mama never doubted! She never lost her courage. Not when Father was taken as a war prisoner by the Turks, not when I became seriously ill and given ten days to live, not during the difficult birth of our Kathy who survived by miracle, not even during her own heart attack... When she used to make the sign of the cross and say simply, but devotedly, "Come, Jesus and Mary!" or "Help, my Vanghelistra, full of Grace!" she knew that help was near! She had faith in Jesus' saying:

> Whoever is thirsty, come to me and drink.

And,

> Whatever you want, ask, and it will be given to you. (John).

Under the Divine Plan, even pains and miseries become ladder steps for our ascent to perfection.

As the Apostle Paul wrote to the Romans:

> And we don't only take pride in the hope of God's story, but we take pride in sufferings, knowing that suffering creates patience, and patience creates testing, and testing creates hope. And hope is not to be shameful about, because the Love of God spreads into our hearts through the Holy Spirit that was given to us.

Yet it is so difficult to believe in the Love of God during our technological age! If I doubted in spite of all my past marvellous experiences and the tangible evidence given to me from "above", it is easy to understand the scepticism of those who have had no extraordinary experiences at all to rely on.

In conclusion, it is evident to me now, that Life is eternal. It is evident to me that all those departed from Earth continue to live in another dimension. A dimension that our senses cannot yet perceive or conceive. Most importantly, it is evident to me that God, our Creator, or Divine Spirit, or Life Energy Force, whatever called, does exist, and is caring for us who, being His creatures, are all part of Him as well (like 'semi-gods' or like "gods" as stated in the Bible and recorded by John) and linked in what some have called "Universal Consciousness". I believe that our life – or lives – follows an evolutionary, educational pattern so that our immortal soul may attain a godlike perfection and be worthy of God our Father. I believe that every single event of our life has its own purpose for our progress, even if it does not appear so to us.

So, if we can have trust like a child, intuitively and without much reasoning, in this so difficult to understand Divine Power which controls our lives, then we can realize that God, Oneness and Immortality of the Soul lie ahead of us.

Yet, I don't believe that our path in this spiritual growth is preset in such a way that we follow it blindly, without any contribution or reasoned changes for its improvement on our part. On the contrary, although our destination is fixed, it is up to us, born with reason and with special gifts or capabilities, to choose the road and the means to get there in the best possible way. "We know the way," (Gospel by John).

Furthermore, I believe, as all scriptures and philosophies hint, that we are also given "Guides" and "Counsellors" to help us during our journey, and we should know by now who and where they are. But again, it is up to us to seek these Counsellors and heed or not their free advice.

At times, when we risk going astray or becoming too discouraged, one or more of these Leaders may contact us. They will be our Leaders to follow and lean onto in moments of crisis. They will act as Guides we trust from our own traditions or religion, whose path we will follow as a beacon, on a dark unknown road.

I also believe that our Divine Guides will act solely as coaches, helping us to reach our potential. Like the super athletic coaches we are familiar with now, they will coach us the same way. Our coaches – in my case Jesus (and His Mother) – are in fact going to guide us, let us know what to expect, indicate how to respond. They will test our endurance. But whether we make it or not, is our sole responsibility.

Because, although our coaches will be watching us and stay by our side, we will have to perform alone. All will depend on how much faith we have in their coaching and in ourselves, on how far we can push ourselves. We will have to face all these tests along this evolutionary path alone and overcome them alone. Our counsellors will just be watching, as all coaches watch their athletes. At times our coaches will just push us or give us support, but in the end we are the ones to do it, to prove ourselves.

Therefore, if we can trust these Guides with all our intuitive self and love, and keep our faith in the Divine Power alight, we will find the sense and purpose of our Being. We will be blessed and fulfilled in this life on Earth – no matter the hardships – while waiting to go on to the other.

And if we are to return to Earth-life again, I believe that it will be by our own volition and for the sole purpose of using our knowledge and experience, to help someone related to us to attain also this state of 'perfection'.

I believe Jesus is the best teacher of perfection that Humanity has had to this day. Yet He is the most demanding with His commands to forgive and love our enemies, to aim at becoming Godlike in helping those in need. All we have to do is follow His example and trust Him.

Luckily, more and more people in our times are becoming aware of His teachings. War, famine and other disasters have brought people of all religious denominations together to helping their fellowmen. Yet more individual growth is needed. If we could apply Jesus' difficult commandment of 'loving and caring for all', everyday, then what bliss Life would be! Without revenge and without bitterness against others! Wouldn't that really be a 'heavenly kingdom'?

Finally, I am convinced that my own family nucleus, like many other families, has Jesus as our divine guide, with his Mother assisting Him. Even though He still has "other sheep" to gather, as He said, so that we all become "One"...

We are lucky that Jesus did indeed choose us to be His "protégés" and His vehicle in helping those around us, in this spiritual evolution. As He says, again in the Gospel by John,

> I chose you...
> My sheep listen to my voice.
> I know them,
> and they follow me.
> And I am giving them eternal life
> and they won't be lost in the eon.

And,

> (...)
> I am the way, and the truth, and life.
> Nobody goes to Father but through Me.
> If you know me, you will know my Father.
> And from now on, you know my Father.
> (...)
> I am the light of the world.
> The one who follows Me, will not walk in darkness,
> But will have the Light of Life.

May your life be lit, my darling daughters, by your Faith in Jesus and His Love!

ERATO EVANGELIDIS SAHAPOGLU

January, 1986

Note: The Gospel quotations are translated from the Old Greek version.

P.S. Could the choice of our own names have any spiritual connotations?
My Father's father was called Anghelis (Angel).
My Mother's father was also called Anghelis (Angel).
My Father's name is Stavros (Cross).
My Christian name is Evanghelia (Good News).
My husband's father was called Gabriel (the Archangel).
Our first born was announced to be called Gabriella (name of the Archangel).
Tito's Christian name is Apostle (the name given to the disciples of Jesus who spread the Good News Gospel).

Finally, my Mother's and our younger daughter's name is Catherine (Purity).

Could all those names have been chosen by simple coincidences? Or is our family, like all other families (and whether they are aware of it of not), united indeed in a nucleus progressing in a pre-ordained divine pattern for the life-fulfillment of its members?

"This is it," I say to Father, closing the manuscript. He had listened to me attentively without interrupting me. "What do you think?"

"First of all, that dream you had with your Mother at that garden... You wrote about it in the Association's bulletin under the title *Only a dream?* I told you then, it was only a dream; the result of your own subconscious wish to see your mother well..."

"And now?"

"Now, I don't know... Difficult to conceive... But I have to admit that there is something there... There are strange forces in our lives... There are communications... I believe it was Einstein who said that there is no time ... That past, present and future merge... Mysteries... As I told you some time ago, when I pass over, if I feel... if it is ever possible, I will try to communicate with you and let you know what I find... " he adds with a mischievous smile.

I try to smile too.

"Anything you wish me to change?" I ask.

"Well, I find the conclusions a bit too didactic. You could stop at the dream... But, hey, this is your baby; this is about what you believe. You decide what to do with it... All in all, very interesting."

"And do you think Nicholas will find it interesting also?"

"I think so."

I hug him, and leave him with his daydreams...

I believe I made my point, Father...

XII - THUCYDIDES VERSUS ERASMUS

*I*t is a cold, grey, end of February day, the garden clothed all in white. Father is feeling better after Robert has given him his bath and massage. I help him eat some chicken soup with pieces of bread in it, and a stewed pear for dessert. Then I leave him to doze off.

Now it's around 4 p.m. and I come to see how he is doing.

I find him watching TV, on mute, with the captions on. A good sign. He smiles at my approach, turns the TV off and makes a sign with his hand for me to sit by him.

"I want to you to write something for me in the Association's bulletin. It is about the wrong assumption all foreigners have about the pronunciation of the Greek diphthongs. This has to be corrected. I will dictate and you record it and then you transcribe it. The right way, you know, with tones and all."

"Sure, Father, with pleasure" I answer, delighted that he is in high spirits.

"So, push the button of your little machine..."

I do...

THUCYDIDES VERSUS ERASMUS

Erasmus, the great Greek scholar, separates the diphthongs.

Greek writers, following a line of tradition, do not separate diphthongs, and pay no attention to Erasmus' theory.

Yet, Thucydides is clear on the subject in his account of the Spartans and Athenians. He states that when a plague epidemic ravaged Athenians, they remembered the Delphi oracle predicting that "loimos" would defeat the Athenians, that is, as per certain historians:

«Λοιμός Ἀθήνας νενικήκατε...» (Plague will defeat Athens).

And as per Thucydides:

«ἥξει Δωριακός πόλεμος και λοιμός ἅμ'αυτῷ»
(The Doric War will come and with it the plague).

The most significant point about the subject is the following explanation given by Thucydides:

«Ἐγένετο μέν οὖν ἔρις τοῖς ἀνθρώποις μή λοιμόν ὠνομάσθαι... αλλά λιμόν, ενίκησε δε ἐπί τοῦ παρόντος εἰκότως λοιμόν εἰρῆσθαι, οἱ γάρ ἄνθρωποι πρός ἅ ἔπασχον τήν μνήμην ἐποιοῦντο.»

Which freely translates:

"And a quarrel started amongst the people whether the wording (of the oracle) should have meant 'loimon' (plague) or 'limon' (famine, starvation)... but that the word 'loimon' (plague) won on the present subject since people remember whatever makes them suffer."

Thus, if the oracle had pronounced **«λοϊμός»**, *that is* ***"lo-ï-mos",*** *separating the diphthong, there would have been no cause for the Athenians to be doubtful whether the word was "limos" or "loïmos" [and quarrel about its meaning]. That shows that Ancient Greeks did not separate the diphthongs. Yet many did not take notice of this historical fact.*

Ca. 1875 or 1880 (the exact date may be verified in the Greek HELIOS Encyclopaedia), Michael Constantinides, professor of philosophy at the University of Athens, was giving a lecture where he happened to quote this passage from Thucydides. Present at the lecture was my professor Procopios Georgiades – then a student.

And during 1919 – noticeable date because it was the day a Greek battalion entered Izmir – Georgiades, commenting in class on the erroneous theory of Erasmus, remarked: "How come Erasmus did not see the problem since Thucydides himself gives the answer in his explanation? "But", he added, "this is not my discovery. This explanation was given to us by my professor Michael Constantinides of the University of Athens."

Years passed... 1919-1986. And a pupil of Georgiades, Evangelidis (Stavros), remembered the incident.

The honour of the answer belongs, naturally, to Thucydides.

But the problem was explained and analyzed by Michael Constantinides, perpetuated by (Procopios) Georgiades and recalled now by me.

It appears that the afore-mentioned historical detail by Thucydides continues to slip away from many intellectuals and Greek scholars, as much in the universities of Greece as in those in the United States, Canada and elsewhere.

I believe that it is the duty of the Greeks to register this explanatory analysis in the minutes of the Academy of Athens and of the Greek universities so that, in the future, there is no doubt on the subject. This is a debt to the Greek letters, and the lovers and scholars of the Ancient Greek language will honour it."

STAVROS EVANGELIDIS

Note:

If possible, besides the Greek Academy of Athens, the text should be distributed to the Greek journals of Istanbul, to the Athenian journals of Greeks from Constantinople, such as CONSTANTINOUPOLIS of Lambikis, POLITIS, CIRCLE OF CONSTANTINOPOLITANS, and here to the ETHNIC HERALD, and to the universities having a Greek Chair, such as McGill, Université de Montréal, etc. It should also be sent to the Greek Orthodox Patriarchate in Istanbul; to Rt. Rev. Meliton Hatzi, Bishop of Chalcedon; to the Archdiocese of North and South America; and to the Diocese of Toronto. Finally, the text should also be translated into French, English and German.

I transcribed the recording, translated it into French and English, and submitted it to his approval – the German translations would have to wait. He signed the typed manuscripts on the 6th of March 1986. The article was published in three languages on our Associations' bulletin on the 10th of October 1986 (and again later, in 1989, in our Anniversary Album).

I sent a copy to all the establishments Father had suggested, as well as to all universities having a Greek Letters Chair in the United States, England and France. To this date, I received no answer or acknowledgement from any Institution…

Maybe I should repeat the exercise …

Coll. Viollet

Thucydide. (Musée national, Naples.)

ΘΟΥΚΥΔΙΔΗΣ ΚΑΤΑ ΕΡΑΣΜΟΥ.

'Ο Ἔρασμος, ἕνας μέγας ἑλληνιστής, διαλύει τάς διφθόγγους.

Οἱ Ἕλληνες λογοτέχναι, ἀκολουθῶντας μιά σειρά παραδόσεως, δέν διαλύουν τάς διφθόγγους καί δέν δίνουν σημασία στήν θεωρία τοῦ 'Εράσμου.

'Αλλά ὁ Θουκυδίδης εἶναι σαφής ἐπί τοῦ θέματος, ὅταν ἱστορεῖ ὅτι κατά τόν Πελοποννησιακό πόλεμο μεταξύ Σπαρτιατῶν (Λακεδαιμονίων) καί 'Αθηναίων, ἔγινε ἐπιδημία πανοῦκλας ἐπιφέρουσα συμφορά μεταξύ τῶν 'Αθηναίων. Τότε οἱ 'Αθηναῖοι θυμήθηκαν τόν χρησμόν (κατά τούς μέν τόν τοῦ Μαντείου τῶν Δελφῶν, λέγοντα: "Λοιμός 'Αθήνας νενικήκατε....", κατά δέ τόν Θουκυδίδην):

"Ἥξει Δωριακός πόλεμος καί λοιμός ἅμ'αὐτῷ".

Τό κυριώτερο, ἐπί τοῦ θέματος, εἶναι ὅτι ὁ Θουκυδίδης δίνει τήν ἑξῆς διασάφησι:

"'Εγένετο μέν οὖν ἔρις τοῖς ἀνθρώποις μή λοιμόν ὠνομάσθαι...ἀλλά λιμόν, ἐνίκησε δέ ἐπί τοῦ παρόντος εἰκότως λοιμόν εἰρῆσθαι· οἱ γάρ ἄνθρωποι πρός ἅ ἔπασχον τήν μνήμην ἐποιοῦντο" (I)

'Εάν λοιπόν ὁ χρησμός ἔλεγε "λοϊμός" (διαλύοντας τήν δίφθογγο), δέν θά ὑπῆρχε ἀνάγκη νά εἶναι ἀμφίβολοι οἱ 'Αθηναῖοι ἄν θά ἤτανε"λοιμός" ἤ "λιμός". Ἄρα, οἱ ἀρχαῖοι Ἕλληνες δέν διέλυαν τάς διφθόγγους. 'Αλλά αὐτό τό ἱστορικό, τό αντιπαρῆλθον πολλοί.

Στό I875 ἤ I880 (2), ὁ Μιχαήλ Κωνσταντινίδης, καθηγητής φιλοσοφίας Πανεπιστημίου 'Αθηνῶν, ἔτυχε σέ μία διάλεξή του νά πῆ αὐτήν τήν περικοπή τοῦ Θουκυδίδη. Καί ἦταν παρών, μαθητής τότε,,καί καθηγητής μου ἀργότερα, ὁ ἀείμνηστος Γεωργιάδης ὁ Προκοπεύς.

Καί κατά τόν 'Απρίλιο τοῦ I919 (ἡμερομηνία ὅπου εἶχε βγῆ ἑλληνικό ἀπόσπασμα στή Σμύρνη), ἀναφερόμενος στήν λανθασμένη θεωρία τοῦ 'Εράσμου, ὁ Γεωργιάδης παρατήρησε:
" Πῶς τὤπαθε ὁ Ἔρασμος καί δέν πρόσεξε τό πρόβλημα, ἀφοῦ ὁ ἴδιος ὁ Θουκυδίδης δίνη τήν ἀπάντηση, στήν ἐπεξήγησή του;".
"'Αλλά", πρόσθεσε, "δέν τό βρῆκα ἐγώ αὐτό, δέν εἶναι δική μου εὕρεσις. Αὐτό μᾶς τό εἶπε ὁ καθηγητής μου,τοῦ Πανεπιστημίου 'Αθηνῶν, Μιχαήλ Κωνσταντινίδης".

Πέρασαν χρόνια... I9I9-I986.

Ἕνας μαθητής τοῦ Γεωργιάδη, ὁ Εὐαγγελίδης, θυμήθηκε τό περιστατικό.

'Η τιμή τῆς ἀπαντήσεως ἀνήκει βέβαια στόν Θουκυδίδη. 'Αλλά τό πρόβλημα τό διευκρίνησε καί τό ἀνέλυσε ὁ Μιχαήλ Κωνσταντινίδης, τό διαιώνησε ὁ Γεωργιάδης καί τώρα τό ξαναφέρνω ἐγώ στήν ἐπιφάνεια.

(I) ΘΟΥΚΥΔΙΔΗΣ- 'Επιστημονική 'Εταιρεία τῶν 'Ελληνικῶν Γραμμάτων, Πάπυρος, ἐν 'Αθήναις, I954. Τόμος I, 'Ιστοριῶν Β', -54 (Σελ. 404).

(2) 'Ακριβής ἡμερομηνία δυνατόν νά βρεθῇ ἀπό τήν 'Εγκυκλοπαίδεια ΗΛΙΟΥ.

Καί αὐτή ἡ ἱστορική λεπτομέρεια τοῦ Θουκυδίδη φαίνεται νά διαφεύγει πολλούς νοήμονας, ἑλληνιστάς, τόσον στά Πανεπιστήμια τῆς 'Ελλάδος, ὅσον καί στά Πανεπιστήμια τῆς 'Αμερικῆς καί τοῦ Καναδᾶ.

Νομίζω ὅτι εἶναι καθῆκον τῶν 'Ελλήνων, νά ἀναγράφουν αὐτήν τήν ἀνάλυση στά πρακτικά τῆς 'Ακαδημίας 'Αθηνῶν καί τῶν Πανεπιστημίων, οὕτως ὥστε εἰς τό μέλλον, νά μήν ὑπάρξη καμία ἀμφιβολία περί τοῦ θέματος. Εἶναι μιά ὠφειλή πρός τά 'Ελληνικά Γράμματα, καί ὅλοι οἱ φίλοι καί μελετηταί τῆς ἀρχαίας ἑλληνικῆς γλώσσης πρέπει νά τῆς ἀποδώσουν φόρον τιμῆς.

6 Μαρτίου 1986 ΣΤΑΥΡΟΣ ΕΥΑΓΓΕΛΙΔΗΣ

- Μεταγραφή ἠχογραφήσεως-

Erasmus, oil painting by Hans Holbein the Younger, 1523, in the Louvre, Paris

Σημ.: Θά ἦταν εὔλογο, ἐκτός τῆς 'Ακαδημίας 'Αθηνῶν, νά σταλῆ ἀντίγραφο στά Πολίτικα φύλλα, στά 'Αθηναϊκά φύλλα Κων/λιτῶν ὅπως "Κων/πολις" τοῦ Λαμπίκη, "Πολίτης", "Κύκλος Κων/λιτῶν", κι 'εδῶ πέρα, στόν "'Εθνικό Κήρυκα" καί στά Πανεπιστήμια πού ἔχουν ἕδραν 'Ελληνικῶν, ὅπως MCGILL, UNIVERSITE DE MONTREAL κλπ. Νά σταλῆ ἐπίσης στήν 'Αρχιεπισκοπή 'Αμερικῆς, 'Επισκοπή Τορόντο, στό Οἰκουμενικό Πατριαρχεῖο, στόν Μητροπολίτη Χαλκηδόνος Μελέτιον Χατζῆ. Καί τέλος, νά μεταφρασθῆ τό κείμενο στήν Γαλλική, 'Αγγλική καί Γερμανική.

XIII- An Omen?

*I*t is a bright, quiet, Sunday morning. The sun reverberating on our snowy landscape makes it hard to look at. For sometime now, we do not go to Church… Too painful for Father to move out, and I do not want to leave him alone… I check to make sure my votive flame burns faithfully in our iconostase… I make the sign of the cross and pray…

Tito will sleep till noon to recuperate from the late hours he puts working on his computer. Kathy will get up late also.

I want to use my free time to prepare something nice for Father's breakfast. I remember the "comfort" nutritious delicacy of my childhood. I beat an egg yolk with seven spoons of sugar till it becomes a fluffy whitish cream.

"I prepared you something special this morning," I say to Stavros, trying to sound enthusiastic, as I put the tray with the sweet café-au-lait and the cup with the beaten egg delicacy by his side table.

"He called my name!" says Father, haggard.

"Who? What?"

"The Angel of Annunciation! He came in my dream. He called me three times: 'Stavré! Stavré! Stavré!'"

"How do you know it was the Angel of Annunciation?"

"I just know…"

"And then?"

"Nothing… He dissolved…"

I shiver… An omen? Will it be soon? I try to sound positive.

"Well, he is usually an Angel of *good news*, isn't he? Let's take it this way. Next time we go out, we will stop by a Church and light a candle to the Icon of the Annunciation… In the meantime, try this sumptuous dessert. It's delicious."

Stavros eats it, absentmindedly, without any comment. *Are his taste buds affected or is he still thinking of the Angel?*

XIV - Despair

It is a gloomy, grey, March day. High snow banks cover the glass patio door half way up. Just the two of us, in the house… My heart is heavy, compressed.

I go down to see if Stavros needs anything. I find him standing, in front of the couch, shaking forcefully trying to do his personal toilet. He is out of balance. He curses, his forehead pearled in sweat.

I hasten across the room, to help him. He flashes, gives me a desperate look. I hand him some towels…

Finally, Stavros sinks onto the edge of the sofa-bed. He grasps his head in his two hands and starts to sob… Tearless, blusterous sobs…

"Why, Mother, why? ... Why did you bring me into this world if I had to face this? Why? Cursed was the moment of my birth! Cursed were you! Damn you, Mother! Damn…" cries Stavros, his chest shuddering…

Tears streaming down my cheeks, I hug him, take him in my arms, put his head slowly, tenderly, on my shoulder. "Shush…" I whisper as I strike his hair and his frail bony back. I rock him gently, like a baby… *God, help us!* I pray. This is worse than any physical pain... What can I do? How can I help?

I continue to rock him, silently, until his sobs subside.

Then I look him straight in the eye. "Please, don't feel bad. Don't ever feel ashamed, Father. At one point in our life we all need some help. You took care of me when I was small… Now it's my turn… You taught me that life is a cycle… How can we make things better, tell me?"

He lifts his hands, in resignation, lowering his eyes.

I cup his head in my hands and try to meet his desperate gaze. "Is there anything you think that might help? Tell me, Father…"

"There is nothing…"

"What about a trip?"

"What trip? I can't even get out and walk on the snow! I can't stand on my feet..."

"You can travel in a wheelchair..."

He shrugs his shoulders, discouraged.

"Would a trip to Istanbul make you feel better?"

"No one left in Istanbul," he whispers.

"Greece then? Or you hometown in Eastern Thrace? You may find some distant relatives there?"

"No one left... friends, relatives... All gone..."

"What about Bonita Beach?"

That stirs him.

"Bonita?"

"Yes... The sun, the warmth, the sea... Would a trip to Bonita help? The sunny climate would change your mood for sure..."

"The sun... the beach... the sea... Hippocrates believed in *thalasso-therapy*... But I am too sick to travel... I cannot walk anymore... I..."

"I will first check with the doctor to see if you can travel. Then, we will get a wheelchair. Maman Amélie, always travels in a wheelchair because of her bad legs. And she has a good time every time she comes to visit us, remember? We take her everywhere with us and she enjoys every minute of it... And Mr. Bond, in Bonita, has lived for years in a wheelchair and very happily as you know... If you agree, I will start the proceedings and look into it..."

He shakes his head doubtfully, but now a glimpse of hope plays in his wet eyes.

Am I crazy? *Another false hope for him, Erato? Don't do it! It is almost impossible for him to go to Bonita. Stop it!* I don't want to listen to reason. I know the most difficult task will be to find plane reservations. March is the high season for Florida. After some futile phone calls to airlines, I call my friend Lefki Dodwell at the House of Travel. I knew, from my days with British Airways, that Lefki could make miracles happen.

"My father has terminal cancer. This is his last wish, his last trip.Can you do something, Lefki? Can you find us two seats to Florida?"

Lefki is moved.

"I will try my best, Erato. It will have to be full fare though. It will be impossible to find an excursion fare now... And your father will need a doctor's certificate allowing him to travel."

"OK." I say. "You work on the reservations I will work on the doctor's certificate."

I ask my cleaning lady if she can come and watch my father while I am away for an hour or two. She can. When she arrives, I get a taxi, and go to see Stavros' chest specialist at the hospital.

"Are you crazy?" he exclaims. "The last X-rays show the cancer has filled all his thorax cavity. By now it must be going to his brain. There is no way he can get on a plane. He will die in mid-flight. His lungs will explode from the pressure. He will never reach his destination!"

"He IS DYING anyway! This is his last wish. It's better for him to die happy than in despair."

"You are insane! No airline will accept him on board in his condition!"

"People travel in stretchers! I know; I worked for an airline. And my father is not a stretcher case. He can travel with a wheelchair," I protest, trying to keep my composure in the face of his ignorance and his negativity.

"Even if they did accept him in a wheelchair, did you think of the implications? If he dies on board, the aircraft will have to be re-routed for an emergency landing. Can you pay the cost? It would be hundreds of thousands of dollars... And not counting what would you do with the dead body... From what I know, you are not a millionaire and you've gone through a great deal yourself. It could have been done at the beginning of his illness. Not now. It's insane! No, I will never sign a certificate!"

I left him, trembling with rage but determined to find a way.

I managed to contact Dr. Balfour Mount, at the Royal Victoria Palliative Center. He told me it could be done. They had had patients travel to and from Australia on a stretcher, and since my father was not at that stage yet it would be easier. But, due to the condition of his lungs, it would have to be a direct flight without any stop in between and be a pressurized jet aircraft, a 747 type, with oxygen on board. He promised to visit Father at home, the next morning, for a full assessment so that he could write an appropriate report. His words were a balm to my heart.

Back home, I called Lefki and asked her to concentrate on direct bookings of a 747 aircraft with oxygen on board and a wheelchair at both terminals. She suggested Air Canada, direct from Montreal to Fort Lauderdale.

That was acceptable to me. I could hire a taxi from Fort Lauderdale to Bonita.

Lefki called me back stating that Air Canada, beside the doctor's report, were also asking for an authorization of "no resuscitation" in case the worst happened during the flight, so that the aircraft would not have to be re-routed or emergency procedures initiated. I agreed, willing to settle this matter with Dr. Mount tomorrow.

Then I called Noella, our wonderful liaison nurse, and explained what we were planning. She told me her husband was an Air Canada pilot and that she would talk to him to see how we could facilitate and rush the proceedings. God was on our side…

Now I explained to Father that Dr. Mount was coming to examine him the next day, and we would follow his recommendations.

I also decided, from now on, to sleep in the reclining chair in the TV room since Father was shaky when he stood up.

That night, after dinner, all excited, I explained my plan to my husband and told him everything I had done during the day. He looked at me as if I were an alien creature.

"Are you out of your mind, or what? He is in no state to travel!"

"He is. With a wheelchair! Dr. Mount is coming to assess him tomorrow…"

"Did you ever stop to think about the consequences? What if his lungs explode in mid-flight, as the lung specialist said? Can you envision this? The turmoil in the cabin? And how are you going to cope with your Father dead, beside you?"

"This is the worst scenario…"

"But a plausible one! And are you sure the aircraft pilot will not do an emergency landing to get rid of a dead body? Who is going to pay for the expenses? We don't have that kind of money!"

"Stop it, Tito! Father is not dead yet!"

"Stop it yourself! This trip will cost a fortune, even if he makes it to Bonita. A regular return fare; a taxi to move you around; living expenses in Bonita… What if he has to be hospitalized there or sent home in a stretcher? Do you have any idea how much that would cost? Or to fly his body back to Montreal if he dies there?"

"I will have the body cremated and bring back only his ashes… I will sell all my jewellery, take a loan, use our credit card, our bank credit line… Whatever it takes… I have to do this Tito, it's Father's last wish…"

"A last wish that you suggested… You just refuse to let go.

"You are crazy, Erato! What do you expect to achieve for your father with this trip?"

"Some hope of pleasant days in the sun. Take all the despair away..."

"And what about you? Erato, you know I cannot come with you. We just lost our best contract and we are trying to stay on our feet. I have to be at work. So, you will be all alone for this ordeal. You cannot cope with it. You will crumble! Remember when your mother died? You went into a terrible depression... I won't let you do it!"

"That was different. I was shocked then and felt guilty at Mama's death. Now I am prepared and I feel good about it. I will not be alone. There are people in the condo, Mrs. Bond and others. Our condo belonged to a paraplegic, so it is adapted for a wheelchair. I will find help if I need any—"

"No, this is final. I will not let you do it."

"Tito, why are you so mean all of a sudden? This is really vital for me."

"Erato, this trip is something I cannot face, I cannot deal with, both physically and emotionally. Nor can you... I love you. We need you. What if something happens to you? What about me? Our children? Your first responsibility is to our children..."

"You are all adults! You don't need me! And I will go with or without your approval. I don't need your permission—"

"I will do anything in my power to stop you. And you are not to touch our business account or our Visa account, or our bank credit. We cannot afford it, it would bankrupt us. And I will not give you a penny."

"I will find a way..." I answered, in tears.

Tito slammed the door, and left for his office.

When my sobs subsided, I went to sleep in the TV room, close to Father.

Next morning Dr. Mount came to see Father. Stavros' eyes gleamed with hope as he tried to explain to him, writing in his note pad, how good he knew the sun and the sea air would be for him. He asked if he could stay in the sun, if he could go to the sea. The doctor patted his shoulder, reassuringly. "You can do anything you want, depending on how you feel," he wrote back. Stavros was beaming...

"Your father can travel, all right," he said to me, once we were upstairs, in the living room.

"I will write a report and an authorization of 'no resuscitation'. Just let me know to whom I should send it. But I can reassure you, he will make it to Florida.

"And if I were you – and if you can afford it – I would let him end his days there... It will be less painful. But you will have to protect yourself. You will have to call the Sheriff's department the moment you arrive, explain the situation to him and ask what are the laws of Florida in this regard. They may have to send their own doctor to examine him. So that when the end comes you are not accused of a euthanasia attempt or any other crime. This is important, do you understand?"

"Yes, I do... Thank you for warning me."

"Also, we will prescribe some painkillers to take with you. A kind of morphine in pills. If he has pain and the pain becomes too strong, you can use them at your discretion..."

I could have kissed him! I squeezed his hands with gratitude.

"You are a good and courageous daughter. He is lucky to have you," he said, his hand on my arm.

Now, I had to start working. First the money issue. I called our friend Haïk Manoukian, a jeweller, who had also appraised my jewellery in the past for insurance purposes. I told him about my plan to take Father to Florida and that I did not want to use any money from our business account or use our Visa, and that I had no time to apply for a loan. I asked him if I he could sell my jewellery if I left it with him on consignment.

There was silence on the other line. "When do you need the money?" he asked after a while.

"As soon as possible, the latest in a week?"

Silence...

"Well?" I asked.

"I am thinking. Erato, you have exquisite jewellery pieces. But they wouldn't sell in a week. It could take many weeks, or even months. Since you need the money immediately, I was thinking... I have some money. What if I lend you the money in advance, without interest? You spend as much as you need, and you pay me back whenever we sell some of your jewellery to cover the amount spent."

"Thank you so much, Haïk! I may take you up on it. I will let you know," I said, trying to swallow my tears. Such a kind and loyal friend!

Next, I called Lefki. Yes, she had found two seats, with oxygen and all, but needed to issue the tickets within twenty-four hours if I agreed. I did. She said she would go ahead and issue the tickets and I could send her the money later. What a gem of a girl!

I promised to send her a cheque in the next few days.

Then I called Noella. Yes, she had gotten from her pilot husband all the coordinates for the Air Canada executive to whom Dr. Mount should send his report. But there was another catch. Air Canada asked me to make funeral arrangements in Fort Lauderdale, for a service to be available on call, if the "worst" happened on board the flight, so that the crew would know to whom to deliver the corpse… I shivered. And they wanted the coordinates of this funeral service. *My God, Father is not dead yet! Help me!*

I immediately called Moshonas, the local Greek funeral service on Park Avenue, explained the situation and asked how they could help me. Very helpful, they gave me a telephone number in Fort Lauderdale.

The people in Florida were really efficient and very kind. They explained I didn't need to book their services in advance, that they were very close to the airport and that upon a phone call they would be at the airport within minutes. And of course, I could give their coordinates to Air Canada.

Finally relieved, I called Mrs. Helen Bond, in Bonita, told her I was coming down with my father and asked her how I could book a wheelchair. As the angel on Earth that she is, she told me she would take care of everything and would see me the moment we arrived. And she gave me her personal taxi service number so that I could arrange for the driver to meet us at Fort Lauderdale Airport and drive us to Bonita.

Thank you, God, I know you are by our side now…

That night, I related to Tito, matter-of-factly, what I had done. I added that our friend Haïk would advance me the money I needed, without interest, taking my jewellery on consignment.

Tito looked at me in disbelief… He paled. Bit his lips. Then without a word, he rose, slammed the door and stormed out of the house…

I sank onto a chair, bruised by his attitude, my heart pounding…

He returned half an hour later.

He came straight to me, hugged me, kissed me.

"I apologize for my behaviour, Erato. I know I did hurt you. It was because I love you. I was afraid, because I can't be with you. I was afraid you would crumble and I would lose you. But I see now how determined and strong you are. So, count on me. Tell Haïk you don't need his help. Write a cheque, tomorrow, for the tickets, from our account. I will raise the limit on our Visa for you to use freely. I will also raise our bank credit limit, if you need to take advantage of it… And call me if things get rough. I will quit everything and come…"

His voice was low and muffled with emotion as he stroke my hair.

I hugged and kissed him, my face bathed in grateful tears…

XV – The Trip

After I gave the good news of "We go ahead" to Father and saw his eyes glean with pleasure, I told our daughters about our plan.

"Good, if you can cope with it…" answered pragmatic Kathy. "Don't worr about Dad, I will help him." *Yes, my Darling, you need care for yourself, but ar always so willing to help…*

"Great, Mother! Excellent idea! It will do you both good. Are you sure yo can manage, alone, though?" exclaimed on the phone my ever enthusiasti Gaby.

"I'm sure I will, I feel good about it," I reassured her.

"Then go ahead!"

The eve of our departure a huge bouquet of red roses arrived for Stavros.

"Have a safe trip and a wonderful time in Bonita! With all my love. Your Gaby."

"She is so special, my Gaby…" sighed Father, wiping away a tear. He kisse the roses and hugged the bouquet in his arms as if hugging Gaby, his firs grandchild, though he adored Kathy just as much.

Next morning, before our departure, Stavros feverishly asked me for a not pad and a pen: "I have to write this down. Strange! It's a voice asking me t write this down, it's very important!"

> *In the year 2000 there will be no great catastrophe as some prophecies let us suspect. There will be no end of the world. Do not be afraid. There is only going to be a solar eclipse. A simple solar eclipse. That's all…*

"The voice is the one of Laplace[1], the great French astronomer of the 18 century… I don't know how it reached me. You have to publish this!

---

[1] Laplace (Pierre Simon, marquis de) French astronomer, mathematician, physician (1749-1827). Wrote about celestial mecanical and probability calculations. Famous for his cosmogony (1796) where the solar system would be issued from a nebula. (as per Académie française, mentionned in Larousse).

"It's very important! Send it to Mary!" concluded Stavros, all excited.

"I will," I promised.

I called Mary Kalipolitis and asked her to publish it in the short notices columns of our Association's bulletin. She agreed.

We kissed and hugged with Kathy and then Tito drove us to the Airport.

When we checked in at the Air-Canada ticket counter, an employee approached us with the wheelchair. We pre-boarded and all went smoothly after that.

Father was completely transformed, happy, beaming with hopeful expectations. Even his trembling stopped. He devoured his whole breakfast, without my help, hands steady: bacon and eggs, croissants, jelly, butter, orange juice and coffee. I was flabbergasted. It was the second time during his sickness that I had witnessed the beneficial transformation of his mind power over his sick body. The first one had occurred months ago during our Association's afternoon tea-dance, when he was singing and clapping hands with enthusiasm…

Upon our arrival at Fort Lauderdale, Father accepted without fuss the wheelchair offered by the ground hostess. I guess he was in a hurry to move on. In the lobby, I spotted someone brandishing a card with our name. It was Mr. Micelli, the taxi driver from Bonita. Short, strong, with dark olive skin. Efficient. He helped Father to the car, loaded our baggage… Outside, it was sunny and the hot Florida weather hit us with its warm breath… After a swift drive through Alligator Alley, we reached Bonita Springs. We stopped at a *Cash & Carry* and I shopped for a whole week of supplies. Then we drove on to Bonita Beach. When we stopped in front of Casa Bonita I, the sun was still up and the air was wonderfully balmy.

I saw, with relief, Helen Bond come towards us pushing a wheelchair. She must have been watching for us. We chatted, exchanging news about our families. "Call me if you need anything…" she said, patting my arm as we moved towards the condo entrance.

Mr. Micelli insisted on helping us into our second floor apartment and with unloading the groceries. The apartment had been opened up by Helen Bond (What a thoughtful friend!), and the sun was pouring in from the balcony door, opened to the sea… Stavros, impatient, holding on to Mr. Micelli with both hands, walked straight to the balcony, and sat in a rocking chair, breathing in the fresh sea air.

When I shook Mr. Micelli's hand, showing my gratitude for his kindness, he said, simply: "I understand how you both feel… My father had lung cancer… I will be completely at your disposal. Please call me any time you need me. I will set aside all other calls and come." I thanked him, deeply moved.

Then I went to hug Stavros… He was beaming… I put a blanket on his shoulders, and left him to enjoy the fiery Florida sundown… Next I called Tito to tell him how well everything had gone, beyond all expectations. I also called the Lee County Sheriff's Department. A very polite policeman said the sheriff would be in next morning.

Finally I started to unpack and prepare a light dinner.

"She did it again. This woman is remarkable," said Stavros over the juicy macaroni mince-meat-tomato dinner I prepared.

He was talking about Helen Bond.

Mrs. Bond was very special. When my mother had died, about ten years before, we all came to Bonita for a short vacation, following Dr. Egeli's advice; a beneficial change needed for all of us, he had insisted. It was just Christmas Time. As we opened the door of the condo then, we were surprised to see in the sunlight flooding in through the open balcony doors, a small decorated Christmas tree on the dining room table, a plate of Christmas cookies baked by Mrs. Bond, and small gifts for both kids and adults. Little cards spread on the table were inviting us for a series of afternoon tea-parties and dinners at our good friends throughout the building. As Gaby and Kathy started to scream with joy over their gifts, I had to brush away my tears and try to smile at so much kindness.

There was something extraordinary about this place. A feeling of goodwill and heavenly blessing… All thanks to the people that lived there…

Father, who was used to having me around, asked me anxiously now if I could sleep in the same room with him. I obliged, and prepared the portable cot, beside the comfortable electrical hospital bed, the bed the condo had come with from its former paraplegic owner. I raised the head of Father's bed and left the balcony door open to let the sea air in. It felt good. I slept, lulled by the gentle rhythm of the waves lapping on the beach.

XVI – The Sojourn

The first thing I did the next morning was to call the Lee County Sheriff and explain our situation. He was very understanding and compassionate. He gave me the name of a doctor on Bonita Beach Road who should see my father as soon as possible so that I had no problems when the inevitable happened. He ended our conversation with some comforting remarks. God bless these good hearted Floridians!

The doctor's clinic was really very close. I booked an appointment for early afternoon.

At about 10 a.m., after a balcony breakfast that Father, surprisingly, seemed to enjoy, I helped Stavros change to his boxer bathing suit, put his captain's denim cap on his head, took two large towels, got him into the wheelchair and we took the elevator down to the beach through the condo's side passage. It was a bright sunny day, about 28 degrees, with a caressing light breeze. The sand was still cool under my bare feet; the strong sun was just warming the skin, not burning yet, and making the sea sparkle with ribbons of diamonds.

Stavros looked around with delight. He opened his mouth and took a few deep breaths of the sea smelling air and remained silent, a contented smile on his lips. His gaze embraced the few bathers: some mothers with kids screaming with joy as they splashed in the choppy waves, two young girls trying body-surfing, a middle-aged man swimming vigorously towards the open sea… a school of small birds… a few seagulls in the sky shrieking to each other, circling and diving into the sea, and, not far away, the white solitary beautiful heron that welcomed us every time we had come here after Mama passed away…

"Nice," said Stavros after a long while, "let's go in," motioning to the sea with his chin.

I helped him out of the wheelchair and we walked to the edge of the water. But there we saw that the tide had caused a sharp ridge, over three feet deep. With the strong choppy waves, it was not easy to get into the water. Father put one foot in. "It's cold!" he cried. But he could not touch down. He tried to sit on the sand bar and let himself glide down to the water but a strong wave hit him almost flattening him.

My God, his knees are so weak. How is he going to get up? I wondered with anxiety. I rolled the wheelchair over by his side and helped him get himself up while he held onto it with one arm. It was a struggle. All the joy was gone from Father's face. But he did not want to give up.

"Give me your arm, I will try to jump in," he said, grasping my forearm.

"Father, the waves are very strong today. I don't know how to help you get in the water. I am not strong enough to hold you against these waves. And you know I can't swim…," I said loudly to be heard over the splashing waves.

Stavros bit his lips and, resolute, tried again. In vain. The splashing hit of the foaming waves was too strong, making him sway at every attempt.

"Damn it," he exclaimed bitterly. He dropped into the wheelchair, an angry and painful look in his eyes.

Oh, Tito, how I wish you were here now! …

"I will bring down a pail and a sponge, and I will sponge you with sea water," I proposed. "It's the sea water that counts, isn't it? We will still have its benefit. Wait for me here," I said trying to sound cheerful.

I put the chair brake on, and ran to the condo, without waiting for an answer.

I came back with two large plastic pails and a sponge. I filled them with sea water, while getting soaked by the waves. Then I started to generously sponge-bath Father with this salted water that Hippocrates held as great medicine. Stavros shook his head and let me do it, without uttering a word, resigned but sad. *Oh God, so sad…* I knew the futility of my gestures, but Father believed in the benefit of sea water, and, having experienced the miracle of positive mind power, I was ready to do anything to maintain it.

But the charm was broken… Later, Father hardly touched the appetizing lunch I prepared and served on the balcony. I forced myself to cough excessively (I always had a little allergic cough, triggered by air conditioning and many other allergens). After a while, I said to Stavros that I had made an appointment with a local clinic to get medicine for my cough, and I proposed he come along. A second opinion on his condition would do no harm, would it? He only shrugged without answering.

The doctor was young, smart and understanding. While he examined me, I explained Father's situation to him in a low voice. Finally I turned to Father and said that the doctor had agreed to examine him also.

Stavros let him do it, then asked for his opinion. The doctor explained in a loud voice, that it was a lingering pneumonia case which really took time to get better at Stavros' age. Father could also take my cough medicine if he needed to… Yes, he could go to the sea, but not stay for too long… And yes, he could sunbathe with a sun protection cream… The doctor offered to prescribe a manual breathing pump if Stavros desired… Father shook his head. He didn't like inhalators…

The doctor gave me his card, jotting his home telephone number on it. "Call me anytime, even in the middle of the night. I will come," he said. Then he wished me "good strength" and gave us both a strong hand shake.

"Nice chap," commented Father as I wheeled him out of the office.

"Come on in," invited Mrs. Bond, when we returned to the condo entrance. She was just in front of 105, their ground floor apartment. Her door was open and she was chatting with Ken, the building maintenance manager.

I thought seeing the Bonds might lift Father's spirits, so I gladly accepted. Their home, in pristine white with Delft blue accents, was cheerful.

Mrs. Bond's knitting was lying on the white couch – she was always busy making scarves or afghans for her friends as Christmas gifts. Khalil Gibran's *The Prophet* was on a side table. Mr. Bond was sitting in his wheelchair, a throw covering his lap to conceal his amputated leg. Years of heart ailment and bad blood circulation had ended in this amputation. But the Bonds were always joyful, always ready to help others, participating in all the condo's social gatherings. Their home was open at all times and their love continuously and steadily poured on us all. We all loved and admired them for their strength and their faith in dealing with life's hardships; they were our role models.

Mr. Bond had been a petroleum company executive in Aruba. A weak heart condition had forced him into an early retirement and they had settled at Bonita Springs. He enjoyed boating, and, in the past, Tito and Father had enjoyed some pleasant boating afternoons with him. When father's hearing was better, he used to enjoy some lively interesting discussions with Mr. Bond.

Mr. Bond welcomed us with a big smile. This time I did most of the talking. Father was mute and brooding throughout the visit. We left with their wish "The Lord be with you," echoing in the air as Mrs. Bond squeezed my shoulder in empathy.

Because the head of the electrical bed could be raised, Father slept better and coughed less. The handy bathroom next to the bedroom, with the built-in seat and movable shower head, made our life easier. The only effort Stavros needed to make was to get into his wheelchair. He could even roll it himself to the bathroom and then stand up if he had to.

The days passed but the sand ridge and the strong surf did not subside. During the next few mornings Father asked to have his "sea water" sponge treatment inside, in our bathroom... However, he agreed to a daily morning promenade on the beach, in khakis, shirt, sweater (March was still cool despite the sun and Father was frail). And always his blue captain's cap on.

In spite of the fresh sea air Father's appetite diminished. He didn't want to eat, claiming he had difficulty swallowing. So we were back to soft boiled eggs, soups and purees, grilled fish that I served almost mashed, and custards with soft fruits.

Stavros would spend the afternoons rocking himself on the balcony, watching the bathers and the birds, the occasional sighting of a porpoise family leaping in line not far from our shore. And finally the magnificent sunsets. Sometimes Father would hum old songs from his childhood or youth, as if he wished to retreat completely in the past... I would cover his shoulders with a light throw when it got chilly and sit beside him holding his hand and hum the songs with him. I consoled myself that this was a hundred times better than what Father would have to live through back in Canada.

"Can we go to the Point?" asked Stavros Saturday morning. It was another beautiful March day, the sun blinding and hot, the sea shimmering, the surf foaming with a caressing murmur on the sand, the flocks of birds chirping, some pelicans flying low, families picnicking on the beach with seagulls circling above them hoping for a feast, but very few bathers.

The Point was at the end of our peninsula, some two miles down the white beach, bordered by mango and eucalyptus trees and with sharp high rocks here and there advancing to the water; rocks that we usually had to detour in swimming to continue towards the tip. Until a few years ago, we used to go fishing or shelling there with Tito, Gaby, Kathy and Stavros. There were some bird nests and consequently flocks of birds hopping gently, "learning", on the wet sand, and an incredible variety of shells washed up by the waves. The girls used to make crafts with them after we cleaned and boiled them: mirrors framed with big shells, napkin holders, animals, painted sand dollars, necklaces, earrings.

I estimated it would be impossible to reach the Point all the way along the beach with a wheelchair.

"It will be easier if we go through BBC, the Beach and Breakfast Club," I said to Father. He pouted.

I pushed the wheelchair on the asphalt side road to the BBC entrance gate. The Hotel-Club was built close to the tip of the peninsula. At the iron gate, I explained to the guard our purpose and asked permission to go through their premises. He was very understanding.

"But you won't be able to reach the Point. After the last storm, we built a protective wall with boulders. I'm afraid the only access to the tip is by sea", he said.

What a pity, I thought. Well, it was better than nothing.

We wheeled through the gate to their tennis court and along their beach sidewalk facing the Point passage. The boulders were not very high, half submerged in water, but made walking through impossible.

"We can't go any further by land," I explained to father. "The Point is only accessible by sea now…"

Stavros shook his head. "Nothing is the same… Everything is changed. Nothing is the same, anymore…" he whispered, a deep sadness in his voice.

Nevertheless, the view was still magnificent. Our gaze could embrace the crescent of the beach terminating at the Point. Behind it, the shores of Fort Myers Beach were clearly visible. A white heron, some dried washed-out tree trunks and driftwood in front of the Australian eucalyptus pines, seagulls circling and breaking the deep silence with their cries mingled with the caressing murmur of the surf…

Stavros, mute, stayed there for a long time … Hugging all this with eyes wide open, perusing, inhaling the revivifying sea air…

I sat on a sea-shell bed beside him and looked at him. *What are you musing about Father? The times spent here with Katina, with our whole family? Your whole life? Your sickness? The end? …*

Father's gaze seemed turned inward but also outward too. He was deep in thought, almost in a trance… It seemed to me that I read resignation and acceptance on his face, acceptance of the inevitable, of all things coming to an end but also gratitude for having being here, for having lived all this… It was as if he was in communion with nature, with creation, with the universe… transcending time and place…

I didn't dare utter a word…

After about forty minutes, Stavros looked at me. "Let's go home," he said without any comment, in a voice devoid of any emotion…

This morning I made a reservation at the *Roof Top* across the street, for their famous Sunday Brunch. I reserved a table by the large bay window. The view from the second floor, covering the whole bay, was extraordinary. When the waiter placed his wheelchair in front of this panorama, Father finally had a gleam in his eye. We had had many pleasant family Sunday brunches here in the past; the girls were always excited about the variety of the dishes – especially the sweets and exotic fruits – and the friendliness of the waiters who loved pampering kids. Kathy, when she was about five, was smitten with Billy, the youngest and always beaming young waiter, and she had declared solemnly she would marry him when she grew up…

My head full of happy memories, I went to the buffet and prepared two plates, one for me, one for Father. The restaurant's waffle machine was broken, so I chose pancakes instead, covered with scoops of strawberries, mangoes, papayas and topped with ice cream and chocolate syrup.

"They have no waffles," I explained to Stavros, "We will have to be content with pancakes, and then eggs and sweets—"

"No waffles? You know I came here for the waffles!"

"Their waffle machine is broken. The pancakes are very good as well, try them. We can go to a Waffle House this afternoon, to have some waffles if you wish."

"No, it's not the same thing!" He pushed his plate aside, without touching it, chewing on his lips, very disappointed.

I tried to swallow my tears, saying to myself that the sickness must have started making its way up to his brain, affecting his thinking, as the doctors had warned me months ago.

Stavros did not take a bite of food that morning, and he brooded non-stop. I hastened to finish my plate and we left. He refused to go to a Waffle House, "It's not the same thing," he repeated stubbornly…

The week passed with the same routine of indoor sea-water sponge baths, morning wheeled promenades along the beach, lunch and dinner on the balcony facing the sea, short chats with the Bond's. Stavros brooded at times but he seemed to enjoy the magnificent flaming sunsets over the sea, the seagulls' and pelicans' flight, and the usual porpoise family swimming close to the shore.

"You know, Mr. Bond told me that wherever there are porpoises there are no sharks. That's why we have no sharks in Bonita Beach," Father explained to me, his gaze following the dolphins' plays in the shimmering sea.

As a ritual now he would rock in his preferred chair and hum old songs from his past till the sun dipped into the sea. I would listen to him, often joining his humming if I knew the tune or the words.

I would either sit in a chair beside him, my arm around his shoulders, or stand behind him and put my arms around his neck. Then his eyes would shine, he would raise his voice a tone and pat my hands. These sunset meditative contemplations were the sweetest times of the day. I wondered why he preferred these very old songs from his youth and childhood. Was it a wish, a daydream, to return to this happy period of his life? A flight from the present? But I just went along with him, without any questions, afraid to break the spell. His health was not worsening and his mood was finally getting better. Now he smiled more often and ate without help the soft food I lovingly prepared for him.

The second Saturday of our stay, Stavros woke up all excited, "We have to go to the Annunciation Church tomorrow," he said, eyes flashing. "I dreamed again of the Annunciation Angel, Gabriel! As before, he called my name three times. 'Stavré, Stavré, Stavré!' Like that..."

I shivered. "I'll see if I can find an Annunciation Church here, Father—"

"The one on Fort Myers is an Annunciation Church, I'm sure. The icon at the right, in the narthex, always depicts the saint to whom the church is dedicated. And I remember from past visits during the Easter service that the icon depicted the Annunciation, with Archangel Gabriel announcing the good news to Panaghia."

"I'll arrange for the taxi to take us to the church tomorrow," I promised.

I called Mr. Micelli and reserved his taxi for all day Sunday.

Mr. Micelli arrived promptly around 10 a.m. He helped Father to the taxi, folded the wheelchair at the back, and once at the Church's courtyard, he helped Father again into the wheelchair. He would meet us there at noon, after the service.

The moment I wheeled Stavros to the narthex, the entrance hall of the church, I saw the large icon of the Annunciation of the Virgin, on the right icon-stand as Stavros had remembered... We each lit a candle, then I wheeled him to the back of the *solea*, the main church, and I stood beside him.

When the priest raised the Chalice inviting the worshippers to Holy Communion, Father stood up.

"I want to take Holy Communion," he said.

I motioned the wheelchair.

"I will push you," I whispered.

"No, I will walk," he answered. He refused my arm, and walked straight up the middle aisle, to the priest, without any help...

I stood in awe, for a moment, then left the wheelchair there, and followed him.

The priest looked at us intensely...

Father took Holy Communion solemnly. The priest, Father Kontinos, was visibly moved. Did he recognize Father from last year's Easter service? Or even from earlier times, years back, when he conducted the Mass in a trailer, the first Greek Orthodox Church in Fort Myers? Father Kontinos knew all his parishioners by name and noted all newcomers. And he might have had a glimpse of Father in the wheelchair as we came in... "God be with you," he said and blessed Stavros. Father returned to the back of the church, straight and without help, and then sat quietly in the wheelchair...

Mr. Micelli was waiting for us with his taxi at the end of the service. He drove us to *Fisherman's Wharf*, for lunch. Anghelos Letsos, the Greek owner, was an old friend. We had met him years ago when he operated a humble hamburger stand at the same location and we became friends. Our girls, very young then, loved to play waitress and helped serve on many occasions. Now he had a beautiful glass-walled fish restaurant, tables covered in blue-and-white chequered tablecloths, comfortable leather chairs, fish nets, and paintings and photographs with Greek themes adorning the walls. Anghelo was thrilled to see us. A bit astonished to see Father in a wheelchair he helped him get out of it, and hugged us both. He offered us the best table, at a window corner, and sat with us to inquire about the latest family news. His wife Joyce and their two boys, Vangheli and Peter, joined us. They just happened to be there this Sunday noon. Angelo asked with his eyes what was wrong with Father.

"You have to show me what you have done with the kitchen," I said, and I walked with him to the back of the restaurant. When I explained to him the situation with Father, he was shattered. He scolded me for not letting him know earlier. He loved my father. He always called him Papou. We came back to the table together, with a plate of Greek salad and a bottle of ouzo. There were very few patrons yet. Anghelo brought a portable radio-cassette player, placed it on a chair, put on upbeat Greek bouzouki music and turned the sound to maximum.

Father beamed, happy. "Live long, *Palikari mou,* my brave son," he said patting Anghelo's arm.

Anghelo smiled, and filled Father's glass with ouzo and ice that turned the liquor into a milky white. Father, to my surprise, ate the salad with appetite and started to sing along the songs he knew, ignoring the patrons' amused stares. Anghelo joined in, and me too. Soon a waiter came with a huge plate of grilled sea-bass, all cleaned and basted in lemon-oil-parsley vinaigrette. Father finished every bit of the portion in his plate! Joyce offered him a cigarette, a Pall Mall.

"Oh, that's nice, but I long for a Salem. Filtered," said Stavros, taking the cigarette anyway.

Last photo of Stavros with Erato, Anghelos Letsos and his kids.

Father liked Joyce very much; Anghelo's American wife was also her husband's business partner. She was smart, simple and kind; and a beauty. Of middle height, slim, with wavy blond hair, sincere large hazel eyes and a wide mouth always wearing a warm heartening smile. She had converted to the Orthodox Church and had learned Greek in order to raise their two sons and daughter "properly," as she explained.

Joyce excused herself from the table. She returned in a few minutes with a pack of filtered Salems for Stavros...

Father took one out, lit it from her cigarette, and inhaled with delight. I thought he couldn't smoke any more, that smoke would burn his throat and make him cough. He had been refusing Tito's cigarettes lately… But he enjoyed this long Salem, leaving it dangling from his lips with obvious pleasure…

Now Anghelos put on a cassette with Greek Tsamiko – war dances. He removed two neighbouring tables and their chairs and he started to dance. Wow! Tall, thin, muscled, his black hair waving, his black eyes flaming, twirling, his feet stamping to the beat, his feet high almost touching the ceiling, he was the war god, Aris, personified.

Father was thrilled. His mouth was open in a continuous smile, he clapped his hands and stamped his feet to the tempo and he put his two fingers in his mouth to whistle with enthusiasm. "*Ya sou leventi mou, na zissis! Hara stin Mana pou se ghenissé!*" (Hail to you my brave one, live long. Joy to the mother who brought you to the world), he shouted, moved.

I was flabbergasted with the change in Father. A miracle started this morning in the church with the Holy Communion and perpetuated now thanks to Anghelo and Joyce…

"Promise to come again. Any time," said Anghelo when we left, as he helped Father walk to the taxi. "And call us if you need anything. Really. Even in the middle of the night…You know I will rush over," he insisted, squeezing my arm. I knew he would… We hugged.

"God bless you," I said.

"God be with you two," he answered seriously, and stayed outside, waving till we pulled away.

That afternoon, Father, was silent as he rocked himself on the balcony as usual. He seemed to meditate, his gaze embracing the flaming sunset and its shimmering reflection on the sea. A sailboat silhouetted in mauve light glided silently far away… A flock of pelicans flew low with cries in the red sky… Then silence… broken by the soft kiss of the waves on the dark sand… And the motionless white heron, as if keeping vigil…

I covered Father's frail shoulders with an afghan and, standing behind him, I locked my hands on his chest and put my cheek on his head. He patted my hands with his and then his hands gripped mine. "I want you to know that these days spent with you here are the most beautiful of my life…" he whispered. "It was worth being sick to experience this happiness. I bless the sickness that brought you so close to me."

I bit my lips. I was glad I was behind him and he could not see the tears in my eyes. "They were happy for me too, Father," I said.

He started to sing a favourite song of his, the "*Voskopoula*":

I fell in love with a shepherdess…
I was a non-speaking child, a ten-year old boy…
I told her, my Mario, I love you,
I am crazy about you.
She grabbed me by the waist
She kissed me on the lips.
And she told me,
'You're still young for love's whispers and pains'…

I knew the song well, we used to sing it all three of us with Mama. I accompanied him in a soft voice.

Continuing to hold my hands Stavros now started singing Mama's beloved song:

A heart without love,
Is like a faded spring flower.
A heart orphaned by love,
Is like an abandoned, spider-webbed church.
It is like a dark night,
Where all hope for it is lost…

I sang with him, trying to control my shaking voice.

When the sun disappeared into the sea and the sky turned to purple, we went inside.

After a light supper, Stavros sat upright on the bed. "Come, bring your note pad, and sit close to me," he invited me.

I took my note pad and sat on the bed, beside him.

"Now, ask me whatever you wanted to know about your Mama," he said with a grin.

"You must have loved her a lot… Did she love you as much?"

"Not as much as she loved you," he said with a smile. "From the moment you were born, you were everything to her… There was nothing she wouldn't do for you… Our life revolved around you. You came first… And when you became sick, she used her strength for both of us. She had an unshakable faith in God… And you healed."

"Did you resent me for Mama's love and attention to me?"

"No, no! I loved you the same way. I just wanted some more special times alone with her, just with her, for her and me… You understand, you're married now… But she wouldn't have anything without you, away from you–"

"Not completely true, Father. When you were in hospital, in Sparta, she left me with your mother and Ismet Hanoum and she came to see you."

"Oh, yes. She did, indeed. Crazy girl! Travel alone in the middle of Anatolia in such difficult times..."

He sat silent for a while, reminiscing, his gaze turned inward in a tender gleam. Then he looked at me seriously but with smiling lips: "Now, take this down. We have not much time. The only advice I will ever give you is this: Put your husband first, in your life. I know you adore your daughters, but kids grow up, fly away, build their own nests. Your husband is the one to be with you to the end... He is a great guy, Tito. You two will have skirmishes and misunderstandings for sure; this is part of living. But never, never, hurt his ego. A man's ego is... Think before you talk. Or say nothing. Even if it's painful. It will pass. Fight for him, with him, be there for him, support him during difficult moments... Now, anything else you want to ask me?"

I shook my head, swallowing his words. Why did he say, 'We have not much time?' What did he sense or foresee?

Stavros rubbed his heart with his palm.

"Are you hurting, Father? Do you want some pain killers?"

"No. We had a great vacation here. That's enough. Now it's time to go home. Tomorrow!"

"Tomorrow? I don't know if I can find plane seats for tomorrow."

"Try!"

I was startled. I began to realize that he knew the end was near and wanted to return home to end his life there... I tried to persuade him to stay a few more days, another week, but he persisted.

"Tomorrow!"

I went to the phone and dialed Air Canada's 24-hour number. Yes, seats were available in tomorrow's noon flight. I reserved oxygen on board and a wheelchair at both ends, and called Mr. Micelli for an early taxi ride to Fort Lauderdale. Then I called Tito to let him know of our arrival. He warned me he had a morning meeting with our best client and might not be at the airport. "Take a limousine, I will be home by the time you arrive," he said.

I told Father we could fly home, tomorrow. He nodded with a wide smile. He rubbed his heart again, but he refused my offer of pain killers. I adjusted the bed to a high back, and started to pack.

Stavros was singing now in a loud voice hymns from the liturgy of the dead!

"My soul glorifies the Lord..."

Then, hymns from Easter:

"It's the day of Resurrection. Enlighten Peoples! ..."

I listened, dumbfounded, not knowing what to say, not daring to say anything... Was he singing to suppress physical pain? Was he singing to silence an internal voice? Or to express an internal voice? Or to formulate a prayer?

I laid on the cot, next to his bed. Every now and then he raised himself on his elbow and looked at me as if to make sure I was there, that I had not gone away.

"Do you want anything, Father? May I help you?"

"Nothing, nothing, go to sleep," he would answer, lying back.

Finally at around one in the morning I heard the regular rhythm of his breathing. He fell asleep. I didn't...

The flight home was terrible. We were caught in a severe storm turbulence that shook and bounced the airplane from all sides. All flight attendants were strapped in their seats. The two of us occupied the front bulkhead seats where an oxygen tank could be hooked up. The violently shaking plane disturbed Stavros. He became pale and had difficulty breathing. The flight attendant noticed it and helped me put on him the oxygen mask. I usually am afraid of flying and become sick if there is turbulence. This time, surprisingly, I managed to stay very calm, for Stavros. I kept pressing the oxygen mask to his mouth and nose, held his hand, "It is only a storm, Father. The captain announced it could last 45 minutes, at the most. Take deep breaths and try to relax," I said to him, and forgot all about my fear, concentrating to comfort him and make him relax. It was a very bumpy flight for the whole three-hour trip and the severe turbulence lasted not 45 minutes but two whole hours.

At the Montreal airport, I missed Tito terribly. The ground hostess helped Father in the wheelchair while I pushed the cart with our bags stacked in. Father's condition had deteriorated unexpectedly, maybe due to the flight conditions. He was too weak to hold on to the wheelchair's armrests. At one point going down a ramp, he slid dangerously from his seat. I stepped in front to stop him from sliding further and protected him with my body and arms. The ground hostess suggested we strap him in for protection. I protested. "Just hold the wheelchair bending backwards, like that. Or, take hold of the luggage cart and let me do it," I said. She refused the laggage cart, but followed my suggestion. We made it safely to the taxi stand. But by now I was really annoyed with my husband for not being there. Couldn't he cut his meeting short? Was it more important than us?

The moment the taxi turned into our garage drive, Tito stepped out of the house. There was icy snow on the ground. At a glance he saw Stavros' weak condition. He asked the driver to join hands with him to make a seat for Stavros and that's how they carried him up the few steps to our front door and all the way up into our split level guest room. They placed Father in a freshly made electrical hospital bed, adjusting the back for comfort. I looked around, amazed. The room, close to our own bedroom, had been emptied and rearranged. Besides the hospital bed, there was a wheelchair, a portable closed toilet seat, Stavros' own reclining chair, the TV set on a portable table across the bed, and another armchair on the other side.

I looked at Tito with surprise and admiration as he came back to the room after paying the taxi driver. "How did you arrange all this in half a day, since I called you late last night?" I asked him.

He looked at me without smiling. "Noella!" he said – the marvellous liaison nurse between CLSC and the Royal Victoria Hospital, who had helped me get Stavros on the Air Canada flight. "She is a true professional. She managed to have this bed delivered this morning through CLSC and advised me where to rent the rest. We also arranged for two retired nurses to come and take care of your father on a 24-hour basis. Mme Lambert and Mme Bouchard. It will be easier for you. Mme Lambert will arrive tonight at 8 p.m. so that we all have time to settle, in privacy. And Mme Bouchard will be here at 8 tomorrow morning."

I stared at him with mixed feelings of awe and gratitude. This was Tito's swift and thoughtful reaction to crisis… And he was also claiming me back to our bedroom… I kissed him with all my love, fighting back my tears.

"This is better than downstairs," exclaimed Stavros in a feeble voice. "You arranged all this?"

Tito hugged him, and explained he had thought this arrangement would be better for Father's comfort. And he explained that a private nurse would come later. Stavros made a pout with his lips. He did not appreciate being cared for by strangers, but he must have realized his forces were weakening. He did not protest. "Well, this will be better for Erato, also," he said, "she won't have to run by my side all the time."

"I'll be with you all the same, Father. And at nights, our bedroom is a few steps away now. I will leave our bedroom door open," I reassured him.

Father smiled, resigned, and laid his head on the cushions.

"What would you like to eat?" Tito asked him.

"Pizza. And Tito, please look at the lottery tickets you bought for me. I have a feeling we might have won something."

"Done!"

It was a tearful reunion with Kathy when she came back from university. But as I expected, Stavros, seated on the armchair, had only a single bite from the pizza: it was too hard for him to swallow – what a reversal from yesterday's meal at Anghelo's! But the ready-made vanilla custard was OK.

No he didn't want the TV on. But did Tito check with the lottery ticket?

"Yes, we have," I answered. He had won ten dollars.

"We won?"

"Yes."

"How much?"

"Ten," Tito squeezed my shoulder, to stop there.

"Thousand?"

Tito's squeeze became stronger as he answered, "Yes, ten thousand..."

Stavros smiled, happy. "I knew it. Finally! After so many years of buying lottery tickets... At least it will pay for all my care and all this..." he said motioning to the bed and the rest.

"Most of it is free; Canada's Health Care gift. And you know you should never think about money," said Tito, patting my father's shoulder.

Father put his hand on Tito's, with affection. "Well, we are lucky to live in Canada. This country is blessed. Such care does not exist in the old country. Anyway, this lottery win makes me feel good, all the same. Happy to contribute a little. And listen, if there is any money left... give it to the girls."

Madame Lambert came at 8 p.m. sharp. A short brunette, sympathetic, with an intelligent gaze behind her rimless spectacles.

Father had a disturbed night. By morning he really had difficulty getting up, even with us supporting him.

Madame Bouchard arrived at 8 a.m. An athletic, grey haired plump lady, looking efficient and competent. She helped Stavros with his toilet and suggested changes to make his bed-stay more comfortable.

I realized with surprised sadness how fast Stavros' condition had deteriorated.

He was really weak now, didn't want to talk and preferred to sleep. Although I stayed with him most of the time I wondered whether the "hospital" look and care were factors in this deterioration. Maybe they invited Father to let go... Feelings of guilt for changing his environment, even for the better, overhelmed me. Madame Bouchard motioned me to leave the room with her, then she explained that this was the cancer doing. "It has flared up, going to the brain. It is a foreseeable, sudden, effect. And it is fast. Be prepared for the worst within 24 hours. Trust me. Unfortunately, I know…"

"What can I do to help?" I asked, devastated, although I should have been prepared for the outcome after Father's Sunday night behaviour.

"Not much. Let him sleep. You may be close to him, if you wish. In any case, I promise to call you the minute he wakes up," she told me, touching my arm.

Stavros refused to eat. Just juices and other liquids.

Our friends the K's stopped to see us early that evening. They had prepared a slide show about Istanbul, to cheer Stavros up. We arranged him in a sitting position, and put the slide show on. As he started watching, I joined my friends in the dining room. They had brought take outs from *Calypso*, an Armenian restaurant in Laval whose owner was from Istanbul. How nice of them! I prepared a plate of pureed eggplant salad and fish-roe dip (Tarama) for Stavros but as I expected he did not want to taste any of the Turkish delicacies.

After about ten minutes, the nurse came to tell me Stavros was asking for me.

"Turn this thing off," he said in a weak voice when I walked to his room. "Nice, but too many colours. They tire me. I want to rest."

I did as he asked and with the help of the nurse we arranged him for his night rest. I kissed him, he waved…

The nurses changed shift at 8 p.m. Father was already deeply asleep. I kept his door open.

I was awakened in the middle of the night by Father's loud voice. I ran to his side. He was in a kind of delirium. "Go forth, Androutso mou! Go forth, my brave. And you Diako! Thanassi mou! We are all behind you. We follow you. I follow you. *Aïdé*. I'm coming with my bare sword. *Eleftheria*! Liberty!"

He was in the middle of the battle of Greek Independence! He was fighting the Turks alongside the heroes of 1821 and before. His arm was making big sweeping motions above his head as if brandishing a sword.

I leaned forward, caressed his cheeks. "It is only a dream, Father. You are having a nightmare. Hush… Shush. I'm here now," I said in a soothing voice, trying to calm him down.

"He doesn't hear you," motioned Madame Lambert in silence.

In fact, Stavros opened his eyes, but his gaze was fixed past me, above me, in the void.

I kept caressing his face, his hair, his hands, putting my forehead against his. Finally, after a long while, he calmed down.

In the morning Stavros seemed to be in a deep sleep but he moaned weakly from time to time.

Noella came to see how he was doing. She took me out of the room. "It is the end, Erato. Do you want me to arrange a transfer to the RVH Palliative Centre and call for an ambulance?"

"Palliative Center? No! He wanted to be home. He wants to end his life at home. I'll keep him here!" I protested.

"It's your call. But it may be long and very painful. At the hospital they can ease his pain and his breathing with medication. You can't do this at home. If he were my father I would not hesitate to transfer him. You will still be with him. They are very kind and discreet at the Centre. It is not like a hospital ward. Besides, your father hears you but has lost all sense of time and location. He may not even recognize you. He is half gone. And as you see he is in pain. It can get worse…"

I bit my lips. "I don't know what to do…" I murmured.

Tito put his arm around me. "It's your decision, Erato. But Noella has a good point. And experience. If you don't want him to suffer…"

Trembling, I returned to the bedroom. I leaned toward Stavros. "Father, Father!" I called to him loudly, trying to wake him up.

He moaned, did not open his eyes. His breathing was difficult, very laboured now.

"Well?" asked Tito, squeezing my shoulder.

"Call…" I said to Noella.

I declined Tito's offer to come with us. I knew Father would prefer that I be alone with him. I promised Tito I would call him.

The room was large, sunny with many windows. The nurses were very efficient. They placed Stavros by a tall window. They were very gentle with him, put a pillow between his legs to avoid any painful contact. A young doctor examined him. "He has a nice tan. Were you down South?"

"Yes, we were in Florida. Came back Sunday," I replied.

"In this condition? Such care is very rare. He is lucky to have you…" he said.

Lucky to have me? Where was the luck? ...

The doctor prescribed an injection every four hours, or at shorter intervals, if needed. "Do not let him suffer," he instructed the nurse. "This will stop the pain and ease his breathing," he explained to me. "You can wipe his mouth and let him suck on these 'lollipops'. Do you want a Valium or something for yourself?"

"No. Thank you."

"There is a fully equipped kitchenette with a coffee machine and a lounge, next door," a male nurse informed me after giving Father his first shot.

They asked me to go to the Nurses' Post. Tito was on the phone. "You didn't call," he said. "All is OK, they are taking good care of Father. He is resting. No pain. Go to bed. I will call you if I need you," I said. "Are you all right? Are you sure you don't want me there?" he insisted. I was certain. He must have sensed it in my voice, as he seemed a bit more reassured.

I returned to the ward. I looked around. There was another patient across the way. He was sitting upright in his bed chatting joyously with his wife, two daughters, and his son.They were recalling past events and laughing with him. He waved at me. "Your father?"

"Yes."

"What is he suffering from?"

"Lung cancer, generalized."

"Mine is kidney. Suffering for almost fifteen years. I'm glad my kids are visiting today," he said with a wide smile, his hand on his wife's. "From Nova Scotia," he added with pride.

"What would you like to eat, Pa?" asked his son. "I'll get it for you. Just name it. Sweets? Chinese? Shell fish?"

"Oh, a hamburger. Just a plain double hamburger, all dressed. And French fries. That would be nice. And a Bud."

"Right-O," said the young man and off he went.

I didn't know how I felt. Stavros' breathing had eased now, he had stopped moaning and his hand responded to mine as I caressed it. He kept his eyes closed as if sleeping, but he was not.

"Are you thirsty?" I asked him.

He nodded, too weak to speak.

I dipped the 'lollipop' in the liquid that the nurse had brought and that looked like orange juice. Father sucked it avidly, like a baby sucking a pacifier. Strange, he really looked like a baby in his cradle! I combed his hair with my fingers.

"Any pain, Father?"

He shook his head.

"Want anything?"

Shook his head again for "no".

"Want to sleep?"

He nodded.

I let him rest. I made myself comfortable on the wide armchair and opened my Missal.

Soon, the other patient's young son returned with a hamburger for his Pa and a six-pack of Budweiser for the whole family. They clinked the beer cans and drank and joked with more laughter. The father finished his hamburger and fries with delight. He seemed tired. "Want to rest a bit" he said. The eldest daughter put a pan-flute concert by Zamphir on the CD player, after asking me whether it would disturb me. I reassured her it wouldn't.

They all stepped out to the lounge and let the old man to rest.

The music was beautiful, poignant and soothing at the same time. I closed my eyes and let it lull me.

I opened my eyes after a while to check on Stavros. He was relaxed and asleep. Then I gazed toward the old man. A smile was on his lips but he looked inanimate! I went closer. He was not breathing! I ran to the lounge to warn the family. They looked at each other, mouths open.

"Do you want me to call the nurse?" I asked.

"No," said the mother, calmly. "It's a blessing that he passed like that, peaceful and happy, in his sleep. He suffered for so long..."

They held hands, then they walked into the room. They circled the bed, talked to their man in whispers, as if he could listen to them, kissed him tenderly. Finally they walked calmly out, waving at me.

I stayed there, moved, in awe of their calm acceptance of the end of the life of their beloved. I wondered whether I could have half their strength.

The music had ended by now. A doctor came in to check the old man. He closed the curtain around him. After a while an orderly came in and wheeled the bed with the old man out...

I was all alone now in the large room with my father. The night nurse, a smiling, tiny, helpful brunette, came to see Stavros. She gave him another shot.

"If he moans, or expresses pain, call me. I can give him another one," she said.

Then she asked me if I needed a pill to relax. I declined.

She came back after a few minutes pushing a bed-chair. "This is more comfortable for the night," she said, arranging a pillow and a blanket for me. What a thoughtful young woman!

"How can I help him?" I asked her, motioning towards Father.

"Just hold his hand. He will feel it. And talk to him if you want. He may not respond but he will hear you. Hearing is the last to go," she said. Then she glided out to her post.

I knew Father could hear me. I recalled my out-of-body experience at the church in my youth and how I heard Father calling my name while I was watching from the ceiling…

I went through the CD box supplied by the hospital. I found a Brück violin concerto with Isaac Perlman. I put it on. The sweet melody, under the magical bow of Perlman, filled the room. Stavros stirred, opened his eyes. I leaned over him, caressed his forehead.

"When I was a little girl, you played the violin for me as a lullaby," I whispered in his ear, my hand holding his. He smiled, squeezed my hand… Closed his eyes again, beaming.

In a while, he opened his eyes again. Looked at me, then ahead, past me, behind me.

"Katina!" he cried, excited. *Was Katina behind me? Or did he take me for Katina?*

I leaned forward, caressed him, put my head on his forehead, then my lips on his cheek. "I'm here… I love you," I whispered, squeezing his hand. He looked into my eyes, then behind me again, squeezed my hand, smiled, closed his eyes and took a deep sigh… He stopped breathing… His hand squeeze weakened… His fingers left mine… An indescribable calm and serenity covered his face. A faint smile stayed on his lips.

"This is it," I murmured in his ear. "Let yourself fly up. You will see darkness around you but a light will twinkle at the end. Follow this light. I went to it and came back in my youth, remember? Follow Katina, she will lead you to the light. To the creator of this light. It is a beautiful all embracing, all loving light. Once you pass through its threshold you will find there all your loved ones who arrived earlier. Katina will be with you. Remember how she described this new world to us? Life will continue. I won't see you but you will see me. You were a great father. A precious grandfather. You taught us to live for the moment, to enjoy the moment…You taught us honesty, courage, love, faith in the goodness of all men and forgiveness. I love you. You will come to me. In my dreams… You promised that once. I will expect you… Till we meet again…"

I had no tears... The violin was still playing… The caring nurse came in, checked Father's pulse, nodded to me in compassion. "Can we stay here till morning?" I asked.

"Yes, till nine o'clock," she said. She came back with a cup of strong coffee. I thanked her and opened my Missal to the funeral hymns Stavros had sung in Florida. I read aloud: *"My soul glorifies the Lord..."* And the Easter hymns he liked: *"It is Resurrection Day. Lighten up Peoples..."* and *"Christ is risen. He won over death and offered life to the entombed ones."*

The dawn found me still praying. I called Tito at 7:00. By 7:30 he was by my side...

* * *

Father's funeral was on the day of the Annunciation to the Virgin, the 25th March 1986. I had put the Icon of Archangel Gabriel - Announcing the good news to the Virgin Mary - under Father's crossed hands... Our family ended the day at *Molivos*, Stavros' favourite Greek fish restaurant, drinking ouzo to his memory and talking about his life.

AFTERWORD

Gaby, who came for the funeral, asked me to leave with her in three days and spend a week in Toronto with her. "It will change your mind. Will do you good," she insisted.

I did go, after the traditional ninth day 'soul prayer' liturgy for Stavros.

Gaby was great with me; she arranged visits with friends and also a 24 hour stay in Niagara Falls. The magnificence of the falls, the boat trip under the great flow, the *Mist,* made me feel alive and wondering at the magnificence and beauty of our World. So many years in Canada and we had never been "under" the falls. Father would have liked that.

Such a thrilling sensation! Pity we had never thought of it…

The night I came back to Montreal I had a strange dream.

I was in front of a large fish bowl. A single orange gold-fish was swimming in it. It turned around and came to rest his mouth against the glass. It became bigger and bigger and finally its head morphed into Stavros' face! His lips moved saying something. The bowl was transformed now into an empty theatre, and I found myself beside my father. But I could not "see" myself. Only Father sitting in the first row… No one else… Then he was on the stage, directing himself to act. Then he was behind the stage, as a decorator. Next he became the actor on the lit stage and finally appeared as the viewer again in the theatre seat… Now Father was talking to me voiceless, telepathically:

"You see, there is no death. Life is a play, Erato. Your play. You are the writer, the director, the technician, the decorator, the actor and the viewer all at once. The beauty of it is that you can change the plot and the background any time! Anyway you want. Most people don't do it, because they don't know. But now you know…"

I woke up with a strange feeling. Was this Father's promise to let me know, once on the other side, whether there was anything there and what it was? The secret of life? I was not sure but I fell under the spell of this dream. And from that day on I did try to "change" things in my life…

Father appeared a few more times to me in my dreams.

One was years after, during Gaby's early stages of pregnancy. Stavros went and sat beside her in a royal blue throne-like armchair. I interpreted it as Gaby going to have a baby-boy. Her first born is indeed a boy; Marc…

The other dream was a few years ago. We were in a nice room, Tito, myself and Gaby (Chris, Gaby's husband was not around). Suddenly, walked in Stavros, in springing steps. He was young, in his mid-thirties, handsome, athletic, tanned, in narrow jeans moulding his athletic legs and thighs, and in denim top. A diamond ring was dangling from his left ear. Stavros with a diamond ring! Imagine! He came to sit between Tito and me, beaming with pleasure.

"What are you doing here, Father?" I asked.

"I live here."

"And where is Mama? What did you do with her? Where did you leave her?"

"I did nothing. Your Mama didn't want to join me. She is very happy where she is. And I am very happy here. Life goes on…"

The dream looked like a puzzle to me. Was Stavros warning us of something impending and a reassurance that "life goes on"? Was he "reincarnated" on Earth? What?

A few months after the dream, Chris, Gaby's beloved husband, succumbed to a rare form of cancer. Before leaving us after a long and brave battle, he expressed his love to each one of us and asked Tito to watch over his kids and take care of them. He was only 37… The family survived the pain and the loss. Chris also appeared to me, both in my waking moments and in my dreams, to tell me he was OK and to let his kids know that he is with them and is watching over them… Thanks for your love, your courage and reassurance, Chris…

Yes, life goes on – thanks to the unconditional Love that guides and drives us all. Thanks for your life, Father. Thanks for your teachings and the sweet memories… And thank you Mother for all your love and testimonies that fortified our faith and brought us hope…

Erato Evangelidis Sahapoglu
23 September 2003/2008

ERATO EVANGELIDIS SAHAPOGLU was born and raised in Istanbul, Turkey. She migrated to Canada in 1964 with her engineer husband and her family. She holds a degree in art history and her short stories appeared in *Spinetingler* magazine and others. She is actually working on short stories and two novels, all inspired by real life. She lives in Brossard, Quebec, by the St-Lawrence river and close to her daughters and their families.